GOVERNOR HENRY HORNER,

CHICAGO POLITICS, AND THE GREAT DEPRESSION

To Bob

Happy Birthday!

Best wishes

[illegible]

GOVERNOR HENRY HORNER, CHICAGO POLITICS, AND THE GREAT DEPRESSION

CHARLES J. MASTERS

Southern Illinois University Press / *Carbondale*

Printed in the United States of America

10 09 08 07 4 3 2 1

Library of Congress Cataloging-in-Publication Data
Masters, Charles J., 1939–
Governor Henry Horner, Chicago politics, and the
Great Depression / Charles J. Masters.
p. cm.
Includes bibliographical references and index.
ISBN-13: 978-0-8093-2739-3 (pbk. : alk. paper)
ISBN-10: 0-8093-2739-2 (pbk. : alk. paper)
1. Horner, Henry, 1878–1940. 2. Governors—Illinois—
Biography. 3. Judges—Illinois—Biography. 4. Illinois—
Politics and government—1865–1950. 5. Chicago (Ill.)—
Politics and government—To 1950. 6. Depressions—
1929—Illinois. 7. New Deal, 1933–1939—Illinois. I. Title.
F546.H67M37 2006
977.3'04092—dc22
[B] 2006018598

Printed on recycled paper. ♻

The paper used in this publication meets the minimum
requirements of American National Standard for
Information Sciences—Permanence of Paper for Printed
Library Materials, ANSI Z39.48-1992. ∞

For my favorite son, Ben

Contents

Illustrations

Preface

By its nature, an omission is always silent. Therefore, some piece left out of the historical record does not raise a ruckus. A lapse in the record does not grab the attention of someone leafing through the indexes of book upon book about the important and fascinating topics of the Great Depression of the 1930s and the groundbreaking New Deal. The governor who served from January 9, 1933, until October 6, 1940, and saw Illinois through this crisis, a man whose epicenter was the prominent city of Chicago (so vivid a symbol of the urban Depression-era experience), is simply not mentioned in the indexes of most of these major works. Where is Governor Henry Horner? Most people have never heard of him. And yet, his story is remarkable. His rise to power in Illinois is a dramatic tale, full of political intrigue and twists of fate. Many around him thought that he lacked "toughness," yet he survived and even prospered in the hottest political seat one could imagine. And when the highest office in the land stood by while he became the target of a political slaughter, he emerged the lion. His story is dramatic, despite all the silence that surrounds it.

This book tells the story of Henry Horner's career, the history and politics of Chicago, and the Great Depression in Illinois. Horner (b. November 30, 1878) died in October 1940, but his voluminous papers were not opened to the public until 1962. Horner left two major collections of papers to what was then called the Illinois State Historical Library, now the Abraham Lincoln Presidential Library. The first of these, the Henry Horner Lincoln Collection, consists chiefly of Lincoln items collected by Horner himself that came from his estate. The second collection, the Horner Papers (1899–1940), covers 191.3 linear feet, containing 443 boxes and 39 oversize bound volumes. It deals with his law practice and his term as judge of the Probate Court of Cook County (1914–1932) as well as his governorship. All the documents are well-indexed and well-inventoried, but to go through all of them would take years. Fortunately, a more selective use of his personal and gubernatorial papers can be enlightening and can reveal much about Horner as a governor, administrator, politician, and human being concerned with the state of Illinois and its citizens.

Thomas B. Littlewood, a well-known journalist, was among the first to utilize the Horner Papers at the Illinois State Historical Library in writing his biography, *Horner of Illinois*, published in 1969. Brief biographies appeared in *Who Was Who in America* (1942); the *Encyclopaedia Judaica* (1971); and the *Biographical Directory of the Governors of the United States, 1789–1978* (1978). The most complete of the short biographical sketches is by Paul M. Angle in the *Dictionary of American Biography* (1958). Robert P. Howard also dealt with Horner in two books: *Illinois: A History of the Prairie State* (1972), particularly chapter 26, "The Great Depression"; and *Mostly Good and Competent Men* (1999).

The best evidence that Horner has been forgotten despite the Littlewood biography and the short accounts mentioned above is that the twenty-four-volume *American National Biography* (1999) omits him completely. No full-scale treatment of Horner has appeared in over thirty-five years. The most recent history of the state, Roger Biles's *Illinois: A History of the Land and Its People* (2005), has only four paragraphs and two other references devoted to Horner. References to a number of other articles and short studies may be found in the bibliography. It does appear that the time has come to reevaluate Illinois's Depression-era governor, his career, and his administrations, along with his connections with Chicago and its history.

Those writers who include him in their historical narratives offer oddly contradictory and dismissive characterizations of Horner. They call him "weak," "lacking guts," and "a rubber-stamper" and then criticize him for being "too independent," "a troublemaker," and an "obstructionist." The most frequent of the criticisms is that Horner was *"not a politician."* Clearly, he *was* a politician: he held an elected office most of his professional life. However, this particular characterization is astute on one level. He was not a typical politician, and perhaps that was the problem. He went against the grain of the politics of the time, and so it is not surprising that other politicians would describe him unfavorably—calling him weak when he went along with them, and a troublemaker when he did not. However, this political sniping has bled into the historical record and would undoubtedly bleed into the popular consciousness, if there were any popular consciousness of this remarkable governor of Illinois. This perception of Horner as a weak servant of the corrupt political machine does not square with his actions. He took on the political machine so brazenly that its leaders launched a desperate attempt to unseat him from office. His strength became evident when he stood nearly alone against the whole Chicago Democratic machine, as well as the White House, and still managed to stay in office and put the entire machine in its place.

Horner steadfastly believed in having a friendly relationship with the average citizen and had an almost obsessive determination to do the right thing in situations. He stood up for honesty and, what is more remarkable, *won* in a political climate that made honesty a liability. Horner's historical reputation is greatly out of keeping with the facts of his life and his career. With his decidedly apolitical style of governing, he reinvented the politics of his era. He ran the statehouse in a singular manner, and it would be a challenge to find another political figure who withstood so much adversity.

Had Henry Horner gone the route of the zealous reformer, he would never have become the governor of the state of Illinois. He would, therefore, never have had the opportunity to right the sinking ship, oversee the feeding of thousands of hungry mouths, intervene between the farmer and the banker with a foreclosure notice in his hand, or quell the revolution that was brewing in the state. Horner was his own breed of reformer. He simply refused to do things in the crooked manner that was expected of him. He refused to "go along" with the political expectation of the day.

Although not confrontational by nature, he soon showed the state that he was nobody's window dressing. This book seeks to fill out the historical record and illustrate how politics, corruption, and greed can railroad even a strong and principled individual. When Horner was railroaded, so were we all. When Horner refused to sidestep the oncoming freight, the rights of the common people were also being tested. Horner's dedication to the common people helped him to withstand it all.

Henry Horner's career has some things to teach us. It shows statesmanship put to the test against political machines that have become self-sustaining entities having little to do with service or stewardship of the public good. Horner's style of leadership has its roots in the original ideals of a country shaking itself free of tyranny. Frequently, we have to be reminded of the power of such ideas. Horner may, in fact, be largely absent from the record for that very reason—he was a man of ideas. He did not rise to prominence propelled by an imposing presence or a charismatic personality. He was not a showman. The city of Chicago at the turn of the century was a city of "big men" who were bold, arrogant industrialists crushing the competition. They were ward bosses, impervious to the law, and gangsters, whose tough-guy personas earned them power and local celebrity. These were the men who fill the history books and create an entertaining saga. But the "good guy" has a role to play as well. In a system of bullies and corruption, the kind, gentle, and honest figure becomes a renegade. How does such a renegade rise to power? And how does his unique style of governing disrupt and remake the system around him? Is there room for the genuine "good guy" in the world of politics? Although the governor's mansion in Springfield, Illinois, was not a comfortable place for a "good guy," Horner settled in there for a time, and no other governor has occupied that house in quite the same way that he did.

My interest in twentieth-century military history, particularly World War II, led me to discover Henry Horner, whose story, I have gradually become convinced, is a hidden gem of Depression-era history. As I sorted through this period in my mind and in research materials, I searched for a structure through which I could explore this period in a new book. I became interested in the relationship between the economic and social events of the 1930s and World War II. Economics and war are always inextricably linked, and a study of one requires an understanding of the other.

Many historians have suggested that if an "official date" for the end of the Great Depression were established, it would most likely be December 7, 1941, the day the Japanese bombed Pearl Harbor. In reality, September 1939 would be a more accurate choice, because the beginning of World War II in Europe, which was twenty-seven months before Pearl Harbor, set the industrial machinery in the United States moving, and the war orders that poured into the United States helped to revitalize the economy. Millions of American men who were hard-pressed to find jobs in the 1930s were either drafted or enlisted in the armed forces because of the enormous manpower needed to fight a global war like World War II. The war did for the American economy what a profusion of New Deal work programs could not quite accomplish—it created real work for millions, opened up employment opportunities at home, and created an increased demand for American products that would support the war effort. With the men gone, women composed a significant part of the workforce, now essential in meeting new production demands, and there were abundant opportunities to earn a paycheck. The capitalist system and America's industrial might were finally unleashed from the difficulties that, only a decade earlier, seemed poised to bring them crashing to the ground in chaos. It has been reported that one year after Pearl Harbor, the United States was producing more war matériel than both Germany and Japan combined. Thus, a fascination with World War II and how it transformed the American economy led me to consider the perilous era that preceded it. How chaotic and uncertain those times must have been when American leaders attempted to invent a way out of economic disaster and to shore up the remains of a system in which the nation had placed all of its most idealistic and noble hopes.

As I read about the 1930s and the Great Depression, I remembered stories recounted to me as a boy by my maternal grandmother, Josephine. She had told me about her mother, Sarah Levy, who was a cousin and friend of Henry Horner. According to family lore, when Horner was a boy, he attended Sarah's wedding, on October 18, 1893, at 226 Ewing Street in Chicago. My grandmother had saved a wedding invitation from that event that she gave to me. She also wrote me letters about Horner, one of which is still in my possession.

As I studied the crushing events of the Great Depression and the bleakness of those years, I began to think about Horner. What would it have been like to be the governor of one of the most populous states in the nation during the darkest period in American history? The situation was made even darker because of the severely divergent positions of the northern industrial and southern agrarian interests in Illinois. It is impossible to imagine a more unsettled time and place, with people questioning the fundamental order of things. Was the great American experiment failing? Was the system destined to completely break down? Some Americans thought that socialism, communism, or even national socialism (Nazism) offered a better way.

I envisioned Henry Horner as a political figure with whom I had a tenuous family connection. Horner, a bachelor who craved harmony and goodwill, had won the governor's seat in the midst of the worst global economic depression in history, at a time when Hitler's Germany was going down the ominous path of Nazism and the seeds of World War II were stirring in the soil of discontent. Questions began to heighten my interest and my research activity: What would it have been like to be elected one of the first two Jewish governors in American history at a time such as this? What were the political and economic dynamics Horner was forced to reckon with at this unique historical moment? What was his relationship with Franklin Delano Roosevelt? Suddenly, it seemed a story well worth pursuing, especially when I encountered the relative absence of the story from the historical record. What I discovered was even more astounding than I had originally envisioned. Horner not only had the Depression and international crises as a backdrop for his two terms as governor, but he also contended with one of the most riotous local political scenes that one could imagine. He held the welfare of the state in his hands and beat back the ever-present threat of revolution, while at the same time dodging political arrows from interests in Chicago that plotted his downfall. How did one man tolerate such a burden? And why is it that his efforts are so easily dismissed?

A genial, well-spoken man with a pince-nez and a moustache, Henry Horner was the picture of the ideal grandfather. He was a prototypical workaholic who took his responsibility to others very seriously. These attributes were unfashionable in the Roaring Twenties, when he was a young man. Indeed, he drew his inspiration from an old-fashioned, unfashionable source: Abraham Lincoln. He was an avid Lincoln scholar as well as a man who couldn't take time away from his duties to party, to invent an amusing persona for himself, or even to marry. Horner must have seemed a rather odd type of individual to those around him in the 1920s. However, the mood of his city, his state, and the country would soon change. As the Great Depression that seized the country came to Illinois, Horner became the man of the hour.

He attacked his job with a methodical fury of hard work and fairness. Like an enormous vacuum, the political machine in Chicago tried to suck him up and make him part of its corrupt structure. With a naïveté often apparent in the most honest of people, Horner held on to his independent, objective appraisal of each situation he confronted. Even though he was buffeted by greater political pressure and retribution than most politicians of the era, indeed any era, he came through it all with a remarkable reputation. At his death, even his political opponents had to acknowledge that Henry Horner was a man who exemplified good government and a heartfelt concern for the people under his jurisdiction. The popular image of the "square dealer" seemed fashioned in Horner's honor. But soon after being lauded by his colleagues and the people of Illinois at his death, Horner disappeared from the popular consciousness. He was erased from our memories of old Chicago, eclipsed by more colorful and larger-than-life figures. Henry Horner did not make a historical character of himself. He was too busy working. But his story is dramatic, interesting, and instructive, and it deserves to be reintroduced into our lore.

I want to take this opportunity to thank those who were kind enough to help me bring this book to fruition: Lain Adkins, Director of the Southern Illinois University Press, whose extensive publishing experience, wisdom, and steady hand was always there for me; Dr. Karl Kageff, Editor-in-Chief, whose advice, guidance, and suggestions proved invaluable; Bridget Brown, Editorial Assistant, who took the time to go through every chapter with me; John K. Wilson, my copyeditor, whom I was so pleased to be working with on another book; Dr. Rand Burnette, for his wonderful research assistance and for being a delight to work with; Pat Burnette, for her editorial assistance; and finally, my son, Ben, who always patiently helped me organize my computer data and research.

GOVERNOR HENRY HORNER,
CHICAGO POLITICS, AND THE GREAT DEPRESSION

1

Muddy Beginnings

When Chicago emerged into history in 1833, it had a population of 350. Trappers, traders, Indians, rough-and-tumble entrepreneurs, and immigrants disoriented in a new world forged an uneasy coexistence in the marshy landscape off Lake Michigan. The city was little more than a cluster of tall and narrow, white wooden structures dotting the wet prairie, forming an elongated cluster around the mouth of the river where it opened into the great lake. The wind howled and the mud lapped at the feet of these early residents. Still, there was a feeling of excitement in the air. The nascent city was perfectly situated to benefit from westward expansion and trade, and those adventurous spirits who took advantage of the new opportunities imbued the area with a particularly American kind of upstart energy despite the hardships.

At that time, there were already signs of the gangster Chicago to come: the town was wild, brash, and lawless, and its muddy parameters set the scene for a rapid exchange of pelts, guns, blankets, prostitutes, and whiskey.

The first Henry Horner, grandfather of the governor, was greeted by this rather dismal and shocking landscape in 1840 when he stepped down from the stagecoach. A Czech from Bohemia, he was one of the first permanent Jewish settlers on record in Chicago. Like other young immigrants who began to show up on a regular basis in the new town, Horner had a background at odds with the Wild West rowdies and Indians that peopled what was nicknamed "the mud hole of the prairie." These new immigrants came from more established communities in Europe. Many had respectable, well-to-do backgrounds, and many of them were intellectuals. The Jewish immigrants, especially, were often from families who had deep, long-standing connections with the great intellectual traditions of Europe. Their fathers had been professionals, and their mothers were esteemed women of the community.

The early history of Chicago was greatly influenced by a wave of Jewish immigration from Germany in particular.[1] Despite a continual and ever-changing history of harassment, persecution, and relocation, the Jews of Germany had been able to create influential and flowering intellectual and philosophical traditions. After the fall of Napoleon, however, a renewed nationalism, a condition of mind that always spelled terror for the Jewish people, resulted in an increase of anti-Jewish activity. Conditions were especially bad in Bavaria, where the pressure on Jews to convert to Christianity was organized and sanctioned by the government. Those who did not comply were *strongly encouraged* to emigrate to America. The Jews who remained were increasingly harassed with restrictions on marriage, domicile, and employment. They were also subjected to special taxes that only applied to them. As life in Germany became increasingly uncomfortable for them, many who could afford to do so departed for America. These early immigrants encouraged a generation of young dreamers still in Germany with letters detailing life in a land of transformation, rife with opportunity, and lacking any history that would ride upon the back of a Jew. As a result, between 1830 and 1855, a second wave of German Jewish settlers came of their own will, with a little money in their pockets to start up something. They brought some order to the rollicking Chicago scene, but their resources were minimal at the outset. Many of them had spent most of their money on passage. So, many of the early German Jews in Chicago began as peddlers who entered the mercantile scene of the city carrying their wares on their backs. But soon the opportunities of this harsh, unsettled world opened up to them, and they opened storefronts on Lake and Clark Streets and lived above their stores.

The first Henry Horner, bringing with him an education, a library of books, and little else, entered the early trade of Chicago as a clerk in a clothing store. Soon, this enterprising and intelligent young man opened a wholesale and retail grocery store on the corner of Randolph and Canal. His business grew steadily, as he catered to the needs for merchandise of a growing stream of westward wanderers. The rich farmland surrounding the little city of Chicago provided a steady influx of grain, produce, and meat that made its way into the city on flatbeds pulled by horses over the uneven, unpaved, and muddy roads. Soon, Horner was a solid member of the business community.

Meanwhile, a young woman living in the village of Zeilhard, located in the central Hesse region of Germany, was contemplating an uncertain future. Hannah Dernberg was now the sole Jewish resident of Zeilhard. At nineteen, she was newly orphaned, and any ties that had kept her near home were gone.[2] She was a tall, substantial young woman with broad shoulders. Nothing about her evoked the stereotypical image of the delicate orphan girl at the mercy of a ruthless world portrayed in nineteenth-century novels. She was capable, energetic, and independent. She had grown up in an educated family, one with a distinguished and prosperous history. Her great grandfather had been the rabbi of Hanover. The Dernbergs had been an integral thread in the scholarly fabric of Jewish German history. Her upbringing was full of books and refined conversation in a secure home. As a young woman, Hannah had set her sights on becoming a teacher. Her childhood had been relatively free of anti-Semitism, but as a nineteen-year-old, she felt history starting to encroach upon her. A revolution was about to hit the old and stable aristocratic order, and this revolution would unleash a backlash that would forever haunt the Jews of Germany. Hannah saw these signs and felt uneasy about her future in Zeilhard. It soon became clear that an influx of new restrictions, aimed at reasserting power over those who questioned the status quo, would never allow a young Jewish woman the option of a teaching career. And so, she left.

When she arrived in the city of New York in 1848, Hannah had left a revolution destined to fail behind her in Germany and moved on to a small, emergent community across the Great Lakes that was waiting to embrace her. She arrived in Chicago, an unmarried, young Jewish woman, traveling alone. Less than a year later, Hannah Dernberg married the up-and-coming young businessman Henry Horner. And so, the existence of a future governor of Illinois was sealed. The introspective and intelligent young Henry Horner found a good mate in the statuesque Hannah Horner. Her energy, leadership, and powerful personality relieved much of the burden of his business. She stepped into the establishment that he had so remarkably quickly built and immediately saw what she could do to make it better. Rather than being territorial about his creation, he was pleased with her industry and handed over a good deal of responsibility to her.

Together, the Horners built a prosperous life for their heirs. Their mercantile legacy began in a store on the West Side that was stocked with pelts and produce from outlying farms. Their business grew rapidly in the flourishing economic climate of the 1850s. The growth of business in Chicago gave political power to many of the immigrants who, just a few years before, had been lowly peddlers ducking the gunfire while diverting a little business here and there from the more powerful saloons and traders. These European immigrants now began consciously shaping Chicago, a city that was in a unique position to experience rapid economic growth. Situated on Lake Michigan as well as near the land passage to its south, the city had the advantage of access by either rail or waterway, making it a natural center of trade. The wild, marshy environment of the city was being tamed and urbanized. Planks raised throughout the city became the wooden streets and sidewalks of Chicago, elevated above the swampy land. The new forward-thinking residents were determined to make a world-class city of their mud hole.

Hannah and Henry Horner became active participants in the development of Chicago. They were pivotal in forming some of the early Jewish organizations in the city, and Henry soon became a prominent businessman in both the grocery and the banking industries. When the city became flooded with immigrant Jews fleeing from the Russian pogroms, Hannah displayed leadership and acted in ways that assured she would be remembered for a long time. She was a charter member of the Johanna Lodge, a Jewish women's organization. Giving a hand up to young Jewish men and women in the community was always her major preoccupation. She found them employment, lent them money, and often acted as a matchmaker for them. She presided over their weddings and felt a deep satisfaction when they became independent and functioning members of the community and set up shops and households of their own. These young families went on to form the prosperous German Jewish community that long resided on the fashionable South Side of Chicago.

Amazingly, while she was an active businesswoman and a tireless charity worker, Hannah Horner also gave birth to a steady procession of children. The first of her eleven children was a daughter, Dilah, born on April 15, 1851. Any time that Hannah was well enough to be on her feet, she was seen haranguing her underlings to make certain that every penny was laboriously documented, while holding her latest baby over her shoulder. This tendency to micromanage would also be a striking characteristic of her governor grandson.

As the daughter of a prominent family in her community, Dilah was considered a desirable match for an up-and-coming lucky young man. Of course, Hannah, a matchmaker by nature, carefully scrutinized Dilah's prospects. The older women of the close-knit Jewish community conspired to see their offspring married, forming families of their own and building a prosperous community in Chicago. It was in this spirit that a woman in Hannah's social circle asked for permission to introduce Dilah to a young man, a nephew of marriageable age, that she thought Dilah should meet. The woman did not mention to Hannah that her nephew, Solomon Levy, was suffering a broken heart. Nevertheless, in early 1871, Levy entered the lives of the respectable Horner family. He was considered very handsome, and Dilah may have been greatly flattered by his attention. He was also worldly and considerably older than Dilah. Hannah, however, immediately saw Levy as a threat. Only nine years her junior, he threatened to impinge on her authority over, and relationship to, her daughter.

Solomon Levy's young life was marked by change, success, and adventure. He immigrated to the United States from Bavaria as a young man to find a new life, away from the restrictions against Jews in Europe, and joined his extended family in Kentucky, where he was put in charge of a family clothing business at the age of thirteen. But Levy took leave of his family and headed out to California with hordes of others sniffing after the scent of gold. He landed in San Francisco after a long and arduous journey that included a shipwreck. From there, the young man went on to Sacramento, where he stayed for some time. He quickly became an established part of society there, making a name for himself as a successful cigar merchant. He accomplished all this before he was twenty-five. At the top of his game in the cigar business, Levy sold out to a brother and moved to San Francisco to get in on the diamond drill and cutlery business. Clearly, this enterprising and mature young man had accumulated a great deal of business experience before he ever set eyes on Dilah.

Solomon Levy, like Henry Horner, was a great reader and prized his personal library. But, unlike the reclusive and introspective intellectual who became his father-in-law, Levy was gregarious and liked to apply knowledge to the wide world. He taught himself four languages that he practiced on frequent buying trips throughout Europe and Russia. Having established himself in business and enjoyed his young bachelorhood to the hilt, Levy needed just one piece of the puzzle to complete his rich existence. He found that final piece when he fell in love with the daughter of a longtime business associate and family friend. Jubilantly, he headed off on a business trip to Europe, stopping in Paris to buy a trousseau for the seventeen-year-old, whom he had determined would be his bride. However, when he returned to the United States, he was devastated to discover that she had taken ill and died. Despondent, Levy could not bear the sights of the city that he had planned to share with his betrothed. And so, he made the pivotal decision to take some time away and visit an aunt in Chicago. Therefore, it can be fairly asserted that Solomon Levy married Dilah Horner impulsively and on the rebound. The marriage was not a good one. The couple immediately began to argue. Recovering her wits after the birth of her last child, Hannah grew to despise Levy and viewed her daughter's marriage to him as a serious mistake. Solomon moved Dilah away from her family's estate as soon as he could, and they established a household of their own on South Michigan Avenue. The temporary relocation of her household was perhaps the only lucky thing about this marriage for Dilah.

In the early hours of October 9, 1871, the Horners, along with the rest of Chicago, experienced a shock and a dramatic change of fortune. The Great Chicago Fire decimated the Horner family home and their businesses. The family was able to flee to safety, although it is said that Dilah's father experienced such a great shock that he practically had to be dragged from the scene, leaving his cherished library behind him. All told, the fire destroyed approximately 18,000 buildings, so that nearly one-third of the people in the city now found themselves without homes. Its houses, streets, and sidewalks being made almost entirely of wood, the city was the perfect tinderbox. A spark from an overturned lantern in a barn, fanned by a typical Chicago wind, spelled a disaster for the city that should have been anticipated. For quite some time, people labored in the ashes and looked to their savings to determine the immediate future. Many, like the Horners, recovered and went on to prosper again, but all those who survived the fire had experienced an unimaginable shock. Our historical understanding of this event is limited because most of the eyewitnesses agreed that the horrors that surrounded them on that night were simply indescribable, that language did not have the power to capture such terrifying imagery. Although disastrous for the people of Chicago, the fire was actually a turning point for the city. The rebuilding after the fire reorganized and modernized what had once been "a walking city." Chicago began becoming an industrial powerhouse with a centralized, commercial downtown, an efficient organization of public transit, paved roads, and updated building materials such as stone and brick. While not yet the skyscrapers that would soon define the city, buildings were reaching higher toward the sky, with the downtown center now visibly differentiated from the residential areas that spread out around it. And so, after the fire, the city moved rapidly into the industrial age.

The Horners began the process of rebuilding and reorganizing almost immediately. Henry decided to give up the banking activities of the Horner enterprise. Hannah relocated the store on Randolph Street. They lived for a time above the store until they were able to purchase a house at 14 Park Row, near the South Side—a prosperous and picturesque area of tall, narrow brownstones on a tree-lined street, now paved, rather than covered over by the hazardous wooden planks. After the fire, the prosperous Jewish community began a relocation pattern that would mark the next few decades. They spread southward into the suburbs, while the eastern European Jewish immigrants who soon overwhelmed the city took up the areas that they had deserted.

The Horners focused their remaining reserves on modifying their enterprise from both wholesale and retail to specializing entirely in the wholesale end of the grocery business. And so, the Horner business empire, diminished somewhat, survived into the twentieth century. Henry Horner never fully recovered from the losses incurred in the fire, perhaps because of his sudden realization of the tenuous nature of all that we build in this life. His peaceful interior space had been compromised and his library lost. The smoke may also have damaged his lungs, because he was increasingly subject to asthma attacks in the years following the fire.

Dilah and her husband, their apartment spared from the fire, were experiencing sparks of their own. In March of 1872, amid sad resignation and rebuilding efforts after the fire, Dilah gave birth to her first child, James. A year later, another son, Sidney, joined the Levy family. It was during this time that it became evident that the Levy household was in turmoil. Dilah and Solomon, having entered into marriage hastily, were not compatible. Aware of the tension between the two, Hannah found herself in a power struggle with her new son-in-law. Initially, Levy worked in the Horner business. But as a mature thirty-two-year-old who had fully established himself in the business world, he resented having to bend to his mother-in-law's authority. Then, shortly before the birth of the Levys' third son, Dilah's father, Henry, died, at the age of sixty, of a brain hemorrhage. He had been a powerful and intellectual man, an entrepreneur who had made his mark on the emerging city of Chicago. On November 30, 1878, Dilah and Solomon Levy welcomed their third son. Although this child never knew his esteemed grandfather, he would bear his name. He was called Henry Levy, and he drew his first breaths in a troubled home.

Shortly after Henry's birth, Solomon decided to start his own export business, an enterprise in keeping with his experience and interests. However, this break with the Horner business interests did not smooth things out between him and Dilah. The fighting continued. Like her mother, Dilah was not the stereotypical sufferer-in-silence, and, in August 1883, she took her three sons, went home to her mother, and engaged an attorney. Possibly the way that Dilah successfully found peace and restitution through the courts inspired young Henry Levy, now four, to pursue a legal career in later life. In the divorce proceedings, Dilah's brief married life became a matter of public record. Although divorce was frowned upon at that time, especially in the Jewish community, the evidence demonstrated that the marriage was beyond repair, and the judge issued a decree of divorce, finding in favor of Dilah. Despite the ruling by the judge that Levy was "guilty of extreme and repeated cruelty," James was awarded to his father's care.[3] The legal precedent that the firstborn automatically went to the father was too strong for any exception to be made. The other two sons, Sidney and Henry, went with Dilah to live in the Horner household. Hannah took them in on one condition: that the children's surname would be changed from Levy to Horner.

As the prosperous and influential community of Jews to which the Horners belonged was inventing itself, the immigration pattern was changing radically. What was once a manageable trickle of immigrants into the Chicago area was now a flood, and these newer immigrants were very different than their predecessors. Among them were eastern European Jews, many of whom were fleeing for their lives from violent Russian persecution. They were departing Europe with little more than the clothing on their backs. Unlike the prosperous Horners, these Jews had long been accustomed to deprivation. They had been poverty stricken and taxed nearly to starvation and were accustomed only to rural life. In the old country, they had been haunted by persecution, but when subjected to unexpected and capricious onslaughts of violence, they took their chances and allowed themselves to be stuffed like sausages onto steamships. They landed at Castle Garden, where their bodies and pasts were scrutinized. And when they were finally fumigated, they were dumped, usually penniless, into New York City. They stayed with relatives or friends from their old villages until they were able to establish themselves in tenements with jobs as peddlers, street merchants, or laborers in sweatshops. They didn't own much, but they did have their traditions and their convictions. And so, the character and the atmosphere of the city began to change.

The affluent Jewish community in which the Horners lived thrived. A short distance now separated the brownstone houses from the business establishments that funded them. The streets were now paved. Trees, still saplings at this point, inhabited plots of dirt in front of each house. In time, they would tower above the sidewalks, giving shade to the luxurious carriages parked in front of the comfortable dwellings, drivers tending the horses quietly, waiting for the occupants of the houses to request conveyance. In this atmosphere, Hannah made her rounds to the store and to her various relief meetings. When she traveled further north, and all indications suggest that she occasionally did, she would have encountered the Maxwell Street area. Originally, this area contained three-story buildings with large apartments on each floor that housed Jews who were rebuilding after the fire. When these prosperous Jewish residents, like the Horners, migrated further south in the city, the vacated apartments were subdivided and leased out to an increasingly destitute type of tenant. Eventually, the eastern European immigrants re-created in this area a kind of urban village, preserving much of the character of the rural communities they had left behind. The streets became filled with an uproarious market—a profusion of hastily arranged wares available for sale on the street. Some of the wares were in motion, as the long tradition of the Jewish peddler continued. Other wares were displayed in a kind of chaotic and rather unsanitary market, where the customer could buy anything imaginable, from live animals to toilets, trinkets from the homeland, and foodstuffs reminiscent of the European peasant origins of the people. It was a lively sight full of the sounds of Yiddish and the smells of fish and a multitude of equally fragrant wares. The housing conditions grew more and more deplorable as the size of the immigrant population increased dramatically. People were tumbled on top of each other, as the living spaces grew ever smaller. It was common to see an entire family renting not an apartment but a tiny bedroom within one of the tenement apartments.

The established German Jewish community did not immediately know how to respond to the new Jewish population. The German Jews were now staunchly reformed, and they viewed their much more orthodox kin with a mixture of sympathy and disdain. They were concerned about what the visible uproar of their "greenhorn" neighbors might do to their standing in their adopted nation. And in the reverse, the eastern European Jews of the ghetto viewed the relaxed practice of Judaism of the South Side Jews with shock and disapproval. Many prosperous Jews, like Hannah Horner, set to work to aid the assimilation and the material betterment of the Jews of the emerging ghetto. And there was plenty of work to do. The relationship between the affluent South Side and the West Side Jews spawned a legion of Jewish women activists who would set a precedent for the unusually large number of Jewish women labor activists in the Depression era. The Jewish women's community established itself as a force in Chicago.

Dilah's son, now Henry Horner, was a bit smaller than other boys his age, but he was boisterous, energetic, and filled with purpose. Perhaps it was seeing this quality about him that so mirrored her own nature that led Hannah to consider Henry one of her favorites within the large brood of grandchildren. In fact, Hannah commissioned an artist to paint a portrait of her favorite grandchildren to be placed right over her bed so that she could gaze upon them when her eyes first opened in the morning. The picture depicted Henry and two of his cousins resting on a bank of clouds, as if to suggest that they were angels.

Life at the Horners was crowded and busy, but it was a good home. On Friday night, all the relatives crowded into the house for dinner. Dilah and Hannah, now both without husbands, worked out a nice domestic arrangement whereby Dilah presided over the hearth while Hannah concerned herself more with business and charity work. Dilah had become a legendary cook, and on Friday nights she delighted the large crowds of the ever-expanding Horner clan. After dinner, the family sang songs and curled up around the fireplace, with Hannah as the centerpiece. After Dilah and her children had taken up residence, Hannah decided to move the family to a new house on South Michigan Avenue that boasted eight bedrooms. In their very young years, the children were educated in evening sessions around the fire by Hannah herself. When they reached the appropriate age, Henry and his brothers and cousins would attend the neighborhood public school. Henry was not a stellar student, but by all accounts he was quite a remarkable young man.

The last years of the nineteenth century in Chicago were filled with tension and excitement. Just as the city seemed to be on the verge of imploding on itself with a menagerie of burdens, it reached up from the depths to grandly assert itself. The Columbian Exposition—or, as it was more commonly known, the World's Fair—was coming to Chicago. The year was 1893. At this time, America was feeling cramped by its reputation as a young, upstart, Wild West country and wished to establish itself in the world as a setting of prominence, where the future was being invented. In other words, America wanted to be introduced onto the world stage. Therefore, in the latter half of the century, the federal government had begun talking about an elaborate exhibition that would introduce America to the world in a grand manner.

An early try, the Philadelphia Exposition of 1876, had been a disappointment. This failure persuaded the federal government to propose that a much grander exposition take place to honor the 400th anniversary of Columbus's discovery of the New World. The setting would be none other than Chicago, which was seen by the rest of the country as one of the most promising and quickly rising cities in the nation. The growth of industry there and the burgeoning skyscrapers, an emerging art form, were seen as the perfect backdrop for the introduction of the new America to the world. And so, away from the soot and grime of the city, magnificent Grecian-style facades with imposing white columns arose to house the exposition. Additional cable cars were built to convey the visiting throngs into the fair to view exhibits demonstrating and extolling new developments in such fields as manufacturing, agriculture, machinery, and transportation. These and other displays placed American achievements alongside the great innovations of world history, such as the pyramids of ancient Egypt. People from all over the world received an introduction to the city during the weeks of the World's Fair. One can imagine that Chicagoans must have been overcome with their city's reasons for pride and for shame.

Henry Horner was almost certainly among the boys who flocked toward the exposition gates in excitement. Photographs of the era show the cable cars brimming to capacity with young boys clinging to the tops. Horner's smallness was giving way to a sturdiness that was reminiscent of his mother. He was an affable young man, usually to be seen on the streets with a small cluster of boys around him, talking, telling stories, making the others laugh, and perhaps once in a while getting into a little scrap with one of them. Around him, Chicago was lurching into the industrial age, the fever of productivity and the hum of engines setting the rhythm for the busy city. And the Columbian Exposition was the crescendo of that song. With the new emphasis on factories in Chicago came a pair of new historical characters: the exploited factory laborer and the resulting labor activist. By the mid-1880s, the streets crackled with tension over the increasing labor unrest. Insurrections by the severely repressed laborers who protested low wages and hazardous working conditions were met with severe reprisals by a law enforcement force fueled by the alarm of the upper and middle classes. The anxiety of the old guard in Chicago over this new class of people—the workers—commingled with a general fear of the foreign immigrant. The early labor movement was attributed to some diseaselike, highly contagious "European" ideas, the spread of which had to be decisively stemmed.

And so, the voices of the old order and the new order began a contest for public opinion on the streets. Every street corner became a political stage dramatizing the sparking social tension. Impromptu speeches, rallies, and debates were put on by unions to publicize the plight of the worker, while police and local politicians tried to characterize these union activists as troublemakers and thugs whose ideas were not to be countenanced. An issue that raised tempers especially high was the availability of housing for laborers. Workers strongly resented that, despite their hard work, they were unable to find affordable housing in the city. This situation was worsened by a restriction on inexpensive building materials because of their flammability. The workers saw these restrictions as another way in which they were blocked by the government in the fulfillment of their American dream. The upper and middle classes saw the workers' desire to use these materials as just another sign of how the new population threatened their own material safety.

In an additional personal insult that was also an attempt to silence the rowdies, the city began to enforce a code that had been long ignored—the Sunday ban on alcohol. Because a large number of the workers were German and Irish immigrants for whom having a cold beer at the saloon was a treasured custom, and since Sunday was their only day off from work, this development incited the already disgruntled workers to a heightened level. The early temperance movement, born during the lawless times of Chicago's days as a Wild West trading post, was reenergized when the unionists were characterized as drunken and rowdy. If only the booze were cut off, the argument went, these fellows would settle down a bit. This patronizing theory only incited more unrest.

The young Henry Horner found himself a witness to some of the most famous events in Chicago's history. It has been reported that on the day of the famous Haymarket Riot in May of 1886, he was out in the street playing marbles. Just blocks away, a rally was being staged to protest a police action of the day before that had resulted in the death of several workers. Someone threw a homemade bomb into the cluster of police that stood at the ready, waiting to crush the rally if it got out of hand. One police officer was killed by the blast, and the rest unleashed a hail of gunfire onto the crowd that was soon returned by an array of hidden weapons among the rally-goers. A riot of clubbing and gunfire ensued. Six more police officers died. Henry Horner looked up from his sidewalk game at the sound of the gunfire and tumult. His mother raced outside and scooped him up, fearing that a stray bullet might catch him.

By this time, an economic downturn had remade the streets of Chicago into a continual parade of down-and-outers. Tucked away in an affluent home at night, young Henry roamed streets crowded with the homeless, the hungry, and the dispossessed during the daylight hours. Intermixed with these depressing sights, the young boy took in the rapidly changing culture of the city—changes brought to the city by the immigrants whose unique cultures had been formed in the historical rifts of Europe. The city was becoming intensely multicultural and multinational as it hosted immigrants from eastern Europe, especially Poland, and from Ireland, as well as a steady stream of displaced blacks from the South. The new workplaces of the city became the factory and the sweatshop, and these took their places next to the older forms of mercantile trade. As is often the case during times of deprivation, an underground economy was also beginning to develop in Chicago, and the streets were populated with a collection of thugs and con artists that would metamorphose into the famous Chicago crime scene of the early twentieth century.

Young Henry Horner found his attention drawn away from school and onto the fascinating, tumultuous streets. And when he got tired of the chaos, he returned home and hid away with his books, a genetic nod to both of the absent men in his life—his father and grandfather. He especially loved to read about American history and found plenty of volumes to suit his interests in his grandfather's library. Although he did not exempt himself from any of the normal pursuits of a young man—his studies at school, his worship at synagogue, and his participation on numerous sports teams—at fourteen years old, he had already taken up a profession. He became the editor and publisher of a little weekly newspaper that he produced in the basement of his home on a secondhand, shoddy hand press. Each edition comprised about a page's worth of his naive and boyish views on the insanity of local politics and social issues of the streets. There was certainly a lot going on that merited comment. However, even in those early days, people remarked on the boy's sensitivity toward the oppressed people of Chicago. People in the neighborhood became accustomed to seeing the young man trudging through the streets, distributing his weekly publication. His father, who had himself managed a clothing business at age thirteen, might well have been proud if he had known about it. In these times, Sidney and Henry, who had been remanded to the care of their mother, rarely got to see their brother, James, or their father, who had not taken advantage of the visitation provisions of the divorce settlement. Young Henry lacked a father but would go on to find some remarkable men to consider when putting together his own unique interpretation of manhood.

When his tenure at the Chicago Manual School of Trades came to an end, it became time for Henry Horner to choose a profession. Some options seemed to present themselves in a rather obvious manner. He could certainly go into the mercantile business; after all, it was a family tradition. But Horner had memories of an unpleasant experience when he lived with an aunt and uncle one summer during an internship in their clothing store. The grind of the buying and selling life did not spark his imagination. Perhaps he didn't enjoy being chained indoors to a counter. On the other hand, he certainly had demonstrated proficiency for the life of a journalist. In fact, the workings of the press would be a topic that continually interested him as an adult. Years later, when he served as the governor, he kept careful tabs on the press and would write to praise or to chastise editors, as the situation warranted.[4] Neither of these career options won out in the end, however. Horner had become entranced with the unique political scene. He watched the mayoral campaign of the first Carter Harrison with keen interest and noticed how Billy Loefler, a Bohemian Jew, rose to prominence as a backer of Harrison. This was an important moment for Horner. Previously, he had only envisioned a rather insular professional world of the Jewish community engaged in politics, activism, and even business only insofar as they related to that community on behalf of both the successful and the not-so-successful Jews. But Loefler had broken that boundary. And so, interested in an entry into the widening world of Chicago, Henry Horner enrolled at Kent College of Law night school. In law school, he established himself as a serious student, which he never had done in public school. He became known both as a scholar and as a prominent and charismatic figure.

Horner always found it of the utmost importance to cultivate a social circle. He did this with jovial goodwill and with a remarkable ability to keep up an interest and an involvement in others. As a law student, he took up an internship with Allan Storey, who was the lawyer who had handled his mother's divorce. This detail lends more credence to the theory that his parents' divorce instilled in the young man the idea that the law was a powerful and noble pursuit that could step in on behalf of the vulnerable and the mistreated. Perhaps his experience in a broken home led the relatively privileged Horner to identify with the lost souls around him and to desire to work on their behalf as an attorney. At this time, Horner was a city boy with primarily an understanding of Chicago. However, he would grow to have a philosophical relationship with the rural part of the state, and later, he would descend into that unknown territory and establish himself as a master of building meaningful connections with people. That was Henry Horner's greatest gift.

2

One Foot on the Sidewalk and One in the Gutter

During the last week of the Columbian Exposition, White City, so-called because of the imposing white edifices erected to house the exhibits, was growing a bit grimy and weary from all the excitement. The angry labor activists of the city displayed a frenetic, irrational energy. The down-and-outers had done what they could to siphon any extra pennies from the flood of visitors and were feeling like their streets were as cramped as if they had a houseful of visitors camping out in their drawing rooms. It was during that week that the exhausted city lost its mayor, Carter Harrison, to the bullet of a jilted city job seeker—just one more casualty of a desperate and disgruntled populace.

Before being mayor of Chicago, Carter Harrison had been in a real estate partnership with his brother but later left to buy the *Chicago Times*. When he became mayor, he put his sons in charge of the newspaper. At his death, his heirs inherited the paper and struggled in the family business in their father's absence. The newspaper was faltering. When they finally submitted to its financial demise and sold the enterprise, their fortunes were diminished, but their spirits were greatly revived. Carter H. Harrison, the son of the martyred mayor, took his wife and children and embarked on an adventure through southern Europe, Switzerland, and northern Africa.

However, at the turn of the century, Carter H. Harrison was called back into the rough-and-tumble world of Chicago politics. To the day he died, he wondered whether his genes had driven him down the same path as his father or whether he had been ambushed by bullies and thrust into an undesirable destiny. The younger Harrison held a powerful asset that was vulnerable to exploitation by the powers of the city's underworld and political players—the popular name of his martyred father. Thus, when there was a political vacuum in Chicago, the young man was pressed into service. The city's underground, which had only lukewarmly embraced his father, seized upon the son. His abstract and intellectual "live and let live" policy was just the ticket for the throngs that made their living in ways that would have made the Lake Shore Drive ladies gasp with disapproval.[1] And so, there arose an odd political marriage between the upper-crust intellectual Harrison and the rough bosses that ruled the streets. The contrast was never more apparent than when the announcement of Harrison's candidacy was made. Harrison himself had this to say: "I promise . . . to have a clean and efficient government. It will be a government far superior to that of the present administration, which is hopelessly, unequivocally, and characteristically Republican." When that failed to raise the roof, First Ward boss John Coughlin added the cheer: "We'll elect Carter and we won't do nothing wrong; he will have gambling and let the races run!"[2] One might expect that Harrison was a little uncomfortable with this characterization of his campaign platform. Still, he had learned all too well from his father's experience that ward politics called in the votes, or perhaps more precisely, paid for the votes. So, he had little choice but to hang his hat with the saloon politickers for a time. It was this strange relationship between Harrison and the powers that be at the First Ward, namely Aldermen Michael "Hinky Dink"

Kenna and "Bathhouse" John Coughlin, that created a way for young Henry Horner to gain some early political experience. It is indeed an irony that Horner, who would be elected to the governorship under the slogan of "good government," would get his start with the likes of Hinky Dink and Bathhouse John. Because the Horner family had long been associated with the Harrison campaigns, first the father's and then the son's, Horner was enlisted after he graduated from law school to help Hinky Dink Kenna advance the cause of Harrison's campaign by serving as a precinct captain.

To understand the unique development of Chicago politics and perhaps urban politics in general at this time, it is essential to consider the circuslike atmosphere of saloon politics on which Horner cut his political teeth. Kenna and Coughlin virtually invented the genre, and they lorded over the vice-ridden First Ward from 1890 until nearly 1940. Coughlin was the alderman of the First Ward until his death in 1938—an astonishing forty-six-year term. Kenna remained influential even after that, although he had stepped down from the position as alderman in 1923, when redistricting changed the representation in each ward from two to one. However, as ward committeeman, he retained power over patronage and became known as the wisest of all the Chicago ward politicians. Although the power of Capone would eclipse them and render them somewhat irrelevant in the end, Kenna and Coughlin created the procedures by which the gangland mafia would operate during the 1920s and throughout the Great Depression, and they contributed to the lusty and ribald texture of the Chicago of the early twentieth century. And yet, they seemed like a couple of circus clowns—one playing straight man to the other's buffoon.

And indeed Bathhouse John Coughlin was a buffoon—but one of the most effective buffoons in town. He was a big fellow who talked a great deal, although he could hardly get a complete sentence out, he so lacked eloquence. But because he was friendly and refreshingly straightforward, he was liked on the streets of the First Ward. As a very young man, he believed that he had made it big when he landed a job as a "rubber" in a bathhouse. In those days, a wide variety of men, from pimps to politicians, frequented these institutions where they could have a revitalizing soak and rubdown. The bathhouse was a place to talk with the boys, make rowdy jokes, have a drink, and relax. Coughlin enjoyed his work; he was a loquacious and very sociable young man. In the bathhouse, he made contacts with a wide cross section of Chicago society. There, the underworld rubbed elbows with respectable society, and so he naturally came to envision those worlds brought together.

In 1882, John Morris, a local saloonkeeper, lent Coughlin $800 to purchase his very own bathhouse on East Madison Street. Coughlin was delighted with his new status as business proprietor. He expressed his nouveau riche pride with a very outlandish fashion sense. He began wearing gaudy, fancy clothes—silk waistcoats in fantastic colors, pink gloves, flashy decorations—and he sported a dramatically waxed moustache. He preened like a peacock, displaying the feathers of an up-and-comer, although he looked more like an up-and-coming pimp than a businessman. After a time, he was successful enough to purchase another, more upscale bathhouse and so began to feel himself an established and powerful member of the community. At work and in the saloon, Coughlin was "one of the fellas" and engaged in the lively conversation and debate concerning the issues of the day. He was in the midst of the local political scene, and it was only natural that he would begin to covet a political position of his own. He began to develop a political philosophy that, in part, helps to explain his odd popular appeal. His philosophy was egalitarian, and perhaps he expressed it more effectively than the best educated of social philosophers when he said, "It don't pay in this world to think you're better than the next feller just 'cause you happen to be on top and he ain't."[3] This democratic outlook, combined with a reputation for being as good as his word, propelled John Coughlin toward a colorful political career in Chicago.

When he entered the political fray, he was hailed "Bathhouse John" in honor of his line of work. The political life was not a genteel one. Most interested in politics were those involved with the saloons, the brothels, and the gambling establishments, because it was this world that had the most at stake in the policy of the ward; after all, these establishments were at the mercy of the law and the police enforcing that law. And so, from the beginning, the politicos of this district had smut on their shoes. The First Ward contained the infamous "Levee," a neighborhood that was congested with establishments of vice—gambling, prostitution, and drinking. At the other end of the district, however, was a more respectable section containing large department stores and office buildings. And so, the concerns of the First Ward ranged from protecting vice to supporting the free expansion of business, as well as, of course, protecting the poor, hungry, diseased, and disenfranchised members of the district.

A system for addressing the first two concerns was beginning to develop. The saloons, brothels, gambling dens, and the like were in the informal, and rather voluntary, habit of paying the First Ward bosses in return for police protection. And the aldermen (the heads of the ward political system) were regularly paid by big business and industry either to pass ordinances that would help them expand or to block ordinances that would interfere with business. The exchange was not quite that straightforward, however. It worked like this: A representative from a business concern would pay a visit to an alderman to request a certain action on an ordinance. The alderman would then "suggest" that the representative hire an attorney to better explain the industry's position. Next, the business would hire one of the ward bosses' men and pay an exorbitant fee that would be split among the group. Finally, since the position of the business was well understood, the alderman would promptly act on it accordingly. This system, nicknamed *boodling*, assured that the modestly paid aldermen of the city became enormously wealthy individuals.

At the time that Bathhouse John Coughlin ascended to the throne of alderman, a weak movement calling for reform of these policy-for-sale practices was beginning to develop. The system needed tightening, and the rather dim-witted Coughlin was not the man for the job—not until he partnered with Hinky Dink Kenna, that is. The two became complementary sides of a coin that would be the effective currency in the ward for decades.

As a youth, Michael Kenna was described as an extremely small boy with an old man's face. He began his illustrious career on the streets selling newspapers after he dropped out of school. He delivered papers deep in the Levee and began to become a familiar face on the scene amid the saloonkeepers, prostitutes, and con men. Wandering in and out of the local establishments, he was often called into service to do errands for the proprietors, one of whom nicknamed him "Hinky Dink" in honor of his short stature. Ambitious from the start, Kenna borrowed money to open a regular newsstand and was successful enough to pay back the loan almost immediately. After the fire of 1871, he saw his opportunity. He set up a lunch counter and coffee shop right in the midst of the ruins, profiting nicely from the lack of competition, courtesy of Mother Nature. He supervised one employee twice his age; Kenna was thirteen years old at the time.

As a young man, he grew restless and decided to see the world. He responded to an advertisement and became circulation manager for a newspaper in Leadville, Colorado. However, he returned after two years because, ironically, he had no stomach for the violent gunfighting in the town, a situation Chicago would soon have in common with it. At the age of twenty-four, now back in Chicago, he opened a saloon and soon had the political life of the First Ward under his thumb. Though they did not originally start out as allies, political pressure from reformists and internal factionalism led the savvy Kenna to propose a partnership with the distasteful blowhard Coughlin. With Kenna's vision and planning and with Coughlin's ability to get the word out, the two remade the loose political habits of the ward and created a political machine.

First, they formed a core crew made up of an assortment of characters that included among its ranks a pickpocket, a safe blower, a brothel owner, and several panderers. This crew carefully and self-consciously, with Kenna as the mastermind, formalized and expanded an organization to draw the underworld together as a political force and to take care of business in the First Ward. They built a system of protection and made regular collections. But they were not thugs. A mild-mannered young man would simply appear on the scene of an establishment requesting the protection fee set by the organization. Often, the proprietor would pay up. Kenna and Coughlin weren't all-powerful, but they could step in and provide legal fees or "have a word" with the police chief when a situation warranted it. At other times, the young collector might be thrown out on his ear by a rough proprietor who didn't like to be bossed by the bosses. In those cases, the young man returned quietly back to the organization and the "refusal" of protection was duly noted. After a tidy profit was made by what was now referred to as "the syndicate," the protection money was used to establish a defense fund. The defense fund might feed a hungry family, pay medical expenses for a sick child, help bridge the gap until an injured worker could return to work, or send a consumptive prostitute out to a sanatorium. Kenna and Coughlin were regularly seen in the homes of the destitute, where they listened to people express their righteous indignation over their material conditions, placed the back of their hands on a feverish infant, or delivered a handful of bills to a family with an out-of-work head.

As the syndicate formalized and extended its reach, it began to be involved in the rapid growth of business and industry in the city. It allowed ambitious and powerful men to realize their larger-than-life dreams, unimpeded by the bureaucratic processes created by early city planners. Business tycoons like the infamous Charles Yerkes engaged in audacious corruption in partnership with what were called "the Grey Wolves" of the city council. To build massive business enterprises, competition had to be eliminated. Entrepreneurs bribed council members to obtain franchises. Yerkes even made use of the scandalous power of "professional vamps" to seduce and then blackmail officials. The pursuit of monopoly engendered a corrupt dance, as lawmakers, officials, and opportunists tried to squeeze money out of the single-minded empire builders. A biographical sketch of the utilities and transportation magnate Samuel Insull describes the system in this way: "It would usually work like so: a syndicate would charter a new company to directly compete with an existing street railway or utility company. A competition between the two—to obtain franchises, to get property owner consent signatures—would then ensue. Ultimately, the dummy company would extract some sort of bribe from the existing company, or simply force the company to buy them out, to prevent the chance of competition."[4] It was in such a business climate that Samuel

Insull would rise to prominence and build much of Chicago's famous rapid transit system in the twentieth century.

The syndicate also took an active role in the elections. Hinky Dink Kenna set the pay rate at $.50 per vote, and the First Ward became notorious as an organization that could really "get out the vote" for a candidate who had the funds. The First Ward provided effective support for its favored candidates. It employed such tactics as moving vagrants from polling place to polling place and having them cast ballots all over town. This they called the "Hobo floto voto." While Kenna managed the system, Coughlin continued to play the clown, offering a dash of colorful charismatic leadership to counter the humorless, pinched demeanor of Kenna. As a songwriter, Coughlin penned such popular ditties as "Oh, Why Did They Build That Lousy Lake So Close to That Beautiful Burg?" and "She Sleeps by the Drainage Canal."[5]

In those days, Henry Horner worked as a precinct captain for Hinky Dink Kenna and Bathhouse John Coughlin. A precinct captain may have been on the low end of the syndicate totem pole, but he would still be privy to a gritty and realistic view of syndicate politics. It was the precinct captain who doled out the favors that loyal membership in the syndicate might assure. The precinct captain would notice a hole in the sidewalk outside a merchant's store and offer to have it fixed. Later, that same precinct captain might return to the store and express his surety that the merchant would vote for the candidate favored by the syndicate. The precinct captain understood the relationship between people and power; he was aware of the gap between idealistic rhetoric about poverty and social conditions and the lived experience of the folks under his jurisdiction. As a precinct captain, Horner was called into service running errands for Kenna. He learned the way things got done in city politics; he surely saw transactions and scenes that offended his respectable nature, but he had seen enough of suffering on the streets to appreciate the street-level watch that the bosses kept on their constituents. He learned that politics was about favors and connections; it was a complicated network of alliances and debts to be paid at some unspecified future time. This was the reality of urban politics that took place in the rowdy world of the saloons, where the bosses were one of the gang and everybody had a say; the prostitute had a dollar just like the humble clerk, and they both had a voice. Perhaps Horner's affluent background and his concern for people would have made of him a perfect, passionate, white-gloved reformer had he not had this education in the reality of the streets early in his career. As it was, Horner's relationship to syndicate politics and later to machine politics was complex. But his one foot in the gutter and one foot on the sidewalk would eventually unbalance him.

After passing the bar, Horner partnered up with another young attorney, Frank A. Whitney, and they took up residence in an office in the Securities Building on Madison Street. Whitney's father, Henry Clay Whitney, had been a friend of Abraham Lincoln in the 1850s. The junior Whitney told many stories about Lincoln that fascinated Horner, who, like many in the community from which he came, had a predisposition toward Lincoln from childhood. Whitney shared with Horner some of the prized possessions of his family that reflected their intimacy with the Civil War president. Whitney's father had written a book called *Life on the Circuit with Lincoln* about the times he shared with Lincoln when they traveled the Eighth Circuit Court together through the more rural sections of Illinois in their early days as lawyers. These early exposures to Lincoln's life led Horner down a path he would never abandon. He became an avid student of Lincoln, whose humble beginnings and honest deportment he found inspiring. It could be argued that Lincoln was a greater influence on Horner than the Hinky Dinks of the city. However, they both exerted their own particular example. Reading about Lincoln familiarized Horner, who had barely traveled outside of the city, with the lifestyle, concerns, and philosophies of the rural portions of the state. This perhaps eventually contributed to his perceived ability to be a governor for the full state and helped him to cultivate downstate relationships that would save him in his hour of need.

Certainly, Horner's thorough interest in Lincoln helped to crystallize his philosophy of government. Later on, when the national tide turned toward the creation and celebration of enormously rich, powerful, and egoistic men, Horner resisted such characterizations of success. He held fast to the Lincolnian idea that government's purpose was to serve the people, and that any system that regarded one person's happiness and well-being as more important than another's was misled. Lincoln's core values also seemed to be Horner's. Lincoln once expressed his philosophy of government in this way: "I have never had a feeling, politically, that did not spring from . . . the Declaration of Independence . . . that all should have an equal chance."[6] At different periods in American history, the national mood seems to have disregarded this basic principle. During Horner's early political career, the public-servant model exemplified by Lincoln was giving way to the powerful, charismatic "boss" figure who lorded over his territory. The tyrannical and antihumanitarian character of this type would only get more pronounced as time wore on.

Kenna and Coughlin saw themselves as "lords," but they were connected to the people in their jurisdictions, and they did have a benevolent agenda running parallel to their avarice. However, as the political machine distanced itself from the streets, the rights and well-being of the people seemed beside the point. The machine came to feed only itself, and any human obstacle that appeared in its way was ground in the gears until things ran smoothly once again. Horner was never part of that machine, and while others were buying into the glamour and celebrity of the American tyrant, Horner was reading Lincoln. People who knew him remarked that he was a public servant and not a politician. This made him both stand out from the crowd of power players in the city and fade into the background at the same time, because he refused the flashy, domineering path to greatness.

Horner went on to build one of the most impressive Lincoln collections in the world, one that still graces the archives in Springfield. He entered into a network of other Lincoln enthusiasts with whom he kept in close contact. When members of this circle happened on a Lincoln artifact, even the tiniest scrap of a note from the Great Emancipator, they would call on each other to share it. Horner wrote articles about Lincoln, gave speeches about Lincoln, and counted Lincoln as the most important example for any statesman to follow.

Among the other people who were examples in his life, Horner lost two in rapid succession during his years as a young lawyer. In the year 1900, James Levy informed Horner that their father, Solomon Levy, had died of a stroke. The influence of the man on Horner had been minimal since Levy had chosen not to be a factor in the life of the sons under the care of his former wife. Nevertheless, shades of Levy can be seen in Horner's character—his sociability, his love of books and intellectual conversation, and his competence and success in the world. Perhaps more important, Horner's memory of Levy left him with a certain visceral reaction to bullying—and there were bullies galore that he would encounter in the political world of early twentieth-century Chicago.

As a model of how to be an adult and a community leader, Hannah Horner was someone he could always look to. Thus, while he did not choose to attend Solomon Levy's funeral, young Horner responded to the death of his grandmother with all the dignity and solemnity that the passing of so remarkable a woman should engender. She died suddenly while on a trip to Pasadena on February 15, 1902, when Horner was twenty-four. She had run her business with immaculate care—no receipt or other detail had passed by her unnoticed. At the same time, she had never avoided or resented her duties to the public. She had continually entered into organized and informal charity projects as if they were part of a paid commission. She had never questioned the idea that shepherding less fortunate members of the community was part of the responsibility of having a certain privileged position in society. So, through the organizations she had helped to create, Hannah Horner had given a hand up to a legion of others in need, and in doing so, had helped to build Chicago.

After the death of his grandmother, Henry Horner, his mother, and later his brother Sidney moved into an apartment on the South Side. There they lived a quiet existence, with Dilah Horner presiding over the household scene in her masterful *über*-mother way. Later, Henry Horner would say that if there was such a thing as a perfect mother, he possessed the closest to that ideal available in human form. And so, wearing his trademark pince-nez and dashing groomed moustache, the now handsome and stocky young man emerged from his home, well fed and adored, and went to his offices at the Securities Building. He stayed in partnership with Whitney, developing a close and productive working relationship until 1905, when Whitney relocated to Florida. After that, he partnered with Lloyd Charles Whitman and relocated his offices to La Salle Street. During those years, Horner specialized in real estate and probate law, and he did a great deal of collection work for the various business enterprises owned by the extended Horner family. He showed an early exuberance for receipts and the correct placement of small sums. (Years later, this would cause eyes to roll in the governor's office, but since this penny counting never went to pad his own pockets, the habit was attributed instead to a scrupulously honest nature that he sought to enforce on the world.) By this time, Horner had hired his spunky and competent young sidekick, Ella Cornwall, who would be his personal secretary throughout his career.

After-hours, if he didn't stop at the saloons to talk local politics, Horner would often drop by the Standard Club, an exclusive German Jewish social club. From Hannah Horner, he had learned the value of clubs and organizations. The Standard Club hosted many of the power players of the city. The scene consisted of cocktails and cigars, a card game, and business and political strategizing. The voices of big business boomed there. Horner was a perfect type for membership and leadership in this community. Despite his fairly spotless reputation, he was still "one of the boys," and he soon found himself a member of the board of directors. Realizing that he also needed to branch outside of Jewish circles, Horner became a Mason, cheerfully serving on committees, making phone calls, and circulating among the mixed crowd of the lodge. Many years later, he would become the grand orator of the Masonic Order and would impress everyone with his intellectual, yet impassioned, speeches. He added a variety of other clubs to his résumé throughout his career. More than simply seeing these memberships as politically or economically expedient, he seemed to genuinely enjoy the fellowship and the connections built in the social organizations. Indeed, he did not seem to have much use for solitary time. He craved company and conversation.

It was during this time that a pivotal and yet largely undocumented chapter of his life came to pass. During his twenties, Horner was viewed as a handsome young Jewish man with good prospects. Although his time was consumed with activity, one or another of his connections in the community would occasionally think of him when it came to a marriageable young woman in the family. Horner usually had little time for such awkward introductions, but when he was introduced to the seventeen-year-old daughter of a wealthy Jewish family from the town of Paris, in the east-central part of Illinois, apparently he was taken with this young woman. Perhaps the idea of a domestic life with children appealed to the solid young man who liked children and had an easy rapport with women. Whatever his motivation, he decided to marry and became engaged to the young woman from Paris. But then, as he began to consider the reality of marriage, he thought of his mother. At this time in history, a woman in her position needed to have a man in her life, and Dilah had gone through most of her life without a husband. Horner had honorably stepped in as the protector and caretaker of his mother. It was a responsibility that he took seriously, and in return, his mother lavished her maternal attention upon him. He would often admit that his mother's attention was sometimes overbearing for a grown man in his position, but he accepted it with good-natured humor. His affection for his mother was quite sincere. At the same time, he threw himself into his work and took very seriously the responsibilities of his charitable and volunteer work, such as with the Masonic Order. When he began to consider the implications of setting up a new household with a wife, he grew concerned about his ability to honor all of his commitments. Gripped in a panic over the subject, he called off the engagement. That act set the pattern for the future sacrifices he would make to keep his mind and time focused on those who depended upon him—first his mother, and then the state of Illinois. Later, though, he would admit that he deeply regretted the decision not to marry; he grieved the lost opportunity to have children and grandchildren. As an older man, he always took the opportunity to advise young colleagues to marry.

3

An Honorable Judge in the Age of Whoopee

In the early part of the twentieth century, the light issuing from the Levee was getting redder and redder. The heat was starting to scorch those who stood at a respectable distance. The Levee itself was only a few blocks square, but at its height, it held over two hundred whorehouses. Some were just dives that served a beer and an anonymous flesh exchange, but many others were extremely posh, bedecked with the stereotypical red velvet drapes and pricey antiques in elaborate drawing rooms. There, the power players of the city waited their turn for some of the city's world-renowned entertainment. The streets were lit with a red glow, and the music of the dance halls spilled out to provide a jazz age–style backdrop. People from all walks of life, emerging from chilly Victorian childhoods, were fascinated with the culture that flourished under the protection of Coughlin and Kenna. But at the same time, there was a sense of unease about the whole affair. Just where would it end? No longer were the realities of the Levee "hush-hush." The whole city could be seen watching with avid fascination what was quite a show.

The centers of the spectacle, the crowned jewels of the underworld, were the Everleigh sisters. An important footnote in the history of these times, they were the tabloid royalty of the period. Ada and Minna Everleigh were living testaments to the freedom and opportunity that could be achieved through an unhesitating embrace of vice. Having both fled in their teens from bad marriages in Omaha, they first became members of a touring vaudeville show. Later, at the young ages of twenty-one and twenty-three, the sisters took their earnings to Chicago, settled down, and invested in the world's oldest profession. At the height of their success, they operated the most exclusive brothel in the region. The Everleigh establishment seemed more a luxurious spa than a brothel, and there was a steep price to pay even to enter the doors of the tony establishment. There was a waiting list of prospective prostitutes who hoped to find employment with the Everleigh sisters. Their girls were simply the most beautiful and refined prostitutes in all of Chicago, and they were well paid for their services. The sisters themselves did not present *themselves* as prostitutes, even though that was their bread and butter. They wore fashionable but demure dresses, dotted with diamonds that the ladies of Lake Shore Drive might covet. The sisters and their establishment represented the changing status of the Levee and its relationship with "respectable" Chicago.

Evidence of the institutionalization of vice was never more obvious than at the pivotal First Ward Ball, where Bathhouse John, decked out more garishly than ever, entered the ball with an Everleigh sister on each arm, formally introducing the new royalty of the district. They then went on to preside over the most licentious, drunken, orgiastic display of partying ever seen in Chicago. The rest of the city had had enough. The reform movement was reborn, and Carter Harrison had to rethink former allegiances and his "live and let live" policy. The law practice of Horner and Whitman had prospered and kept Henry Horner quite busy, but he still managed to keep fairly abreast of the doings in Chicago. As a Harrisonite, he enjoyed close proximity to a successful mayor who served multiple terms. Like Harrison, Horner was able to dip his foot occasionally into the Sodom-like insanity of Chicago while still, on the whole, keeping his nose clean and his dignity intact. In fact, he and his mayor, perhaps the last mayor with whom he would enjoy a good relationship, had a good deal in common. They were both from privileged and respectable backgrounds, and yet they were still able to communicate with and understand the logic of the underworld of Chicago. Neither of them felt particularly ruffled by the strange world of the Levee, and yet neither seemed to be corrupted by it. But after the First Ward Ball displayed for all to see the growing audacity of the Levee's vice, Harrison could no longer associate himself with the ward bosses. He cut ties and began to work seriously with the growing reformist organizations in the city. Chicago never liked moral reformers, and so this move spelled his eventual political downfall. In his autobiography, Harrison summed up the relationship he had cultivated with the Levee in this way: "My theory in dealing with the more unsavory individuals, with whom political fate insisted on throwing me, was to exert what I had of skill and intelligence in lifting them to as high a standard of political philosophy as I might, while I held to my standards."[1]

Horner, whose tastes were more akin to Harrison's than to Hinky Dink Kenna's, also began to distance himself from the political saloon scene. Like Harrison, he had shown an ability to cheerfully coexist with a world of scoundrels and bullies, while still maintaining his good name. However, unlike Harrison, Horner did not interest himself in the reform movement. As a strict egalitarian, he felt uncomfortable with the patronizing and sometimes class-inflected tone of reform politics. If the fellow on the street wanted a drink, to bet on a race, or to have some female companionship, Horner saw no reason to interfere with him. He was not a moralist. Horner combined a good personal reputation with an ability to let others live their lives as they saw fit. This combination of a good name and a respect for the lived experience of all classes was one of the factors that differentiated him from the sea of political aspirants in a city filled with power-hungry men who dreamed of organizing the chaos to their own ends.

In the autumn of 1912, Chicago was swept into the scene of national politics. The charismatic outsider Theodore Roosevelt was leading his characteristic charge against big money and Republican orthodoxy, as embodied in the rotund personage of President William Howard Taft. The Midwest was caught up in the revolt, and a pro-Roosevelt furor had taken over the predominantly working-class city of Chicago. This left the Republican Party in Chicago in a terrible state of disorder when they were blown off track by the winds of public opinion. Roosevelt, an adventurous man's man, was poised to defeat the effete, soft, and corrupt Taft, and Chicago was cheering. Fred Lundin, a Swedish immigrant who had begun his professional career selling home-distilled spirits, began to strategize. What was needed, he reasoned, was a Republican candidate for mayor that appealed to the spirit of the times: a charismatic, manly figure that would put a new face on the Republican Party and leave the business of the brain to another, namely Fred Lundin. He found a perfect solution in the person of William Hale Thompson, who would come to enter the historical record as Big Bill Thompson of Chicago. Kenneth Allsop, in his history of gangland Chicago, pulls no punches when he describes Lundin's candidate as "that oafish and grotesque buffoon."[2] And indeed, it is difficult to understand Chicago's attraction to this man who seemed very much like Bathhouse John, but with a meaner edge and without the populist warmth.

Thompson had dropped out of school as a young man; he had no temperament for academics. Instead, he migrated to the West, where he initially worked as a brakeman on the Union Pacific Railroad. Throughout his career, he characterized himself as a former cowboy, but the truth was that he had been employed as a ranch cook. However, as a teenager, he did learn to use a lariat and to shoot a gun, and he drank in the colorful language and the swagger of the Wild West. He wasn't a cowboy long; he migrated back to Chicago just a few years later, while still in his teens, but he savored his newfound "cowboy personality." All through his career, he would act as if he learned to handle a saddle before he learned to walk. Big Bill grew into a tall, increasingly obese man with slack lips and absolutely no ability to edit his thoughts before he spoke them. The result was that his position on issues changed in each situation in which he found himself. This habit had one advantage: he was always able to tell his audience what they wanted to hear. When Big Bill Thompson came on the scene as a newcomer in 1915, Chicago was in for a big change.

Thompson entered politics like a shadow of World War I, sweeping into the city that had long teetered on the edge between innocent oversight of the law and dangerous corruption. With Thompson, Chicago plunged over the edge into darkness. At the time, the spoils system was in disarray, having suffered under the influence of reformist mayor Carter H. Harrison, and more and more corrupt legislators and council members had been replaced by honorable ones. Lundin set about taking over what remained of the spoils system, reviving it, and deepening its impact on the average citizen. Under Mayor Thompson, Chicago went through a period of rapid growth. A personal friend of Al Capone throughout his career, Thompson maintained a close relationship with the leaders of the underworld as well as the scions of industry. He took up with great enthusiasm the inventive practices of Chicago's famous political syndicate. It was a prosperous era, and people were loath to look too closely into the forces behind such prosperity. The power of a good name in the city was now questionable.

Both Carter H. Harrison and Henry Horner had good names and would have to decide how they would fit into the new Chicago. A pivotal moment in Horner's career resulted from a conversation with Jacob Lindheimer. This German Jew from Stuttgart begun as a saloon owner, but quickly worked his way up to a prominent position in the banking industry. Lindheimer became as close to a father figure as Henry Horner ever had. Early in his career, Horner was elected to the position of south Chicago tax collector. This position was an inconspicuous note in his career, since the position was abolished before he could occupy it, but it was, nonetheless, significant because he met Lindheimer, who was the incumbent in that position. Lindheimer was impressed by the young attorney and soon took Horner under his wing and welcomed him into his family circle. Always keeping the career of the young Henry Horner in his thoughts, Lindheimer watched out for opportunities. And when it came time to nominate candidates for the judgeship of the Cook County Probate Court, it occurred to Lindheimer that it could be Horner's time.

The young lawyer was well liked and had good connections. Protective of his religious community, Lindheimer reasoned that it would be good to see a Jew occupy the post. He proposed to Horner that he should run for the position and pledged his support. Long attracted by the good that could be accomplished in public service, Horner immediately liked the idea and threw his hat into the ring for probate judge of Cook County without hesitation.

In the primary, Horner had a formidable opponent in Michael F. Sullivan, the first assistant state attorney. Even though Horner's qualifications were unquestionable, many assumed that he would not win. However, the Irish vote was split among Sullivan and two candidates named Cobern and McEnerny, and in the final outcome, Horner secured the nomination. He threw himself into campaigning and was at ease shuttling about the city to meet with prominent and influential people, making his characteristic good impression, and elevating his visibility in the city. He also tried his hand at populist stumping for votes. And of course, he stopped in at the First Ward. At the Silver Dollar Saloon, he was placed on a ticket that included a variety of Democratic candidates and party leaders. There, he heard a speech by an up-and-coming young figure on the political scene, county legislator Anton J. Cermak, who represented the United Societies for Local Self-Government, an anti-Prohibition organization. Horner was convinced by the young man's stance on the liquor question and was also impressed by Cermak's forthright delivery. After this meeting, Horner and Cermak would go on to become political allies in the city for some time.

When it came time for Horner to address the rowdy saloon crowd, he may not have felt entirely in his element. But he quickly absorbed the spirit of the occasion and displayed his talent for "talking straight" and adapting himself to any crowd. On this occasion, and many others like it, Horner sounded less like a Lincoln scholar and the grandson of a grocery magnate, and more like a bartender wiping down the bar and talking plain sense to the patrons. But he was not playacting or being insincere. Horner would demonstrate throughout his life that he valued people. In their faces, he could see stories, dreams, and material existences. He was unable to turn a sea of faces into a massive prop for his own advancement. Thus, as a candidate, he communicated with each of his audiences in an authentic way. People felt it. That evening, he gave a necessary nod to the political organization, continuing to make his own uneasy peace with the corruption of street-level politics: "What I learned of the practical politics of the city, I learned in the First Ward organization, and I am not afraid to say that I don't care what the men who criticize the democracy of the First Ward say about it." But then he went on to express the basic philosophy that would characterize his entire career: "One thing I learned here is that there is something bigger in politics than holding office. Something bigger than four-flushing about platforms and running after newspaper notoriety in the quest for public acclaim. That thing that is bigger is the true friendly interest of your fellow men."[3]

Because Horner did seem to be motivated by a "true friendly interest" in all his dealings, he had enormous appeal as a candidate. The order of the day for politicians was a commanding presence, a flashy charisma, and a good splash of aggression. Horner's appeal was not of the "big" variety, like the bravado of Thompson or the gangster "Big Jim" Colosimo; nor was he destined to be nicknamed "the Boss." But his "friendly interest" turned out to be more powerful than "the club."

Horner's appeal wasn't all idealism and authenticity. He was also a smart interpreter of the political scene, and he knew the priorities of the First Ward. He needed to give a nod to those priorities without throwing himself entirely into the mix of good-time scoundrels. The residents of the First Ward had seen less of Horner in recent times than in the past, but they did not harbor a grudge against him or feel betrayed by him like they did Harrison. They still remembered the young man as a loyal precinct captain for Kenna and were proud of his success. He paid homage to them in his speech, and his studied mention of respect for "practical politics" showed them that they would not be victims of idealistic reform at his hands. Later in the speech, Horner invoked a "battle cry" for "personal liberty," which, of course, the inhabitants of the Levee took to mean that drinkers, gamblers, and prostitutes would be free to pursue their own particular version of happiness in the city.

Another wise move by Horner was to loosely associate himself with the anti-Prohibition forces of the city. On the same evening that he addressed the First Ward, he introduced himself to Anton Cermak and vowed to keep the man in mind. He had been influenced by what Cermak had said in his speech. While Horner sympathized with the working class, he could not always see their side of things, and Cermak had opened a window through which the future judge could see the issue of Prohibition more clearly. Horner and Cermak would work in concert in the future, but the power dynamic between them would be quite different.

During the same election period, Carter H. Harrison was not having an easy time balancing his own principles of leadership with the prevailing political order. He was torn between the necessities of his own political survival and the pressure from "respectable" Chicago to stop turning a blind eye toward the Chicago underworld. He incorrectly assessed the climate and determined that it was time for change and that the lords of the Levee would soon be demoted. His administration had begun to institute some crackdowns on vice in the city. These early attempts at reform were met with a decisive political backlash. His betrayal of the syndicate that had boosted him led to a steep decline in his popularity. In his bid to run the city for a sixth term, he was defeated in the primary by County Clerk Robert M. Sweitzer. Perhaps it was lucky for the sensitive Harrison that he did not enter into combat for the mayorship with Big Bill Thompson. Any candidate up against Big Bill could expect to get verbally roughed up. Thompson felt no qualms about employing personal, racial, and religious invectives to stir up the uneasy melting pot of Chicago to his advantage. He was a successful, populist rhetorician who would have quickly overpowered the intellectual and genteel Harrison. The *Chicago Tribune* described Thompson in this way: "His old fashioned boon talk is loosely expressed and not carefully thought-out, but his listeners like it!"

It seemed that the bootlegger-Svengali Fred Lundin had found the perfect candidate. Although Thompson was a political nobody who mouthed irrational campaign rhetoric like a drunken sailor, it seemed to be Big Bill's time in Chicago. He was also lucky that the Harrison supporters, bitter about the loss to Sweitzer, threw their support his way.

Thompson's penchant for tossing out meaningless and extravagant promises also tapped into the hopes of the city's black population, which was desperate for things to change for them in the city. Thompson originally came to the notice of Fred Lundin through his association with the Billy Lorimer wing of the Republican Party. Lorimer will go down in history for having organized one of the most corrupt party organizations in history, and it seemed clear that Big Bill would not try to clean things up. Charles Merriam describes the Lorimer system that Thompson helped to sustain as an "organization resting upon patronage and spoils, and flanked by the support of predatory business interests."[5] A vote for Big Bill Thompson was a vote for the Lorimer system of corruption and big money, a Republican ethos that stood in sharp contrast to the ultimately egalitarian social welfare organization of Kenna and Coughlin.

And so, with Harrison finished in local politics, Big Bill Thompson took his seat in the mayor's office. At the same time, Henry Horner found a comfortable seat at the Cook County Probate Court. There, he would reign during the prime of his life, fortunate to escape bullying by Big Bill, who probably could not be bothered with the more practical workings of his government that Horner represented. Horner, now thirty-five years old, found himself in a black robe that seemed a perfect fit. He was a gentleman of hearty tastes, well fed and in good health, but with a tendency to overwork, and his eyes reflected that. And yet, there was a spark of excitement in him. As Judge Henry Horner, presiding over the Cook County Probate Court, he observed the people of Chicago parade past his bench day after day, and with them would come some very fascinating stories. He would leaf through their wills and hear from mistresses demanding recognition. He would reassure orphans before his bench, and with a flourish of his pen, would afford them all the solid protection that could be offered by the law. His life would be filled with grateful widows showering him with the kind of female attention that he so craved throughout his life. On their behalf, he would pick up the phone to make use of the vast network of friendships and alliances that he had created as a young lawyer. It was his world, to rule scrupulously and meticulously. He had learned that the people approved of him and would not try to impose their will upon him. After all, who would concern themselves with wills and deeds and taxes when the city was in a scramble to stay wet? Let the judge scratch in his ledger.

The probate court under Henry Horner was the perfect union of man and occupation. First of all, the court represented a huge administrative undertaking that few could be more qualified to oversee than Horner. An enormous flow of money was organized and distributed in the court. Phillip Bregstone, a contemporary of Horner's who documented his distinguished career in a history of Chicago's notable Jews, noted, "It is estimated that the entire wealth of the county passes through that channel on an average of once every fifteen years."

When Horner was a lawyer in partnership with Whitman, many private concerns had come to rely on his honesty to track and organize their wealth. Like his grandmother, who scrutinized her accounts even from her maternity bed, Horner saw the significance of the mundane details of accounting. He monitored the funds that came through the probate court with a watchful eye. The importance of that practice during his judgeship cannot be overemphasized. At that time, opportunities for graft provided by studied administrative neglect greased the political machine of Chicago. All the budgets were puffed up, and this excess padded a profusion of pockets. Phony money trails zigzagged through the ledgers of the city. Payrolls were fudged creatively, while those in charge applied their wits to brazen "book cooking." Saloons vibrated with laughter at the anecdote of "Miss L. C. Smith," who was on the city payroll for many weeks until it was discovered that "Miss Smith" was actually a typewriter and not a typist.[7] But the probate court was not the territory of grafters and saloon bosses. At the probate court, Henry Horner was the protector of widows and orphans. He slew the dragons that threatened them—not with a sword, but with an account ledger and a sympathetic ear.

Being a social individual to the extreme, Horner enjoyed the lively parade of families and their stories that marched through his courtroom. His work brought out the philosopher in him. Dealing with what human beings made in life and what they left behind in death caused him to consider the nature of achievement and mortality. He saw how relatives squabbled over the fortunes left by family members, while attorneys and court fees ate them up, and he learned that the relationships that were left behind were the most permanent record of those lives. From the bitterness and greed that followed one person's death, versus the carefully planned security of the family that followed another's, Horner began to formulate his philosophy of life. Perhaps it was his experience in the probate court that helped him to continue to see through the allure of wealth and to concentrate on public service. During World War I, his work took on a melancholy significance when he settled the estates of soldiers killed on the front. He saw his role as the defender of widows who had already suffered a terrible blow, and he redesigned the probate procedure to minimize the pain and inconvenience for war widows and also for wives whose shell-shocked or injured husbands could no longer oversee their own affairs. The usually affable judge became a bear on their behalf. He convinced undertakers, lawyers, and bankers to scale down their charges or to provide free services to veterans' families so they would be able to build a new life. His work during the war era did much to endear him to Chicago's people.

Judge Horner thought of his position at the Cook County Probate Court as more of an art than a science. He did not process papers mechanically and looked for ways to make the system work for people. He used his administrative skills to make sure that no one in his courtroom was getting fleeced. He handled the money of those in his court with extreme care and always tried to assure that people were given a fair deal in trying times. Aware that lawyers had a tendency to pad bills and to do "creative" accounting, Horner required full reports of financial dispositions from them. His meticulousness about financial matters made the probate court a refuge from corruption. However, he also knew when to gloss over the details as well. He was ready to dispense with bureaucracy when it threatened the well-being of the survivors before him. He gained a reputation for his scrupulous honesty and attention to detail. He also enjoyed the dramatic spectacle of the courtroom, which included some of the most scandalous stories in Chicago. He oversaw cases involving phony wills and forged letters; he watched mistresses from the red light district tussle with wives from respectable Lake Shore Drive to control the fortunes of departed businessmen; he heard bastard sons declare themselves the secret heirs to fortunes. For a person who enjoyed the endless mysteries of human nature, the probate court was a lively place to preside. Horner tried to remain a sane and objective observer and handled the money of those in his court with extreme care to assure that people were given a fair deal in trying times.

Perhaps Horner's lack of family life allowed him to create some sort of a family out of the whole town of Chicago. The number of his club memberships only increased over time. He joined the Chicago Literary Club, had lunch on Wednesdays with a club called the Bandarlogs, and on Saturday met with the Skeeters. These clubs brought together influential men in a wide variety of disciplines, including leaders of industry, politicians, artists, writers, religious leaders, academics, and other types of men who enjoyed Scotch, bridge, and conversation. Horner created a vast map of associations and was regularly welcomed for dinner or drinks at the homes of wealthy and influential people. As the years passed, the middle-aged bachelor judge became a particular favorite of the wives of his associates. He valued the friendships of these ladies as much as he did the fellowship of their husbands. Although he had decided that as long as he still had his mother he would not marry, Horner did have romantic involvements with various women. Yet, he knew that as a public figure he had to comport himself with discretion, and he never attracted scandal. He still lived with his mother, Dilah, and his brother Sidney, and from time to time he expressed some good-natured exasperation at not being seen as an adult by his mother, who coddled her sons tremendously. Horner told one of his acquaintances, "You never grow up in your mother's eyes. My mother still considers me a little boy."[8]

Although Horner had not developed a relationship with his father, he did stay in close contact with his brother James, who had been a champion bicyclist in his youth and went on to make a great deal of money in the automobile industry. James became a well-known figure in Chicago; he owned a number of car dealerships, including a Buick dealership on Michigan Avenue. The third brother, Sidney, was educated in Paris and later went into the picture frame business. Sidney was known for being an adventuresome individualist.

At the Literary Club, Horner made a splash when he used his profession as the inspiration for a literary project. He wrote a novella in which a deceased soul, who belongs to a club called "The Restless Ashes," is forced to resign from his position when his case has finally been successfully investigated and settled in probate court. The events in probate court often did seem to be the perfect fodder for fiction or Hollywood drama. The personal business of powerful individuals often comes spilling out after death. When heirs line up to claim what they believe to be rightfully theirs, the intrigue that follows is often dramatic and compelling. This drama was part of what Horner enjoyed about the job. He also became quite a fan of the movie industry. He never missed out on the offerings of the local cinema and even made some connections in Hollywood. He was extremely busy, but his life was filled with activities he enjoyed.

With Big Bill as mayor (1915–23), Chicago outdid its own reputation for brash lawlessness. The mayor was unpredictable from the start. There seemed to be no logic to his pronouncements. And so, after winning on a platform that included a "wide open" policy toward alcohol sales and consumption in the city, Thompson's first act as mayor was to cave in to the anticrime activists and close the saloons on Sundays. At this time, the city was feeling increasing pressure from Prohibition supporters to implement dry laws. The most polarizing and central issue in the city was alcohol. The city was divided into the "drys" and the "wets," and Thompson, lacking any understanding of the matter, did not quite know which camp to join. And so, he got caught up in the glamour and the rhetoric of the anticrime movement and ordered the enforcement of the Sunday laws. Bathhouse John sounded the alarm in the Levee by writing an impassioned song about saloons closing on Sundays, and it was clear that the wets were going to work themselves into a fury over the issue. Anton Cermak, representing the United Societies group, paid a visit to Thompson. He enlightened the mayor on the views of the foreign-born voters of the city for whom a Sunday drink was an integral part of the pursuit of happiness after a grueling workweek. He also used his clout as a legislator to suggest that the mayor would have quite a struggle with Springfield if he made moves that seemed to ease the way for Prohibition into the city. Such a position, he told Thompson, would be at odds with the plans of the General Assembly, which was shoring up the state for the expected assault upon their saloons. Not having really thought out the issue in the first place, Thompson quickly forgot about the Sunday ban on alcohol sales.

After his first misstep as a moralist, Thompson did have some success that fueled his popularity. Early into his reign, he successfully settled a big streetcar strike that appeared particularly threatening to the city. At this time, the streets were chaotic and seemed to be vibrating with hair-trigger nerves. Thompson's brash machismo was sometimes effective in this context. He abandoned the course of the reformer and began to enthusiastically contribute to the cultural decay of the city. He was regularly involved in scandals concerning gambling houses and brothels and cultivated friendships with the Italian mafia. He held Big Jim Colosimo's hand as the man ascended the ladder of power in the city, eventually eclipsing Hinky Dink Kenna and Bathhouse John Coughlin. Later, he became deeply involved in and accountable to the Capone empire. He paved the way for the syndicate to be taken over by leaders who won their posts through violence rather than by merely paying for votes. He cut the funding for the Morals Division of city government and then followed up by abolishing it altogether. He did everything in his power to thwart crime-fighting and moralistic reform in the city.

Big Bill Thompson, by virtue of his being so very bad, motivated the women's organizations in the city to put the wheels of a "good-government" movement in motion. The temperance movement had long been the province of a small but active minority. Initially, it was a variety of women's organizations that linked the problems of abandoned and mistreated wives and their hungry and abused children to the issue of drinking among working-class men. These men, it was argued, spent their money and time in the saloons rather than in taking care of their families. And when they returned from the saloons, drunk and belligerent, they were more apt to mistreat their families. The dry movement, at this stage, had little political might. However, during World War I, the drys attached their movement to the sort of xenophobic nationalism that often asserts itself in wartime. Liquor interests, the drys argued, were German. To drink a beer was to give a penny to the Germans. The ethnic make-up of the saloon crowd only enhanced the perception that the wets were serving a foreign master. And so, those who equated abstinence with patriotism leaned toward Prohibition during wartime. By the time Prohibition became an actual amendment to the constitution, however, the perception that alcohol interests were foreign and a threat to the United States had largely died down. Now, it was quite popular and acceptable to be wet. It was estimated that on the eve of Prohibition, Chicago was an overwhelmingly wet town—three to one, in fact. But the wheels were already in motion.

On the morning of January 16, 1920, Chicagoans opened their eyes to a city in which they could no longer have a cocktail legally. The Volstead Act had become law. The era of Prohibition had begun, and the reorganization of power in the spirits industry would cut deep into Chicago's culture. The criminalization of the production, sale, and transportation of alcohol was just the door needed to transfer the power from the ward bosses to the thugs on the street. Big Jim Colosimo took control of the alcohol traffic in the city. The innocent days of saloon politics, vote buying, and kickbacks that had characterized the Kenna and Coughlin era were quickly replaced by gunfights in the streets and a level of corruption that was much more threatening. And still, Horner's life in probate court remained steady and enjoyable. His proximity to the underworld of Chicago waned, and perhaps he was less aware of the internal changes in the "practical politics" of the city. However, his broad network of friendships and associations across the professions of Chicago must have hummed with discussions about the impact of Prohibition upon the city. He surely felt the tension when the petty thugs on the streets began to be seen about town in well-tailored suits with gold glinting around their fingers and about their necks. But Chicago was still a backdrop that inspired hope and excitement for a man interested in the world outside his window. Change was rapid in the city, and there was always the expectation that something good might be around the corner. Even in a social order enforced by gunfire could a man carve a space to make his way in the world.

It wasn't until January 8, 1921, that Horner truly had to confront the consequences of his choice to remain a bachelor. On that date, his mother died of complications from diabetes, and Horner was entirely on his own at age forty-two. He took up residence in an apartment in Madison Park. His new apartment was very much a bachelor's place—he had Lincoln busts and books scattered throughout the rooms and a parrot, about which he liked to tell amusing anecdotes to friends in the club. In his self-deprecating sense of humor, Horner cast himself as the parrot-pecked pet owner rather than a henpecked husband. He kept himself occupied with an overwhelming array of responsibilities in his elected position within the court and with his political work in the Democratic Party. He also might have felt a little freedom from the responsibilities of a devoted son and embraced the opportunity to fully taste adulthood. He stepped out on the town a bit more and, it has been said, enjoyed the company of local singers and actresses. After the death of their mother, his brother Sidney, disgusted with Prohibition, liquidated his modest assets and returned to Paris to live a different and rather bohemian life.

Throughout his first two terms, Big Bill Thompson blundered along, dipping and rising in the esteem of the public, as it responded to his unpredictable behavior. In a city fueled by crisis, he sometimes hit the mark with his forceful personality or sounded the right indignant note about some public abuse. At other times, the papers crucified him for an ill-considered remark and continually charged that he had links with notorious gangsters. It was generally known that his character was about as solid as Swiss cheese, and there at last came a time when the public seemed to care about such issues.

Big Bill finally felt the brunt of the good-government movement when one of its candidates, William Dever, defeated him in 1923. The city, it appeared, had had enough of its corrupt leader. And Mayor Dever did improve the civic standards of Chicago to a small degree. However, he had a formidable job ahead of him. Thanks in large part to Prohibition, the city was in the impossible grip of gangland power. It was the era of the "Big Fix" in Chicago, and it would take more than a well-meaning leader to combat that. Fletcher Dobyns, writing as an apologist for his fellow reformer Mayor Dever, suggests that his efforts were undercut when the Democratic machine "saw to it that Dever's hands would be tied so completely that while he led the people in prayer in the front room, Tammany could escape unmolested by the back door with the silver and the jewelry."[9]

The "Big Fix" was the nickname for the organization within the underworld of Chicago that gained its power when it wrapped its tentacles around the upper world and squeezed. What had been an informal syndicate under Kenna and Coughlin became an iron web controlled by ruthless gangsters. The system included both graft and protection. The graft included the siphoning off of public funds through every avenue imaginable—padded payrolls, phony city contracts, bribery of officials and law enforcement, and the "cooking" of innumerable ledgers in the city. Protection generated additional revenue. Every bootlegger, pickpocket, burglar, shoplifter, stick-up man, confidence man, safe-blower, and gambler paid the syndicate for protection. If they should run into trouble with the law, a professional "fixer" stepped in. Businesses paid for protection from violence and the destruction of property. The lord of this new organization was Big Jim Colosimo, but he was murdered in May of 1920 and replaced by Johnny Torrio, who himself would lose the mantle of power to Al Capone. The old syndicate had been corrupt, yes; but it had been organized, in part, to support a benevolent defense fund. This core purpose of the syndicate shifted radically with the change in leadership during the Prohibition era. Now the driving force was the economic interest of a few corrupt individuals who became wealthy to a degree that greatly overshadowed the boodle-induced wealth of the city aldermen.

When Mayor Dever began his term, he displayed a lack of understanding of gangland culture. The wets were still a strong political force in the city. Politicians tried to outdo each other with rhetoric about the Eighteenth Amendment. The mayor had a certain degree of power to determine how strictly the alcohol restrictions in the city were enforced, and the wets were unsure about Dever. Did his good-government stance mean that he would side with the drys? To mollify the powerful wets, Dever initially pushed through an ordinance that would weaken the enforcement of alcohol restrictions in the city. However, in doing so, he created chaos in the underworld bootleg business and inadvertently started a bloody gang war. After this initial debacle, he followed up with a number of actions and statements that led the people of Chicago to believe that he was really a dry. In crossing the majority of the citizens of Chicago who despised Prohibition, he created an opening for Big Bill Thompson to crawl back through.

Formerly a floater on the issue of Prohibition, Thompson returned in 1927 proclaiming that he was "wetter than the Atlantic Ocean."

He also employed a bizarre campaign plank called "America First," in which he tried to ride on the nationalistic sentiment brought about by the world war. He interpreted nationalism in an odd way, and hearkening back to the American Revolution, he reasoned that the greatest threat to American freedom and culture was the British aristocracy. He regularly threw anti-British invective into his campaigning. Such outdated rhetoric meant little to a city fed up with Prohibition, and still he went on to win the election. However, after the election, he launched an assault on the University of Chicago library and tried to get all books that reflected a British influence removed from the shelves. Horrified by his censorious and anti-intellectual behavior, academics brandished their weapon of choice, the pen, very aggressively against him. He was deeply embarrassed when he found out that the British monarchy had actually benevolently donated a great many of the books to a predecessor school that later became the University of Chicago after the school's collections were decimated by the fire of 1871. A wave of biting and sarcastic lampoons of the mayor's "America First" activities followed. It was apparent that the city that had elected Thompson was getting tired of his antics and of the way power was handled by the flamboyant bullies of Chicago. But as John Bright points out in his profile of Thompson, "he had been elected mayor of Chicago before the storm of laughter broke, and mayor he will remain until 1931."[11]

4

The Bottom Drops Out

Chicago may have been full of hoodlums, and someone occasionally may have had to mop the stain of blood off the sidewalk, but the 1920s were good times for most people. The country was beginning to see some real returns on the American dream, and the opportunities for spinning wealth out of the industrial machine seemed endless. Mass production was feeding a frenzy of optimism and greed. The assembly lines were pouring out products, and the new, cynical field of advertising began setting the tone for the country by selling the idea of American invincibility. Everything seemed possible. The war had come and gone, and what was bad for Europe was often good for America. If they didn't have potatoes over there, why, America could grow them and ship them over there. The lifestyle of the American family was transformed and improved, seemingly overnight. Indoor bathrooms took the place of latrines. Buggies were pushed aside by Ford beauties snaking down the street. Overworked housewives now found themselves with a little more free time on their hands with the help of new appliances—vacuum cleaners, sewing machines—every week a new gadget, it seemed. Voices magically traveled through telephone wires, and radios kept people company around the fire. People gathered in jubilant fascination to witness a new form of mass entertainment: Motion pictures gave them the images out of which they crafted their own new dreams. Industrialists in Chicago and across the country were making millions, and people didn't mind dancing in their shadows. A new form of music, thick in the dance halls and the dive clubs, spilled out onto the streets. It set a rhythm for the feet of Chicagoans. It was a time to let loose a little and have a drink, so much the sweeter for being illegal. Queen Victoria was long gone, and people were feeling sensations that had long been subdued.

Of course, not all Americans were experiencing prosperity. Many were still unable to save anything for a rainy day, let alone to invest, farmers were still struggling not only in Illinois but throughout the country, and not everyone could afford to buy all the new products advertised and glamorized in the motion pictures. But there was a feeling of hope in the air. The culture went through radical changes, worshiping anything new and dismissing with disdain anything that seemed old-fashioned or stuffy. The new haircut was the bob, and it seemed symbolic of a country that had shed half of itself in a frenzy of transformation. But like a haircut, much of the prosperity of the times was more symbolic and speculative than real.

During the 1920s, many came to believe that one need do little else but play the stock market to get rich. More and more people clamored to get involved in trading securities, yet no more than 7–8 percent of the population owned stocks in that decade. Most of the profits made were dumped right back into the market in a frenzy to create more wealth. The stock market ballooned as the nation poured its hopes into the American economy. Those who were too poor to invest in the stock market were also caught up in the spirit of conspicuous consumption. There were so many new products to buy, and if you didn't have any money, why not buy on credit? Surely, even better times were right around the corner. People of modest means thrust themselves deeper and deeper in debt, naive about the nature of credit and debt but wanting to experience the great cultural change that seemed promised in new material goods. Everyone seemed too filled with an optimistic, materialistic greed to see the warning signs. Wholesale prices peaked and then fell sharply, consumption and production stalled, and unemployment began to rise. In October of 1929, the bubble burst. When stock prices hit bottom on the twenty-third, investors went into a panic, dumping stocks in a mad dash to preserve what they could of their wealth. Those investors who had bought on margin, thinking the market would continue to be bullish, were financially ruined with the collapse of prices on the market.

The Jazz Age, alternately nicknamed the Roaring Twenties, had been an age of conspicuous consumption and the pursuit of pleasure. The fashionable personality traits were wit, cynicism, sophistication, and a certain brazen disregard for others. That was Fitzgerald's Chicago. It was also the Chicago of flashy sloganeers like Big Bill Thompson, who were undoubtedly influenced by the glamorous, empty rhetoric of advertising. However, that persona soon became unpopular, and diligent men with compassion, good judgment, and common sense would be most sought after. Henry Horner had not been dancing at parties with the fashionable set. He had not become alienated with privilege and did not suffer from boredom. And he had not expatriated himself abroad. That way of life wasn't in his background. However, it was soon to be his era. His particular set of characteristics would be just what the 1930s demanded. Horner was now a seasoned veteran on the bench, and though he worked hard and had not turned himself over to the aimless gaiety of the era, the 1920s had been good to him. He was establishing a very sound reputation in Chicago, being elected to term after term as probate court judge, and winning each election by a larger margin. Very few of the power grabbers around town dared to cross him. His decisions were inviolable, and he did not violate the trust the city put in him. He was also becoming known as one of the most ardent Lincoln scholars and historians in the state. Governor Louis Emmerson called upon him to help mark historical sites related to Lincoln, to dedicate statues and memorials to Illinois's most famous son around the state, and to speak frequently on the subject of Lincoln.

Horner also took the time to establish himself as a political force beyond the probate courts. However, rather than focusing strictly on candidates and reelections, he threw his support behind numerous causes in the city. He was especially concerned with the vulnerable people of the city, including children, and lobbied for better care in state institutions. In 1926, the legislature voted a raise for judges, and in his characteristically nonmaterialistic style, Horner turned over his raise to a new organization serving the needs of children—the Institute for Juvenile Research.

As the 1920s were coming to a close, Horner stepped out onto the streets of a different Chicago. The most immediate result of the stock market crash was a sudden wave of joblessness, as a large percentage of industry seemed to go under overnight. People set off for work with their lunchboxes tucked under their arms, only to confront boarded up windows with terse explanations scrawled on hastily made signs. The sidewalks were crowded with men with tense faces, milling about with unexpected time on their hands. The newly unemployed lined up outside office doors, chasing rumors of an available job. The men sang sad songs to amuse themselves as they waited. They joked hesitantly with each other on the streets and shared news of plant closings and job leads. The men who had once been respectable breadwinners were becoming unshaven and a little grimy. Some of them turned to drinking and rowdy behavior, their anger spilling out threateningly onto the streets. As time wore on, more and more women were joining the men in their aimless wandering in the city. Many of them had husbands who were now deeply entrenched in unemployment and who stayed at home to watch the baby while they went out to search for work as typists or laundresses in a hotel. Like the men, the women formed lines, uneasy and uncertain about taking on a perilous new role. But what really pierced Horner to the core was the children. The sight of children, unkempt and gaunt, wandering the streets alone, huddled against stoops, begging for pennies—these were the images that would long motivate him.

The mood of the city had changed. As Chicago began to slide into the Great Depression, the attitude toward organized crime shifted. With jobs having evaporated into thin air and the public coffers strained by a taxation crisis and by the huge relief burden, all eyes trained on the stuffed pockets of organized crime. Throughout the 1920s, the gangsters of the underworld had been accustomed to throwing around money in a display of arrogance and insensitivity. Al Capone himself frittered millions on gambling and regularly plunked down a thousand dollars for a round of drinks at a high-priced club. Kenneth Allsop notes that Capone "distributed diamond-inlet belts to his new friends and ruby-set gold cigarette cases to politicians and business associates, whose cellars were also kept stocked with wine and champagne."[1] So, when the Depression seized the city, desperate youth, who might have stayed on the straight and narrow in better times, looked to the mafia organizations for a promise of a better life. Gangster fortunes also went to set up the first soup kitchens in Chicago and to help finance various charitable organizations. But at the same time, the rapid expansion of organized crime destabilized the dynasties that had once held things in check. When rival gangland factions heated up their competition to control the city that seemed to lie at their feet, Chicago found itself at the mercy of a continual round of gang wars.

The gangland-war era reached the pinnacle of spectacle and publicity with the St. Valentine's Day Massacre of 1929. Bugs Moran, a rival of Al Capone, had been alerted that a truck full of hijacked whiskey was going to arrive at one of their secret warehouses on Clark Street on the morning of February 14, 1929. The morning was cold and wintry when members of Moran's gang gathered at the warehouse for the rendezvous. Bugs Moran himself was late in arriving. Five men got out of a car, several of them wearing police uniforms, and entered the warehouse. Moran slipped away. Witnesses reported hearing the sound of machinegun fire and then seeing five men leave. The men left behind a gruesome murder scene. Moran's men had been lined up against the wall and cut down in a barrage of gunfire. The press went wild. Moran attributed the killings to Al Capone, who was in Florida at the time. The city of Chicago had been fascinated by the exploits of their new gangland "celebrities," especially the flashy Capone. However, this bloodbath was just too much for the public to take, and Capone's reputation in the city began to take a nosedive. The glamour was wearing thin, as people worn down by the

Depression found their city reduced to a war zone and their young men increasingly the casualties.

In the meantime, Big Bill Thompson continued to cement his relationship with organized crime, which further eroded his popularity. At the turn of the decade, the two most vilified specters of the city were Capone and Prohibition. Seeing himself inextricably entangled with the first, Thompson did some purely symbolic photo-ops with the police force. However, he concentrated on the second, feeding the public frenzy over Prohibition with increasingly nonsensical rhetoric. He tried to resurrect his failed "America First" movement by claiming that Prohibition was pro-American and anti-British. He proclaimed, "Bourbon has increased in price from a dollar fifty to fifteen dollars a bottle, and King George's rum-running fleet, 800 miles long, lies twelve miles off our coast, so every time you take up a drink you say 'Here's to the King!'"[2] By this time, Thompson seemed to have totally lost his grip on reality. Faced with reelection, he was a drowning candidate who hurled insults to save his life. For example, in a public speech, he attacked Edward Litsinger, now a detractor but formerly a friend, by proclaiming, "Ed Litsinger lived back of the gashouse and when he moved to the north side he left his old mother behind!" Unfortunately for Thompson, Litsinger's sister was in the audience. She stood up and shouted, "Mayor Thompson, you are a liar! My mother died twenty years ago, before my brother moved!"[3] After the woman stormed out, Thompson continued on, seemingly unfazed by the challenge to the veracity of his accusations. While the Republican Party reeled under the embarrassing example of their mayor, the Democrats were getting their candidates prepared for the upcoming election.

During Thompson's term, Anton Cermak had been rising in the ranks of the Democratic Party. And when it came time to fill the slate for the 1931 election, Cermak was the top party man. He filled the slate and organized the campaigns, and the result was a resounding triumph for the Democrats. Cermak had proven himself to be an imposing force on the political scene. Here was a gruff, intimidating man who was completely self-made and who took the business of politics very seriously. When it was decided that Cermak himself would go up against Thompson, the physical similarities between the two men were evident. Both were strikingly large men, though Cermak was muscular and imposing, while Thompson's undisciplined habits had rendered him rather slatternly and obese. But these seeming likenesses were soon overshadowed by their very different political personalities.

Anton Cermak was an infant when he and his parents emigrated from Bohemia to America in 1874. They settled in Braidwood, Illinois, a town just sixty-five miles southwest of Chicago. The family struggled economically, surviving primarily off of their little plot of land where they farmed a mere half acre and kept a pig, a cow, and some chickens. Cermak's father also worked irregularly in the coal mines. The young "A. J.," as he was called, was given some responsibilities on the farm. However, he often sneaked off to go fishing with his friends and, later, to visit "Whiskey Row," where hardworking coal miners gathered to find some relief from their difficult existence and share some social communion. Like many of his contemporaries in the Bohemian sector of Braidwood, Cermak managed to accumulate only a wisp of an education. His attendance was very poor, and like many of his friends in the neighborhood, he managed only about two years of public school education before he dropped out to follow that path into the coal mines that seemed destined for him. But Cermak was a little different than other boys his age. For one thing, he broke out of the ethnic bubble of the Bohemian boys and made friends with a couple of Irish boys in the neighborhood who had previously taunted him. As a result of this new friendship, he changed his circle of friends and became the lone Bohemian member of an Irish gang of boys—and what's more, he became their undisputed leader. Indeed, in every group that A. J. Cermak joined, he soon found himself at the top.

When A. J. was twelve years old, his family moved to Chicago to try to make a better living and saved him from having to go to work in the coal mines. There his father got a job in the lumber business. A. J. also worked in a sash and doorframe mill, but again, he seemed more interested in leading the neighborhood gang of boys. He and his friends were only thugs of the lightest variety—a little vandalism here and there and some mild hooligan behavior—but it was roundly acknowledged that A. J. came up with the schemes. He was disheartened when his family returned to Braidwood before he could really establish himself as a wild Chicago youth, and now he had no choice but to go to work in the coal mines. He got a job opening and closing the trap doors that led into the coal pits and then moved into the mines as he gained a more manly physique. Only seventeen years old, he nevertheless adopted the miner's tavern lifestyle. When he drank, he was known to become mean and aggressive. He did some brawling and spent a few isolated nights in jail. His belligerent nature mingled with his leadership proclivities, and his ambition led him to quit the mines in anger after a minor argument with his superior.

A. J. hopped a boxcar and headed back to Chicago with thoughts of his future. In Chicago, he became a brakeman on the Eastern Railroad, and after a hard day's work, he would head down to saloon row with his friends. As was his habit, he became top man in the saloon crowd in Chicago and excelled at their chief occupations—drinking and brawling. But he also established himself as a man with definite opinions, and when he expressed them, a person was wise to listen. One might have expected Cermak to take advantage of his position and his popularity and continue on in the saloon world, perhaps making a good living among the grafters and schemers of the city. His brawn and his imposing nature made him a success at it, and his background did not suggest any alternatives.

However, A. J. Cermak was never one to let his life be scripted for him. One day he decided to change his direction. On that day, after his usual hard labor, he failed to show up at the saloon. Instead, he gathered up his meager savings and a few items he had brought with him from Braidwood that might make an attractive trade. He went down to visit some men he knew that ran a junkyard. He knew they had wagons there for hauling junk, and he discovered that they were more than happy to part with one for a little cash. And so, Cermak made the first definitive step in the direction of his new destiny. He had a wagon, not a horse-drawn one; his wagon was smaller than that. But he was as strong as a horse, and he could pull it through the city himself. And so, he went into business hauling and selling kindling wood. The young man, burly and broad-shouldered, snaked his way through the neighborhoods of the city, pulling his wagon and selling wood. He made it a habit to stop and talk to his customers and others he would pass regularly, and he expanded his network of acquaintances and contacts around the city in this manner. His business expanded quickly as he accumulated regular contracts supplying wood, and soon he had to hire men and purchase additional wagons. He waited two years, until he felt he was sufficiently established, before he asked his girlfriend, Mary Horej, for her hand in marriage. He embraced her Catholicism, finding it a faith more advantageous to his career than the Hussite Protestantism that his parents had brought with them from Bohemia. He settled into a comfortable domestic scene, leaving his rowdy saloon days behind him. When his prosperity allowed it, he relocated to the more fashionable Lawndale. He made good on his promise to his parents and sent for them, and they lived with him thereafter.

In Lawndale, Cermak joined a myriad of social institutions, achieving his aspiration of becoming a prominent Czech businessman. And so, while Chicago showed itself to the world at the Columbian Exposition, he transformed himself from immigrant laborer "A. J." to Chicago gentleman "Anton J. Cermak." It was just the kind of story that Chicago loved. It was in Lawndale that Cermak entered Democratic Party politics. As usual, he seemed to have a plan. He couldn't rest in one position, however comfortable. Involvement in the party politics of the time brought him back to the rowdy fellowship of his days with the saloon gangs. Indeed, there seemed little difference between the two venues. In the party, he paid his dues canvassing neighborhoods and assisting the precinct captain, and as was his habit, he rose like a rocket through the ranks.

In 1902, Cermak was elected to the Illinois House of Representatives, where he served until 1909. As a representative, he became involved in the developing struggle over alcohol restrictions in the city. He may have left the saloon culture behind, but he never forgot the institutions that had given his life meaning apart from the coal mines and the railroad yards. The ethnic minorities, which he supported (and one of which he belonged to), felt particularly targeted by the dry measures. Their clubs and halls served liquor and beer, and the habit of meeting for a drink, a practice that reached back deep into their cultural histories, was a vital element of the lives they lived beyond the toil that took up six long days a week. After a particularly onerous crackdown regarding closing times in saloons, the ethnic groups banded together for a protest rally. The rally was such a success that they decided to form a permanent organization, the United Societies for Local Self-Government, that looked after the interests of saloons, distilleries, distributors, and drinkers across the city. Cermak would long be associated with this group and the struggle to keep alcohol legal in Chicago.

In 1909, having survived a scandal as a legislator in which he was accused of selling his vote, Cermak became alderman of the Twelfth Ward. And like the other aldermen of his day, Cermak amassed a millionaire's fortune despite the modest salary associated with the position. If industrial leaders wanted to pass an ordinance in the Twelfth Ward, they knew that they had to approach Alderman Cermak with their hats in their hands and large checks in their pockets. And when it came time for an election, Cermak ruled the voting precincts, methodically monitoring and adjusting the ballot boxes to assure that the right Democrat sailed into office. Everyone knew that Cermak was the boss. He was reasonable and listened to his network of party men, but everyone knew better than to come to Cermak barking orders. He listened solicitously to only one man: that was George E. Brennan, his mentor and a leader of the Irish Democrats. Brennan had taken over the Democratic Party after the death of Roger Sullivan. Also a former coal miner from Braidwood, Brennan had very aggressively organized the Democratic Party and stocked its leadership with Irishmen. The party would bear his Celtic stamp for many years to come. As Cermak had done in his youth, he again hung his political hat with the Irish. It seemed that the Czech contingent was not large or powerful enough to threaten the Irish leaders in the party. So, the Irishmen allowed him a foothold, and he soon became Brennan's right hand. When Brennan died, Cermak assumed his position.

Cermak enjoyed, through the 1910s and the 1920s, a successful career as a Chicago politician, a liquor lobbyist, and a Democratic Party leader. And when it came time to take down Big Bill Thompson, he was chosen for the job. For Cermak, it was personal. He despised the undisciplined and foolish leadership of Big Bill. While Cermak was also a bit of a bully, he was a serious and disciplined bully who had the party's interests at heart. He had followed Brennan's lead and turned the Democratic Party into a highly efficient machine. He believed in a rigid form of organization, with careful planning from the bottom up, and everyone doing their part—and if they didn't, they would hear about it, or worse. Of course, party politics in this era had numerous intersections with the underworld, and Cermak carefully maintained these connections throughout his political career. Fletcher Dobyns, fueled by a distaste for Cermak and all that he represented, described this period in Cermak's life and the emerging machine of Chicago politics: "Soon after reaching Chicago, he joined a group of men who were engaged in building a political machine after the model of Tammany Hall of New York. They organized denizens of the underworld and their patrons, political job holders and their dependents and friends, those seeking special privileges and immunities, and grafters of every type; they engaged in political sabotage and entered into bipartisan deals and alliances."[4] Cermak was a key architect in transforming the political syndicate in Chicago into a formidable machine that grew so powerful under his successor that it garnered the respect of even Franklin D. Roosevelt. Cermak held absolute power in the Democratic Party, but he wasn't satisfied. So, for the first time in Chicago's history, the chairman of the Democratic Party in the city decided to seek the mayor's seat.

On the eve of the election, the city was in crisis. The city treasury was empty, the streets of Chicago resounded with the shock of the stock market crash, and crime, fed by the economic disasters, had become monumental in proportions. Horner was doing what he could in the probate court, but his attention was also being drawn into the deplorable condition of almost all city departments. City leaders like Horner were buzzing with concern, strategies, and predictions. In his various clubs, Horner took part in serious discussions about policy and debated the efficacy of various economic measures. He became more active in the Democratic Party as well. He and his colleagues knew that forceful and serious leadership was desperately needed, and Thompson was still playing the fool. Horner, a lifelong Democrat, threw his support behind Cermak. He acted as Cermak's campaign treasurer and energized his wide circle of acquaintances on the Democratic chairman's behalf. Cermak won the Democratic primary by defeating several candidates who maintained that a Democratic nominee for mayor should come from the Irish wing of the party, as was customary. Despite the tension in the primary, Cermak was able to reunite the party after his victory and to restore an uneasy harmony. Horner geared himself up to assist Cermak in the general election.

In the election of 1931, Thompson exploited his favorite nickname, "Big Bill the Builder." He took credit for the good days of the 1920s, and truly, Chicago had experienced a good deal of growth and expansion during the years when he was mayor. He prided himself on having overseen the building of playgrounds, parks, streets, and skyscrapers. However, such wild growth could more accurately be attributed to the bold industrial magnates of the era who were helped along in no short measure by the proclivity of government officials to be bought. Thompson, never one to take the dignified route, stumped with personal and ethnic slurs against Cermak. Thompson called him "Pushcart Tony" in reference to his wood-hauling days, "Tony Baloney," and a "bohunk." The personal attacks alienated ethnic voters, who saw in Cermak a sort of ethnic everyman. Also, while Cermak had organized his party behind him, Thompson had alienated the Republicans. A surprising number of Republican leaders not only refused to line up behind Thompson but also crossed party lines publicly and supported Cermak. Thompson was also at a disadvantage because of the growing public discontent with organized crime. People no longer considered the underworld a necessary evil that in some way stabilized the city and that worked closely with the local government for the good of the neighborhoods. Because of the audacity and bloodshed of the Capone era, organized crime had become anathema to the citizens of Chicago and needed attention from law enforcement. It was common knowledge in the city that Thompson had created a climate perfect for the growth of organized crime. Detractors began to dig up receipts and correspondence that linked him to the gangsters of Chicago.

And finally, Thompson, always the panderer to public opinion, had tested the waters and come up on the wrong end on the issue of Prohibition.

Over the years, Cermak had demonstrated consistently that he was a wet candidate, while Thompson had made a few weak and indecisive gestures in the dry direction. Although some reformist organizations decided to support Thompson, on the whole, Chicago was not interested in that brand of reform. It was a disgruntled and fearful city that scowled in Big Bill Thompson's direction on the eve of the election, ready for a change in leadership. The steady and predictable Cermak seemed to be just what was needed—a forceful man who would take the city in hand. Cermak beat Thompson handily, by nearly 200,000 votes, and the sun set on Thompson's career as an elected official. The rough boy from Braidwood had fulfilled a destiny beyond his wildest dreams. He was now the boss of Chicago.

5

The Wheels in Motion

After his inauguration in May of 1931, Mayor Anton J. Cermak had two foremost concerns. The first, and most pressing to the public, was the crushing fiscal emergency in Chicago that required immediate action. The second, and perhaps the more pressing to Cermak himself, was that now he had to gear up for another election. He had made the controversial decision not to step down from the top position in the Illinois Democratic Party but to fill the dual roles of mayor and party leader. Having had no mentor since the death of George Brennan, Cermak depended on himself for counsel. Of course, various contingents of the Democratic Party began volleying for desirable spots in the upcoming Cermak term.

Cermak decided to appoint Pat Nash chairman of the Democratic Party of Cook County, a position that placed him second in command in the party. Nash was a wealthy man whose family had made the bulk of their money in sewer contracts. Nash had long been active in the Democratic Party, although he had rarely run for office. He was not hungry for the spotlight, but he was well known and very well liked among party regulars. He had a calming, cordial demeanor that helped him to soothe ruffled feathers and bring about agreements. He was also sixty-eight years old and spent much of his time raising thoroughbred horses at a vacation home in Michigan. As an older man preoccupied with a leisurely retirement lifestyle, Nash wasn't likely to insist on being part of every decision. However, he was an active participant in discussing general strategy for the party and had a way of bringing people around to his way of thinking. Cermak wanted someone who wouldn't be overly ambitious in the post and who would go along with his decisions without challenging his authority, and he found just such a man in Nash, whose good reputation bolstered Cermak's leadership. Cermak reasoned that Nash would go his way and encourage others to do the same. Refusing to relinquish his position in the party leadership had been a controversial decision, but Cermak believed that the power in the city still lay in the complex web of organizations that the party represented. The mayor's office would be weak if it did not have the backing of the fifty aldermen on the city council. Cermak was not one of those who believed that a political party was relevant only during election times. He planned to make the machine work for him as mayor and decided that only he could strategically place the cogs and gears of that machine. While beginning to mull over those cogs and gears, he also instituted some emergency economic measures in the city.

By October of 1932, about 750,000 Chicagoans were out of work, while only 800,000 in the city still held jobs.[1] Chicago was one of the hardest-hit cities in the nation. Public employees were simply not being paid. Policemen and firefighters were laid off, while the public school teachers labored without pay, routinely feeding approximately eleven thousand starving children in their classrooms. Any real education ground to a halt. People were getting restless and angry. Picketing and disruptive protests erupted throughout the city. Cermak immediately instituted an austerity program in an effort to temporarily reduce the cost of government and succeeded in cutting over $10 million from Mayor Thompson's budget. He also traveled to Washington to lobby for relief aid before a House committee, proclaiming that the federal government had a choice: "it could send relief, or it could send troops."[2] He was not overstating the severity of the situation.

Throughout the prosperous 1920s, there were two major issues that divided Illinois: the battle between the wets and the drys over Prohibition, and the power struggle between downstate government and the political machine in Chicago, commonly referred to as "the battle over home rule" for Chicago. Concerning the first issue, Cermak made it very clear that the Democratic slate of candidates was to be "dripping wet" and that he would not support any candidate who wasn't. On the second issue, Cermak decided to settle the war between upstate and downstate forces by instituting Chicago Democratic control in Springfield. Although he had just won the mayoral election in 1931, Cermak seriously considered running for the governor's chair in 1932. He felt that the only threat to his own power would occupy that seat, so why not fill it himself? But he and his advisers worried about the public reaction to his abandoning the office that he had just been awarded. Would he come off as power hungry? Concerned about public perception of such a move, Cermak kept his own ambitions for the office under wraps. However, he did not abandon them entirely. Meanwhile, there was pressure on him, as the head of the state Democratic Party, to survey the field for an appropriate candidate to run for governor. The incumbent was Republican Louis L. Emmerson from Mount Vernon, a town in southern Illinois. Emmerson, who was in poor health, did not choose to be a candidate for reelection. He realized that, beaten down by the Depression and crippled by a bankrupt treasury, the state of Illinois would not favor an incumbent, especially a Republican one. President Herbert Hoover's unpopularity was dragging down Republican candidates all over the country. In addition, shortly after Cermak's election, Emmerson made a costly political mistake when he vetoed the highly popular Thomas J. O'Grady Bill. This audacious legislation sought to repeal Prohibition in Illinois under the nose of the federal government. The bill would also eliminate existing search-and-seizure laws, again treading on dangerous constitutional grounds. However flawed, the bill was enormously popular in a state in which the majority despised Prohibition and was feeling aggressive on the crime-fighting front. The bill made Emmerson nervous, and rightly so. He believed that the measure was "nothing short of secession and nullification."[3] Passing such a bill would most likely have opened up such a can of legal worms that Illinois would be in court until the federal repeal of Prohibition came through anyway. However, the existence and popularity of such a bill in Chicago demonstrate just how vehement the populace was on this issue. Many Chicagoans were willing to jeopardize the very statehood of Illinois in opposition to those federal busybodies that had dared to deny them the simple right of a drink. Emmerson's veto of the bill felt like a slap in the face and aroused the righteous indignation of Chicago. He wisely decided not to submit himself to a bid for reelection.

The Republican field was wide open. During his last successful mayoral campaign, Big Bill Thompson had run on the ticket with former governor Len Small. Big Bill did not relish fading into the background, and he felt an ill-will toward Mayor Cermak. Therefore, almost immediately after losing the election, he busied himself pumping up Small, who was then seventy years old, as a candidate to run against Cermak's man. They had a formidable job ahead of them; anti-Republican sentiment was rampant. The Thompson-Small combination seemed an unsavory and worn-out offering to the people of Illinois. Cermak felt that the election would be an easy win for the Democrats, and he looked forward eagerly to an unprecedented degree of influence in the state. He also knew that he would have to be careful when selecting his own candidate for governor. The rest of Illinois looked on Chicago with some distaste, and Cermak knew that he represented everything that made downstate Illinois uneasy. He was a tough city boss who had risen from the streets; plus he was the son of foreign-born immigrants, another attribute the fairly homogenous rural population of downstate distrusted.

Many "downstaters" viewed the power struggle between Chicago and the rest of the state as a battle between evil and good. Cermak knew that times were ripe for a clean, good-government candidate. He wasn't sure that he could pass himself off on that score, but he felt confident in his own ability to win over voters. There had never been a time in his life when he had not risen to the top, like the cream in a barrel of milk, and he could not envision himself losing. He knew that because he was a Brennan man, the Irish would have some ideas about his decision. They would assume that he supported their candidate, Mike Igoe, who obviously expected Cermak to slate him. But Cermak had never been a man to bow down to the expectations of others, and besides, Brennan was gone. Nonetheless, he would have to handle the situation carefully since the most important thing, now and always, was that the party *had to* stick together. He was building a machine and had to manage dissension very carefully. He methodically plotted out a ticket that included the most influential Democrats of the city and state, but he still needed someone at the top of the ticket. Igoe did not suit him. During Igoe's years in party politics, he had been ruffled more than once by Cermak's dictatorial style. It was clear that if he were elected governor, Igoe would seize the opportunity to step out of Cermak's shadow. In order to have full control, Cermak had to fill the one position above him with someone who wouldn't dare exercise power over him. He needed a "Cermak man" in the governorship. Nervous about starting a party scuffle at this key juncture, he decided to keep Igoe and the party in suspense for a time. He let the Irish Democrats assume that Igoe would be the man.

During this time, someone brought to his attention another possibility: Judge Henry Horner. He was familiar with Judge Horner, who had been the treasurer of his own campaign. Horner had gained some notoriety in the party when he had set about returning unexpended funds to contributors after the election. The story of how the noted philanthropist and chief of Sears, Roebuck, Julius Rosenwald, had gotten a "refund check" while he was in the hospital was a source of some amusement at the time. Rosenwald said it shocked him so much that he almost had a relapse. Cermak began to think more about Horner. Everyone thought him a capable man, but not one who tended to make a formidable impression. However, when Cermak thought more about it and consulted with Nash, choosing Horner made sense to him. Who could argue with Horner? Downstate couldn't find fault with him. He was a Jew, and that could be a drawback, but Cermak thought that this obstacle could be overcome. He continued to think on the prospect.

Horner had been readying himself for an elected office outside of the courts for some time. He had once intended to make a run for the mayor's seat against Thompson but had thought better of it. And it was not the first time that someone had mentioned his name in relation to the governor's seat. When he came out as an advocate for stronger sovereignty for Chicago in Illinois, the Illinois Municipal League had mentioned his name, in print, as an attractive choice for governor. In fact, many of the city's wealthy and influential men had chatted with him over bridge at one or another of the clubs and had said in confidence something akin to "Horner, I expect to see you in the governor's seat some day." For his part, Horner expected that Cermak would be an ally in the mayor's office; after all, Horner had worked in his campaign. When approached by Cermak and Nash about running for governor, Horner was intrigued and immediately alerted his closest supporters, including his mentor, Jacob Lindheimer. Horner knew that there had been some discussion about how an honest judge could have thrown his support to Cermak, a man not exactly renowned for honest dealings.

Horner's political orientation was a matter of some speculation in political circles. He seemed as straight as an arrow, and yet he moved with ease about the disreputable political landscape of the city. He was a principled man, but he was also a realist. It was often difficult to reconcile the two sides of his nature. When questioned about his support of Cermak, Horner replied, "Perfection in government is usually reached in campaign speeches and Utopian hopes."[4] Horner knew from his experience in the streets that life in the city could be hard and that the law had to bend sometimes to meet the specific circumstances of the folks under its jurisdiction. With his wide circle of acquaintances in the city, Horner must have known that Cermak was more than just a little shy of perfect. But Horner stuck with a survival strategy that he had learned from Harrison. A man had to tolerate a lot of different types to make it in the city's political scene, but he could still maintain his own standards. He didn't like lying and cheating, and he didn't engage in either, but he knew that as probate judge, he wasn't in a position to tell the politicians their business. Plus, he had a good impression of Cermak, dating back to his own election as probate judge. He felt that the commanding man could make some badly needed changes in Chicago.

Cermak had given Horner clear indications that he envisioned him occupying the governor's seat, but he had cautioned Horner not to discuss it too widely and not to go public. Cermak suggested that he was planning to wait a while and get party matters lined up before making his ticket public. Soon, however, although there had been no formal announcement from Cermak, the buzz began. Many of the most powerful and influential men in the city took to the news with great alacrity. After all, they knew Horner from the club. His affable nature did not create many enemies in his circles, and everyone knew that he was a square dealer. Lindheimer began organizing Horner's people. And yet, the formal announcement from Cermak didn't come. The "Horner team," led by Lindheimer, would prick up their ears with each speech or press event issuing from the mayor's office. *Did he mention Horner?* Whenever Horner would call the mayor to inquire, Cermak would respond vaguely that the situation was very tricky. Since it was important not to anger the Irish contingent of the party at this crucial time, he had to move cautiously. Cermak suggested that he was dealing with Igoe and making him some offers to forestall a fight over the candidacy. The infuriating delay wore on for nearly a year, and the influential men who were in Horner's corner became increasingly restless. They began to pressure Cermak to announce his candidate. In the press, there was speculation that Cermak's choice of Horner was not in earnest, and that he still had plans to take the candidacy for himself. Could it be that Cermak was betting that party leaders would so strongly object to having a Jew as the Democratic gubernatorial candidate that Cermak would be able to step forward to save the day by becoming the candidate himself and reuniting the party? Speculation ran wild. But as time passed and his back was against the wall to announce his slate of candidates for the Democratic ticket, Cermak began to confront the practical considerations that would have been involved in pushing aside

Horner and taking the candidacy for himself. And he began to see the wisdom in settling on Horner.

In a city of bad reputations and shady pasts, Henry Horner stood out like a flower in a field of weeds. With his impeccable reputation as a judge, Horner was sure to please a public hungry for good-government candidates who would end the political corruption that had characterized the Thompson era. Perhaps they could look past the "Jewish issue," Cermak reasoned. But more important, Horner had not, in all his years as probate judge, caused a ripple of conflict in the Democratic machinery. Horner would not stand in his way when it came time to send legislation off to Springfield, and Horner would surely let him run Cook County how he pleased. Plus, the pressure to settle on Horner was simply too great to ignore. The judge had powerful friends and a good deal of financial backing to run the race in style. Cermak finally agreed that he would simply have to run Springfield from Chicago. Finally, he brought out the long-awaited ticket. It was a testament to his mastery of detail and strategy. The candidates represented a careful geographical balance between Chicago and downstate, as well as a mixture of ethnicities that would delicately assure that the melting pot would simmer rather than boil over. Cermak had also carefully maintained relationships inside the party through his selection of candidates. He paid plenty of homage to the ward leadership in his selections. And he was determined that he would have the whole machine at his back; there would be no fractures or antagonisms. Every important constituency was now indebted to him and wouldn't dare challenge his nominations. Henry Horner was on the top of the list: the heavily favored gubernatorial nominee for the Democratic ticket. A deep sigh of relief issued from the offices of many a power player in the city.

6

Judge Horner Runs the Race

As the city sunk deeper into the Great Depression, Chicago once again tapped its greatest resource—hope. Another world's fair was on the way to Chicago. Ideas for the new exposition had begun to percolate as early as 1923, but plans really began to get underway during Mayor Dever's short administration. The new fair would be called "A Century of Progress," and it would be a celebration of the amazing period of innovation that had raised Chicago from a marshy prairie to a world-class industrial city. A good number of men aspired to have the honor of being titled "World's Fair Mayor," but it now looked as if Anton Cermak had won that distinction. The proud mayor looked forward to the 1932 elections with great satisfaction.

It looked to be a great year for Democratic candidates. It certainly wasn't a good year for incumbents. In the spring of 1932, 40 percent of employable Chicagoans were out of work. The entire country was now in the tunnel of the Depression. Herbert Hoover occupied the White House, but he seemed not to grasp the material realities that existed under his leadership. Rather, he seemed to live in a haze of abstract principles and found it unsettling to his political philosophy to take decisive action to respond to the national emergency. Hoover believed strongly that prosperity could only be regained through the activities of the business sector. After all, it was business that was responsible for providing jobs and hence income to the nation, Hoover argued. He felt it would be morally wrong to provide relief to the general population and refused to consider direct economic aid to any interest other than business.[1] An outraged nation looked to the Democratic Party to send in a heroic presidential candidate to rescue them.

Aside from the reversals in state and city government, the first couple of years of the 1930s were momentous for Chicago in many respects. In those years, Chicagoans had to acknowledge that the party was over as they accustomed themselves to the cruel realities of life after the stock market crash. They also felt the tremors when two of the city's giants came crashing down in defeat. Al Capone was the first of those giants. After the St. Valentine's Day Massacre of 1929, intended to wipe out Bugs Moran, Capone escaped legal action, but his role in the spectacular gangland bloodbath was well known by the public. Capone enjoyed his macabre celebrity status and continued to up the ante on his reputation for ruthless exercises of power over his underworld empire. However, the national spotlight backfired on him. President Hoover himself took notice and began to lean on the federal courts to take care of the Chicago menace. Capone seemed to be making a mockery of the entire law enforcement institution. Federal agents developed a plan to corner Capone on charges of tax evasion and violation of Prohibition laws. After a protracted game of cat and mouse, Capone, to his great surprise, was given a sentence of eleven years for tax evasion in 1931. The Capone era had ended.

The second giant was equally notorious for his exercises of power in the upper world of Chicago. On June 6, 1932, amid the hoopla of the election, the dynamic head of Commonwealth Edison, Samuel Insull, resigned from the top position at the Chicago Rapid Transit Company. The careening speculation and overconfidence that had typified the nation as a whole in the 1920s was now having its effects on the great institutions of Chicago. Insull's empire had collapsed, and in October he was indicted on charges of bankruptcy, embezzlement, and fraud. Later, Insull fled America and engaged in a protracted extradition fight. After all that trouble, he was finally acquitted of all charges. However, his great fall seemed symbolic of the condition of the American dream and marked a shift of eras in Chicago. It was becoming clear that the city would have to look to someone other than its powerful and corrupt big bosses to get itself back on track. The era of Thompsonism was over; Capone was dethroned; and the corrupt business barons who had once been above the law were now deflated. The whole state, the whole nation, in fact, was searching for leadership, disillusioned by the old order.

Homer Tice, a farmer and state representative from downstate, expressed the mood of many in the nation after beholding the fall of Chicago's giants: "I am badly worried. For long years we downstate have looked up to Insull, Traylor, and others of their class in Chicago as the last word in all financial matters—as great and dependable authorities. What scares me is that they don't know the way out; they haven't any plan or real remedy. If they haven't a plan to pull the country out of this depression and the state out of this revenue crisis, what can be expected of us ordinary folks who live out in the sticks?"[2] People were beginning to see that corruption among the powerful wasn't something to overlook in favor of a larger stability and order that they didn't understand. The overinflation of a coterie of powerful egos had, in part, created the conditions under which they now suffered. This growing political insight among the general population, as well as their difficulty in imagining an alternative, made the 1932 elections unique. Perhaps for this reason, regular people found themselves looking for explanations and plans rather than empty sloganeering.

Now that it was to be Henry Horner as the frontrunner of the Democratic Party for governor, it remained to be determined who would oppose him in the general election. The state Republican Party was suffering the Hoover backlash, and Big Bill Thompson and his creaky, marionette-like candidate Len Small did not show a great deal of promise in turning that situation around. Realizing this, a number of Republican candidates entered the race against Small, hoping to make a stronger and, frankly, more dignified showing. Among them were State Treasurer Omer Custer and six others who lacked the visibility of the Thompson-Small camp.

As the nominees for the election were being lined up, the good-government movement began to show itself as a major ideological force. With so much suffering afoot, the public had run out of patience with the diamond-cuffed gangsters and the "boodling" political types. Law enforcement was receiving unparalleled public support, and candidates' records were being scrutinized like never before. Chicago had struggled for years under the perceived corruption of Thompson's governance of the city and the evident coziness between the mayor's office and organized crime. Now, good-government societies were scrambling to find suitable candidates that might return the city to the more rational and trustworthy eras of Harrison and his predecessors.

The Better Government Association had backed Cermak as candidate for mayor, but his status as "good" was always questionable, and his relationship to "good government" was a matter of constant debate in the papers. He was certainly different than Big Bill Thompson, but was he less corrupt? Writing in the *Tribune*, Fletcher Dobyns expressed a common strain of public sentiment when he appraised the Cermak campaign for mayor: "For more than a quarter of a century, the good people of Chicago had looked upon Tony as a spawn of the rotten Sullivan-Brennan machine and a low spoils politician. Now they pictured him surrounded by his family; they heralded the occasional sops that he had handed to social workers and reformers to distract their attention; made a hero out of him, and elected him mayor by a large majority."[3] Others questioned how Cermak had managed to accumulate millions of dollars on the meager salary of an alderman and a party chairman. Cermak was not the first alderman to make a fortune outside the context of his official salary. Receiving payoffs for political influence was a long and celebrated tradition. However, he was the first to rise from the saloon political rank to the mayor's office. He was the first of the Hinky Dink Kenna and Bathhouse John Coughlin legacy to sit in with the "high hats," as the upper-crust politicians were called. Cermak had broken a class boundary in Chicago, and he had been able to do so in large part because of his unusually imposing personality. He was simply one of those men who couldn't step into a room without commanding the authority of everyone present. He was also quite serious and hardworking. But still there was some skepticism surrounding him. Was he really fit to be the mayor? And was he really a token of good government to come? The Better Government Association could at least assure itself that it had gotten rid of Big Bill Thompson. Better days had to be in store.

Indeed, they were right, for Henry Horner had not risen from the modest and morally ambiguous atmosphere that Cermak had. Perhaps Horner had the luxury to adhere to the straight and narrow. Would a man of Horner's inviolable scruples have risen from the coal mines to the top of city government? Perhaps not. But Horner was the kind of candidate for which the good-government societies had been searching. In him, the efficacy of Lincoln's principles could be tested in the industrial age.

Cermak could read the signs. He had no intention of reforming Chicago, as some of his backers may have hoped, but he did keep the good-government movement in mind as he selected his candidates. He noted the tougher stance now being taken against the underground economy in Chicago, and he saw that the era of tycoons, whose purse strings had once made him rich, was now ending. Cermak may not have been terribly "good," but he knew that his choice for governor was undoubtedly a good-government candidate, and no one could dispute that fact. And that may even have irritated Cermak a bit as he thought about the more privileged Horner, who hadn't had to struggle to make a living working in a coal mine, now stepping forward to take the position that Cermak wanted. This time of desperation would perhaps be the only opening for a Czech candidate to take the state's highest office. It might well be his last chance, and he would have to hand it over to Henry Horner. Perhaps Cermak still harbored the thought that any man who donated his raise in pay to charity and who returned unspent campaign contributions must be just a little bit of a fool; but perhaps such a man might also be wise enough to step aside when times warranted, Cermak must have hoped.

Those lining up to challenge Henry Horner's bid for the governorship had to contend with his reputation for honesty and diligence. They simply could not argue that he was corrupt, so they settled for arguing that he was weak. After all, if they could establish that he was a puppet for Cermak, then Cermak's enemies would have one more opportunity to get in a lick at the successful mayor. Cermak's Chicago was increasingly being likened to the complex and corrupt political organization in New York named for Tammany Hall. In fact, it was speculated that Cermak wanted to merge the two syndicates. Regardless, it seemed that the general populace of Chicago, unused to Horner's well-bred and civil style of public service, did not quite know how to take him. They had become accustomed to aggressive posturing from their leaders, who were routinely referred to as "bosses." Cermak and Thompson had set the bullying political tone in Chicago. Thompson, a football hero in his younger days, delivered each of his speeches as if it were his half of a slugfest. He ran on macho slogans such as "He cannot be bought, bossed or bluffed."[4] Cermak, dubbed "Dictator Cermak" by Thompson, was equally strong-handed. He established power through a more understated and methodical intimidation, but it was clear that in any group he never was "one of the gang." He was the leader, and that was that, but the gang was everything to him.

Horner, on the other hand, was a different kind of candidate entirely. He was independent, affable, and congenial. He established his influence by carefully cultivating a network of cordial relationships motivated not by political strategy but seemingly by a sincere interest in other people and an enjoyment of society. His leadership qualities were not the byproducts of a forceful or particularly charismatic personality, but rather they were established interaction by interaction, civic duty by civic duty, case by case. When Horner wanted something done, he applied the power of friendship. He could be stern and unbending in moments that required principle, but he never used his strength of character to further his own power. Horner had garnered a great deal of respect among Chicagoans, but of course not everyone knew of his work in probate court. The people of Chicago were used to a louder, cruder style of electioneering. Was the judge's goodness *real?* Whether a Governor Horner would bow down to the demands coming out of Cook County was also a matter of speculation. Many people could not envision any politician functioning as the superior of the intimidating Cermak.

Shortly after Cermak finally announced that his candidate for governor would indeed be Henry Horner, a jilted and angry Mike Igoe announced he would run against Horner in the primary. He would team up with attorney Scott Lucas, running for the U.S. Senate, against Cermak's candidate, William H. Dieterich. Bruce Campbell, a downstate candidate who seemed to be perpetually on the ballot in Illinois, would also run for governor in the primary. And so, the Democratic slate for the governorship was filled, and Horner, with Cermak's backing, was the favorite. In the meantime, Big Bill Thompson was enjoying another chance to perform on the Republican stage as the chief architect of the Len Small campaign for governor. It gave him a chance to rail against Cermak, to attract attention to himself, and to give voice to his peculiar political ideas once again. But first, Len Small had to win the primary, and he did so. Omer Custer came in second, but he couldn't outdo the name recognition of the Thompson-Small pairing or their plentiful campaign funds. On the Democratic side, Campbell and Igoe cancelled each other out downstate, and Horner, as expected, ruled Cook County. Horner sailed to an easy victory in the primary, along with every other candidate that Cermak had carefully placed on the organization ticket.

Since Horner was Cermak's man, there were immediately rumors of election fraud in relation to his victory. William Stuart, a contemporary of Horner's with a decidedly Thompsonist agenda, carefully documented details of the campaign in his book *The Twenty Incredible Years*. Citing the overwhelming results of the Twenty-fourth Ward, where Horner garnered 15,614 votes and Mike Igoe only 241, Stuart suggests that the corrupt ward organization had come out to lean on the ballot boxes in favor of Horner. Also feeding the fire of accusations against the Cermak machine was the victory of Cermak's candidate for U.S. senator, William H. Dieterich, who received more than double the number of votes cast for Scott Lucas. Stuart remarks that Lucas beat Dieterich downstate, suggesting that something had gone awry in Cook County.[5] But suggestions of election fraud were de rigueur in the Chicago of those days, and the election marched forward. Henry Horner, candidate for governor, now fifty-three years old, stepped to the fore.

The governor of New York was also emerging from the shadows to become a presidential candidate worthy of notice. Chicago politicians did not know what to think of Franklin Delano Roosevelt, who seemed overnight to have been propelled from a minor figure to the man about whom everyone was talking. After securing all of the candidates for the 1932 election, Cermak turned his attention to Washington. He had only one issue in mind: not securing federal assistance for his beleaguered city, but repealing the despised Prohibition. He assessed the candidates for the presidency with one question: how wet are you? The people of Chicago at this time were consumed with three issues: fighting their way out of the Depression, opening the upcoming Century of Progress Exposition, and repealing the Eighteenth Amendment and the Volstead Act. Many prudent presidential candidates decided to approach the third issue conservatively. They knew that Prohibition was desperately unpopular and destined to fail, but they also wanted to appeal to the religious types and rural folk who peopled organizations like the Anti-Saloon League. And so, many candidates espoused the adoption of what was called the "Moist Plank." They would, for instance, suggest weakening the restrictions on alcohol, perhaps legalizing beer, but not repealing the Eighteenth Amendment in its entirety. Cermak, however, vowed that he would support no candidate who was not "dripping wet." For Cermak, that meant someone who was prepared to immediately set the wheels in motion to pass an amendment relegalizing spirits and who would see to it meanwhile that a law was passed legalizing beer.

Initially, Cermak was not convinced by Roosevelt's hard-line stance on the Prohibition issue, and he refused to join in with the Roosevelt forces. He criticized Roosevelt's record and his qualifications and touted other candidates, particularly Al Smith, a "dripping wet" who had been the governor of New York before Roosevelt but lost the 1928 presidential race to Herbert Hoover. Cermak prepped his slate of candidates on this perception of Roosevelt before the various candidates discussed national politics in interviews, speeches, and remarks. Horner, who was clearly concerned with more than the Volstead Act, apparently took the party stance to heart and became convinced that Roosevelt was not the best candidate for the highest position in the land. Like Horner, Al Smith had close ties with the business community, and Horner felt that was an important component of reviving the national economy. In Chicago, the former mayor Carter Harrison was a leading Roosevelt supporter, and he tried to get Cermak to join in and assure Illinois for Roosevelt. It didn't work, but Roosevelt was nominated anyway. In the end, when Roosevelt finally adopted a wet plank at the national Democratic convention, Cermak acceded and threw his support to Roosevelt, foreseeing what his support would mean for Illinois under the probable next president.

Horner, however, was unused to such a quick turnabout of conviction. Soon thereafter, in line with Cermak's wishes, Horner's speechwriter included a glowing statement of support for Roosevelt in an upcoming address. Horner informed his writer that he was not a supporter of Roosevelt and asked him to remove the passages from the speech, since for him to make such remarks would be considered hypocritical. Before long, Horner received a call from Cermak. It would not be his first lesson in realpolitik; he had Kenna and Coughlin to thank for that. The next day, he praised Roosevelt in a speech on a campaign stop in Rockford and predicted that he would make a stellar leader for the nation. It was clear Horner had learned that a candidate is wise to pick his battles carefully.

Henry Horner's mother, Dilah Horner. Chicago History Museum, i38732.

William H. "Big Bill" Thompson, 1915. Chicago History Museum, DN-0009693.

Governor Horner with his Lincoln collection, 1933.
Chicago History Museum, DN-0103510. *Chicago Daily News* photograph.

Chicago aldermen Michael "Hinky Dink" Kenna (*left*) and "Bathhouse" John Coughlin, 1924.
Chicago History Museum, i10927aa.

Governor Henry Horner.
Chicago History Museum, i21417.
Photo by Herbert Georg Studio.

The governor-elect, Henry Horner, with Mayor Anton Cermak, Mrs. Floyd Finley, and Tom Courtney, 1932. Chicago History Museum, DN-99346. *Chicago Daily News* photograph.

Cook County Democratic Party chairman Pat Nash (*left*) and Mayor Ed Kelly, 1937.
Chicago History Museum, i13907. *Chicago Herald Examiner* photograph.

Lt. Governor John Stelle, 1940. Chicago History Museum, i38730.

7

A Big Hit Downstate and On to Victory

The campaign underway, Henry Horner boarded his Packard and left the city limits, a small entourage of campaign staff following close behind. Downstate campaigning was a prospect of both possibility and peril for Horner. Away from Cermak's controlling scrutiny, he felt better able to run the kind of campaign he wanted without the constant mandate to "check in."

Horner was a city boy, born and bred, but the scenes of his imagination and the setting for his philosophical musings were often rural. As a child, he had listened to his grandmother talk about how Lincoln had grown up in a log cabin and how he had scratched an education out of the dust. As a young attorney, Horner had thought of Lincoln as a man who could speak to heads of state and farmhands in the same, straightforward language. Certainly, Lincoln must have been a strong presence in Horner's mind as he looked out his car window to behold the Illinois countryside. Horner had convictions and ideas about the farmer's plight in southern Illinois. He knew things were going to be bad; people were suffering terribly. To win the election, he had to convince these people that he was the man that could make it better. He believed in the difference between his career as a politician and the careers of Big Bill Thompson and Len Small—his interest was in public service, not in the power and the hoopla. In approaching the people downstate, he had to make this distinction clear.

There was another issue that lurked in his mind. He knew that people were in an uproar about the prospect of a Jewish candidate for governor, and some would be disposed not to like him. This disheartened him more than it would most candidates. The people of rural southern Illinois were largely from highly conservative Christian denominations. They weren't used to the ethnic mix of Chicago, and they tended to be xenophobic. Their fear of outsiders had been nurtured in the Civil War, which had torn that end of the state in two. They preferred the predictable sameness of their own kind and prided themselves on enforcing their boundaries without any help from the government. Horner had been given word that the remnants of the Ku Klux Klan had already organized their forces for Len Small. He was well aware that the "Jewish issue" had been in the air when Cermak put together the ticket, but this was business as usual for a town like Chicago, which had long been driven by ethnic politics. Still, Horner knew that his being a Jew was viewed by many as the single downside to his candidacy in Chicago, and this would be even more intensely the case in the more homogeneous south. He thought carefully about how to handle this question when it came time to meet face to face with the common people of southern Illinois. He needed to help them see past his ethnicity and convince them that he would be the governor who took action to reduce their suffering.

Southern Illinois struck quite a contrast to Chicago. It is little wonder that power struggles between the two arose, considering that two cultures so alien to one another were expected to be governed by the same body. As he traveled through the state, Horner witnessed the majesty of farm life for the first time in his life. He took careful note of the landscape: large farms owned by businessmen who hired on laborers or tenant farmers, and small farms operated by families who seemed to be perpetually on break on their porches, swatting the flies away on the hot summer days. These farmers made just enough to set their own tables—trying for anything more was futile.

There was also a conservative cast to the politics of rural Illinois. Later, this part of the state would narrowly vote against repealing the Eighteenth Amendment. Politics did not have the same status in this region as in Chicago. While southern Illinois had long political traditions and party allegiances tracing back to the Civil War, the self-sufficient citizens had little need for government interference before the 1930s. However, southern Illinois, like the rest of the country, was in transition in 1932. The way of life that these rural people had become accustomed to for decades was unraveling. Bertie Hunsaker, an Illinois farm woman, recalls a typical experience of farming in this era: "We stayed with it ten years. We stayed with it till 1930, and we were working from daylight to dark and never taking a vacation or thinking about anything but what we were going to do next to try to make a dollar. We'd raise a good crop of tomatoes or peaches or anything else, and the bottom would fall out of the market and you couldn't hardly give them away."[1]

Farmers, accustomed to hard work, found their efforts bore no fruit in the hopeless conditions of the Great Depression. In many instances, it cost them more to produce crops than the crops were worth on the market. In addition to devastating market conditions, farmers found themselves disproportionately carrying the taxation burden in the state. They owned property but often had incomes totaling less than zero; it hurt them the most that the state relied so heavily on property taxes. Farmers like the Hunsakers had to give up the only way of life that their families had known for generations. Horner also took special note when he passed through the coal country that was even then becoming legendary for its chaos, heartbreak, and violence. He saw the refuse of a declining industry and signs of the mayhem. Coal country had the power to transport the beholder to another era, one in which you could not tell who enforced the law and who broke it. Destitute-looking men ranged the land, out hunting—skunks, possums, and rabbits slung over their backs, a supplement to their meager incomes. Despite the agricultural plenty for which this part of the country was known, people were starving.

It was into this economic heartbreak that Horner entered in 1932. If they chose to pay attention at all, people were accustomed to the alienating rhetoric of the Hoover administration. They weren't prepared for the friendly, straight-talking judge whom they were about to meet. The rural political setting was a barbecue at the park. Although people came primarily for the free food, they were also satisfying a curiosity about the power players from the city. They waited anxiously for the judge, with a good dose of suspicion, to see the "Jew from Chicago."

When Horner made his appearance, he took many by surprise. A tall, rather portly man with an open, grandfatherly face, he entered the scene with great energy and familiarity. He did not wear a dark suit or a "high hat." He had his shirtsleeves rolled up, and he treated every voter like a friend—and he believed that the first duty to a friend is honesty. When local Democratic officials stepped forward to greet him and to introduce him to prominent local citizens, Horner would acknowledge each of them with an enthusiastic handshake. One of his first practices at these occasions was to invite the group over to a shady spot to have a quick talk and a cigar. In that context, Horner got straight to the heart of things, confronting the matter of his ethnicity in a friendly and direct conversation:

> I think I know what some of you are thinking and don't want to talk about. You're thinking I can't win this election because I'm a Jew from Chicago and a Jew from any place, even from Springfield, couldn't possibly get votes in this country. Isn't that so?

And choosing an individual from the group, he would go on to reason:

> Well I can see the map of Ireland all over your face. And you didn't have anything to say about who your parents were, did you? Or what religion you were born into? I learned my religion at my mother's knee, and I wouldn't trade it for all the gifts or all the patronage in the world. I believe in the same God you do. I wouldn't forsake

> either my mother or my religion. You're going to hear that my name isn't really Horner. And it isn't. Originally it was Levy. But it was changed to my grandmother's name of Horner.[2]

In this way, Horner turned the awkward silence into an opportunity to relate to, and establish a level of intimacy with, his audiences. He showed a natural knack for rhetoric because he found the commonality between them and himself. Instead of hedging or eclipsing the issue of his being Jewish, Horner embraced it. In doing so, he showed loyalty to his family and his heritage; he did not dishonor his background by relegating it to shameful silence. This was something that the conservative and proud rural population could admire; this family pride and commonsense approach to life were among the traits that they most valued. They had perceived the Chicago politicians as being different from them—slick-talking and slippery when it came to the truth—men who say what they think you want to hear to get themselves elected. From the outset, Horner established himself as someone who cut right to the heart of matters, and this won the admiration of many people downstate.

Having dealt squarely with the one matter that troubled him personally, Horner began to really enjoy his downstate campaigning. The meet-and-greet aspect of campaigning suited his personality very well. He liked talking with the regular people he encountered and seeing the sights that he had so long imagined. His meticulous memory filed away images and impressions that he would conjure up later when he was called upon to make difficult decisions in Springfield. He also took time to investigate some Lincoln material in Paris, and undoubtedly Lincoln was persistently in his thoughts during this period. Horner was gaining momentum as a candidate. South of Chicago, he was away from Cermak and all the pressures that he had borne after his nomination. He found touring the countryside an opportunity to step outside and think, to ready himself for the challenges that seemed destined to lie ahead. He had seen many models of political leadership in his lifetime: Harrison, the ward bosses, Thompson, Dever, Emmerson, and, of course, Cermak. Even his grandmother, Hannah Horner, could be counted in that list. Horner knew the times were such that he would have to exercise a different kind of leadership. But it was Lincoln who would be his most influential model.

In probate court, Horner had the opportunity to stand alone in his judgments and make up his own mind about things. Throwing himself into the treacherous political ring had robbed him of that luxury for a time. It could be argued that the downstate campaign gave him pause to reevaluate his relationship to Chicago politics and to make his philosophical relationship with the southern part of the state into a concrete one. In terms of issues, Horner's speeches were not quite as full of refreshing candor as were his private conversations. They were fairly typical party fare for the time. He focused on the plight of farmers, responding to their unrest regarding property taxes and promising to alleviate the burden. And as was expected of anyone on the Cermak ticket, he vowed to champion the repeal of Prohibition. It is unclear how such a promise went over in front of this audience, but very likely, the issues of equity and relief for farmers made other issues seem irrelevant to the farmers suffering so acutely.

In the south, Horner also concentrated on making a connection with the coal miners who were in the midst of a complicated and contentious dispute. He listened carefully to town mayors, union men, and owners to gain a fuller understanding of the situation. He learned that the struggle wasn't a simple dispute over working conditions between owners and workers. The Peabody Coal Mine Company had a long history of power in the state and strong connections with the Democratic Party, while most of the workers were members of the United Mine Workers, or UMW. However, there was unrest among many of the men because they believed that the UMW was getting just a little bit too friendly with Peabody. After a particularly heated labor dispute within the union over hours and wages, it was decided to take a vote to determine what conditions would be presented to the owners. However, the powerful UMW leader, John L. Lewis, aroused much suspicion when he claimed that the ballots had been stolen and then presented a contract proposing that the workers be paid at the rate of five dollars a day, a rate that the workers had already categorically refused. The miners felt that the UMW under Lewis was no longer an organization that served their interests.

A large number of men withdrew from the UMW and started, in September 1932, the Progressive Miners of America, or PMA, in protest. The owners immediately asserted their power in favor of the UMW and laid off or refused to hire anyone associated with the Progressives. These blacklisted men struggled desperately, most living off what they could grow in their backyard gardens. The anger and desperation grew, and PMA members began sabotaging mines and engaging in violent protests. The owners and the UMW responded with violent retaliation of their own, and the result was more a war than a strike. Horner's campaign strategists worried about his getting involved in such a controversial and highly emotional scene, concerned that he would be forced to take sides and might inflame the controversy and arouse anger that would mar his campaign. However, Horner was adamant that the coal miners, too, had to be addressed in a straightforward manner. He went to Ziegler, a major coal-mining arena, and spoke to a crowd peopled with men from both sides of the dispute. He vowed to bring about a peaceful resolution but took a hard line against the more aggressive union agitation. "If I'm governor there's going to be law and order," he promised.[3] However, through talking one-on-one to the men, he developed sympathy with the Progressives. He despised their unruly tactics but saw that their cause was just.

Just as he had during his early days of campaigning in the saloons, Horner again showed an ability to change his way of speaking, depending on his audience. He used this gift to his advantage in downstate Illinois as well. He wasn't above throwing in some over-the-top colloquial language, such as "Some folks say there ain't no hell, but they ain't farmed so they can't tell."[4] Horner's "down-home" word choice might be dismissed as a typical politician's stratagem; however, considering his honest relationship with the public and his philosophy of public service, such colloquialisms more likely demonstrate his amiable, people-centered personality. People had feared that Horner was not as forceful a personality as might be required for a candidate for high office, but they underestimated the power of the sincere "friendly interest" that he had shown toward others throughout his life. And he surprised quite a few skeptics; he was a big hit during his downstate campaign.

Horner established himself as the frontrunner by leaving no political demographic out of his campaign strategy. He had gone triumphantly into the unfamiliar south and made a strong impression. He had convinced the farmers and the miners that he wasn't a slick "high hat" from Chicago who would be insensitive to their concerns. In Chicago, Cermak's political organization and allies made Horner the overwhelming favorite in nearly every ward. Thompson had cultivated the support of black voters, who had a historical allegiance to the political party of Abraham Lincoln. He also had the support of Italian Chicagoans and enjoyed lukewarm support from antisaloon types. However, Horner's clean personal reputation, despite his wet stance, made it difficult for Thompson to take the higher moral ground on Len Small's behalf as a viable political strategy. Running a campaign rife with bigotry in order to maintain his hold over black and Italian voters, Thompson had to rely on sheer inertia. Through his own connections, Horner had won very devoted support from big business and banking. Known for being an intellectual and for employing reason rather than political rhetoric on most occasions, he cultivated the support of the academic world and was able to send out campaign pamphlets proclaiming he was backed by two hundred academics at the University of Chicago.

During the election, Horner found a strong and vocal ally in Edward J. Kelly, who was then the chief engineer of the Chicago Sanitary District. Like Horner, Kelly was a member of the Fourth Ward. He had long-standing connections with Cermak and worked hard on the Chicago end of Horner's campaign. A convincing public speaker, Kelly addressed Chicagoans on the radio, heralding Horner as a public servant devoted to the public good who was not really a politician at all. Indeed, Horner seemed to combine the attributes of a genteel intellectual and a populist candidate in a very unusual and effective alchemy. He seemed an unstoppable candidate, a situation that Kelly would have to contend with in a few short years.

While Horner continued to gather momentum, the opposition was putting up an odd defense. Her name was *Doris*, and she wound her way up and down the Mississippi and Illinois Rivers, a faint strain of jazz warbling from her decks. Small crowds that gathered along the banks to enjoy the spectacle of the campaign yacht would be invited on board to have a dance and a drink. On board, they enjoyed an impromptu party and a bit of speech making and sloganeering on the part of Big Bill Thompson. Len Small seemed oddly out of place in such a setting, but it didn't seem to matter. The campaign was Big Bill's show. "Len Small is gonna drive out the internationalists, the prohibitionists and the depressionists. . . . Let's vote out the wreckers and the robbers! Let's elect Len Small governor and Calvin Coolidge president!"[5] There was a hushed whisper. But it didn't matter to Big Bill that Coolidge had made it clear back in 1928 that he was not in the running for president.

The yachting campaign grew so notorious that larger and larger crowds began to anticipate the arrival of the *Doris* and the free party that was to follow. During the campaign, the Small-Thompson troupe also stopped here and there for political rallies on dry land. Thompson clearly demonstrated that his primary motive for being involved in the election was a deep and unremitting grudge against Cermak. He largely dismissed the opposing candidate, Henry Horner, and argued instead that Horner's election would be an opportunity for the power-mad Cermak to tighten his grip on the state. As he had done in the 1931 campaign, when he ran unsuccessfully against Cermak, Thompson resorted to calling him names like "Tony Baloney the Dictator" and "Anton the First, Emperor of Cook County." He played on the downstate fear of Chicago taking control of the statehouse by implying that a vote for Horner was really only a vote for big shot Cermak, a character that he knew would not play well to the rural population. Thompson also decided to pull out the ethnic and racial invectives that he had displayed in his struggle with Cermak for the mayoralty. He told farmers, "Elect Henry Horner and the price of pork will go down to nothing."[6] He derisively referred to Horner's *real* surname as often as he could and continued to refer to Cermak as "Pushcart Tony." Many of the political players in Chicago were vulnerable to ethnic slander of one kind or another and, like Cermak, had come from modest backgrounds. They most definitely were not impressed by such thoughtless rhetoric. Colleagues in the Republican Party recognized how damaging this could be to Small's chances and begged Thompson to stop the bigotry. Big Bill countered that it was his responsibility to use every means possible to assure the election of Small.

It was probably a great asset to Horner's campaign experience that Cermak's attention was divided during the election. While he did do a great deal of speaking and campaigning on Horner's behalf, much of his attention was drawn away toward Roosevelt's election. Cermak's reluctance to warm up to Roosevelt did not escape the notice of the future president. Nevertheless, Cermak worked overtime to assure that Illinois would emerge a visible pro-Roosevelt state at the end of the campaign and reap the resulting rewards from the administration. He set about feverishly fund-raising for Roosevelt, which was especially important, since it was widely acknowledged that Hoover had outstripped Roosevelt in terms of campaign financing. As a grand symbolic gesture of support, Cermak organized the National Association of Roosevelt Czechoslovakian Clubs of America and acted as president of the distinctive new organization.

While Cermak was desperately waving a white flag in Roosevelt's direction, Horner had a little more freedom to run his campaign on his own terms. Naturally a sociable man who had an amazing sense of audience, Horner seemed to enjoy the campaign process. But by the end, he was, of course, exhausted. On one occasion, while working on a speech at the home of supporter Dick Finnegan, he fell asleep on the couch, and Finnegan finished the speech for him. But he seemed to be gaining more and more support. Even the *Chicago Tribune*, a strong Republican newspaper, backed him: "In Judge Horner's case, the Democratic organization made a choice so good as to prove an intent to offer the party the best available candidate for the head of the state ticket."[7] Then finally, it was election time, and the real work was about to begin. Horner chose to spend Election Day among friends at the Standard Club. There was little he could do now but wait.

He had done all he could to reach out to every voter. All of Horner's affiliations were understandably proud of their prominent member and looked forward to having one of their own in the governor's seat. The Skeeters wired a poem to Horner that ended "Henry the Skeeter is our state's delight."[8] The early jubilation in anticipation of an easy victory rose to weary elation that evening when the scope of Horner's victory was revealed. Roosevelt's victory over Hoover was by 450,000 votes; Horner's victory over Len Small was by over 566,000 votes. In the Illinois General Assembly, the Democrats now controlled both chambers: 33–18 in the Senate, and 80–73 in the House. The Illinois Democratic delegation to the U.S. House of Representatives outnumbered that of the Republicans 19–8.[9] Horner's half-million-vote margin of victory was the largest in the state's history. Nearly all the candidates on Cermak's ticket sailed to victory that day. Roosevelt too seemed to have benefited from the Cermak machine. In Cook County, though, Horner outshined even Roosevelt, pulling more votes than the popular presidential candidate. Downstate, Roosevelt received higher numbers, but it was nevertheless astonishing that a Jewish candidate from Chicago had even carried downstate. After the election, the sheer magnitude of Horner's connections in Chicago and throughout Illinois became evident. Personal congratulatory notices streamed in. In a postal telegram, James A. Farley, Roosevelt's campaign manager and soon-to-be postmaster general, wrote, "Heartiest Congratulations upon your splendid victory[.] I sincerely appreciate the support and valuable assistance you rendered the national ticket during the conduct of your own campaign."[10] Many of Horner's associates gave him pieces of advice; others expressed their confidence that a good man such as Horner would do nothing less than the best for Illinois. Most pledged their support and offered their help and advice in the months ahead. Horner had only just completed the whirlwind of his campaign and already his thoughts were turned to the serious task that confronted him. Illinois in 1932 could not possibly have presented the governor-elect with a more daunting challenge.

8

Roll Up Your Sleeves, Governor

During the election, Horner's blood pressure had given him some problems. As usual, he had not been too ruffled by it. He blamed it on the pace of an election: the endless meet-and-greets, and the complexity and enormity of Illinois's difficulties as he had encountered them on his travels throughout the state. Dick Finnegan, who had witnessed Horner's exhaustion, wrote him a letter after his election cautioning him not to overtax himself and to pay particular attention to the state of his health. The stress of both a state campaign and an active role in the presidential election had also gotten to Cermak, who had to retreat to Europe during the campaign to recover from one of his bouts of digestive troubles. Of course, Cermak had taken the opportunity to do a good deal of public relations stumping for Chicago during his rest period. He made the case abroad that the violent reputation of the city was unfounded and that Chicago was a world-class industrial economy warranting respect and investment. Both men, now exhausted, retreated for a brief recovery period to French Lick, Indiana, with Bruce Campbell. Once a political rival, Campbell had become a close associate and supporter during the campaign. This turn of events most likely grew from the personal admiration he had developed for Horner during the downstate campaign.

In French Lick, Horner fielded personal questions from the press. Being a bachelor had not been an issue during the election, but now the state was envisioning him as the man in the governor's mansion. The public was intrigued by the romantic possibilities of having a bachelor governor. Some stirrings of matchmaking were even in evidence in the sensationalist press. From the outset not the kind of public figure who thrived on notoriety, Horner immediately quelled these kinds of imaginings. He assured the public that at the present time the situation in Illinois was so grave that his governorship would be entirely about public service. The governor's mansion would simply not need a hostess—these were not the times for a party in Springfield. Horner rightly assumed that he would be a very busy man for a long time. After resting in Indiana, Horner spent some time working with Governor Emmerson on the historical preservation of a Lincoln property. Since they had not been pitted against one another in the election, Horner enjoyed a friendly relationship with the incumbent governor. While Emmerson did publicly reiterate his fear that the Democrats would turn the state over to the evils of the dole, privately he was reasonably satisfied to turn over the governorship to the respectable Horner. His enthusiasm would probably have been less had he been turning over the governor's mansion to Len Small.

The relationship between Cermak and Horner was further confirmed when the governor-elect spent the holidays with Cermak's family. It appeared that Horner and Cermak were going to march into Springfield hand-in-hand, even if one of the hands was going to be reaching from Chicago. In the interim between the election and the inauguration, Cermak also found himself distracted with some rumblings in his own stomping grounds. When the new administration moved in, the underground economy would have to do some shifting to accommodate the changes. It was rumored that Cermak had promised to meet with his underworld "colleagues" after the state elections to discuss the unofficial policies relating to vice. It was also rumored there would be a shake-up and that connections with the syndicate in New York would be strengthened under the new mayor, who favored a Tammany Hall–style political machine. Cermak planned to reign over this empire when he formalized the loose connections between vice and city politics. He had read the signs: Prohibition was nearing an end, and bootlegging was about to lose its punch in the underworld. So, he trained his attention on organizing and controlling gambling in Chicago. Syndicate leaders were apprehensive of the implications for their existing power structures.

On the sunny day of Horner's inauguration, Governor Emmerson introduced Horner as "my personal friend." In a gesture of goodwill, Horner had even agreed to keep on Governor Emmerson's faithful chauffeur. The passing of the torch was amicable and upbeat. However, Horner made it clear with his actions that the first order of the day was not celebration. He assailed the assembled throng, which was in festive spirits, with a serious, forty-page inaugural address that was all business and, frankly, rather boring. However, he wanted to make clear the deeply considered steps that he intended to take on behalf of Illinois. The first item on the agenda showed just how little he cared for public relations at this juncture. He declared that the tax debacle that had plagued the state for years would be the first arena for change. He proposed that a sales tax be initiated as an emergency measure. The citizens of Illinois, already bowed down under financial duress, didn't want to hear about additional taxes. The sales tax was not a popular proposal. But Henry Horner was not one to gloss over realities, a characteristic that had endeared him to voters during the campaign. He was determined to demonstrate that his administration was not going to curry popularity or manipulate the mood of the public. It would be about exercising careful judgment and doing what had to be done. Illinois was in an emergency situation, and the sales tax was a necessary measure.

In his speech, Horner also tackled the second issue that was obsessing the general public. He renewed Cermak's commitment to the repeal of Prohibition, but not as a way of making political hay from the emotional reaction of the people to this issue. Approaching the subject with practicality and seriousness, Horner asserted that when the Eighteenth Amendment was repealed, the sale of alcohol would have to be reinstituted carefully and be made subject to strong state regulatory policies and taxation. Anyone listening to these words could almost feel the hairs rising on the back of Cermak's neck as he listened to Horner publicly adopt a moderate and cautious stance on Cermak's pet issue. Overall, it was not a good day for Anton Cermak. In view of the financial crisis in Illinois, Horner thought it would be in bad taste to throw an expensive, traditional inaugural ball. So, showing gentlemanly taste in escorting the aging widow of a former governor, he hosted a reception in his new home, the Executive Mansion, instead.

The mansion was not equipped for affairs of this size, especially considering Horner's popularity and his legions of connections. Security was tight at the door as the party soon began to swell in size. When Cermak arrived, the beleaguered police officer at the door did not recognize him and was immune to his protestations regarding his identity. A vivid description provided by Thomas Littlewood relates that Cermak finally "ducked through a back laundry-room window, dodged under a maze of pipes, and emerged at the reception in an irritable mood."[1] This comic drama seems a foreshadowing of Cermak's failed intention to run the show in Springfield from Chicago. His candidate was beginning to eclipse him already. On the day of his inauguration, Horner also demonstrated that while he publicly kept the larger picture in view, he wasn't above a little personal retribution. In a symbolic gesture that reflects plenty of forethought, the moment Horner was sworn in as governor, his executive assistant slipped off to the statehouse and got on the telephone. Horner's first executive action as governor was to fire a state trooper who had referred to him as a "Jew son-of-a-bitch" during the election. This action served as an indication that while Horner kept up an amiable demeanor in the most contentious of circumstances, he would fight back when attacked. This quality of quiet determination unveiled itself and startled the political world of Illinois when reelection time came for Horner.

A Chicago man, born and bred, who had never traveled extensively because he was so busy with responsibilities in Chicago, Horner now found himself in Springfield, where he was free of the chill, damp wind spilling over from Lake Michigan and also free from the direct scrutiny of Cermak. In Chicago, Horner had many friends but also many entanglements. There was always someone giving him advice, pressuring him on some matter, or expecting to get something from him. The Chicago political scene was quite suffocating. One can imagine that Horner took the opportunity to take a breath of fresh air when he landed in the flat, sunny expansiveness of Springfield. He enjoyed strolling in the charming downtown area, finding reminiscences of Lincoln on every corner. While he watched his own belongings being hauled into the impressive white building, Horner probably thought of Lincoln watching the construction of the governor's mansion with his sons. Horner didn't have much to move in. He hadn't accumulated a house full of furniture and keepsakes, as some of his predecessors had. In fact, he had little more than his clothing, his sizable library, and his ever-expanding collection of Lincoln memorabilia. His possessions did not fill the mansion, and he took to limiting his use of the estate to a few choice rooms.

One part of Horner's history that he did transport to Springfield was his personal secretary, Ella Cornwall. Looking now like a plump and cantankerous grandmother, she had served as a trusted confidante during his early years as a young attorney and his long career on the probate bench; now she would occupy a prominent position in state government. She handled his paperwork and kept him organized, but she also had an eye out for his personal welfare. She reminded him to stop and eat when he was lost in work, and she even was known to lay out his boots on rainy days. It seems certain that Hannah Horner was in his thoughts at this time as well. She, more than anyone, would have been proud of the achievements of her grandson. Her visionary nature, her work ethic, and her scrupulous honesty must have been in his thoughts as he viewed the majestic statehouse. Later, in a rare display of sentimentality and extravagance, Horner had the portrait commissioned by his grandmother of himself and his cousins laboriously restored from beneath layers of paint and moved to the Executive Mansion in Springfield. And so, Henry Horner embraced a new home and a new set of challenges.

The first major round of work for any new governor is attending to that political minefield—appointments. It is during this time that an elected official must consider who put him or her in office and weigh these political debts against the public good. And that is exactly what Horner did. Although during the election, Cermak had left him somewhat to his own devices, the mayor of Chicago was now hanging over Horner's shoulder quite obtrusively. Seeds of an uneasy relationship, planted during the inauguration, began to take root as Horner carefully made his appointments.

It surprised no one that two of Cermak's son-in-laws found themselves with fairly significant promotions. The first, Dr. Frank Jirka, became state director of health, and the second, Ricky V. Graham, became president pro tem of the Senate. Detractors noted that there were a handful of Cermak's close friends who received plum government jobs as well. But even if he was repaying some political debts to Cermak, Horner himself had the final word. He paid tribute to the assistance and support of the Lindheimer family by appointing Jacob Lindheimer's son Benjamin, a major architect of Horner's campaign, to be chairman of the Illinois Commerce Commission. Horner also honored several of Lindheimer's preferences in making other appointments, indicating that he valued Lindheimer's role in his election nearly as much as he did Cermak's. Cermak had expected Horner to feel some degree of indebtedness to Lindheimer, but he was irritated when it became clear that Horner was consulting advisers from outside the mayor's office on the matter of appointments. Horner's own set of priorities did not match the organizational chart on Cermak's desk. The mayor felt openly defied when Horner appointed Joseph J. Rice as the state director of finance and Ernest Palmer as the head of the State Insurance Office, because these appointments were contrary to his wishes. The mayor had put up with enough. Horner's independent streak was beginning to worry him.

One city worker recalled overhearing Cermak talking to the governor on the phone: "Well, goddamn you, you're governor in name only. Who the hell do you think you are?"[2] Apparently, Horner thought of himself as governor of the state of Illinois. Overall, he showed great independence in making his choices. He refused to depose qualified Republicans in favor of Democrats, and some of his new appointments were Republicans as well. Mindful that party politicians were frequently accused of appointing connected "hacks" to positions requiring a good deal of expertise, Horner called numerous academics into duty. Some were reluctant to take on the demanding life of public service. When economics professor Simon Leland turned down an appointment as head of the State Tax Commission to take a vacation in Italy, Horner admonished him: "That's just the trouble with you fellows who are always telling us how things ought to be done. Then we give you a chance to do it and you're always too busy, you've always got something else."[3] Horner shamed Leland into service, just as he had pressured undertakers, attorneys, and bankers on behalf of the people when he served as probate judge.

Many politicians, especially downstate ones like John Stelle, were leery of including these intellectuals in their circle. Horner received a good number of letters protesting the "fatheads" that would be coming to Springfield. Stelle, a lifelong Democrat, was also furious about Horner's employing Republicans. Horner had assembled an administration in which each member was qualified for his position, but he had not crafted a cohesive or harmonious group. He had career politicians, businessmen, Democrats, Republicans, and university professors all huddled under one, uneasy roof with a daunting task ahead of them. Time would tell whether qualifications could mitigate the potential chaos of such diversity. As can be expected in politics, Horner received his fair share of criticism for his appointments. He could not please everybody. Some hopefuls didn't like the suggestion that they were not the most qualified for the job. Democrats shook their heads at the Republicans on Horner's team. Many had hoped that their support would translate into a position and were disappointed when it did not. And, of course, Anton Cermak had expected something quite different from "his" governor. Many politicians would have relished the chance to throw their power around and show who was boss, consequences be damned. But Horner was not the typical politician. He genuinely wanted to be liked, and it was a strain on his kind nature to disappoint anyone. This was a habit of mind that would wear on the governor.

The governorship was quite different, he soon discovered, than the probate bench. There he had ruled with an unquestioned sovereignty, and very few dared to challenge his decisions. In the governor's chair, each and every decision he made was met with a cacophony of protest and debate. Everyone seemed inspired to try to influence the new governor. After the appointments were made, Horner turned his attention toward healing rifts. When Cermak angrily called a final time and railed against his latest appointment, the mayor worked himself into such a rage that he actually slammed the phone down. Although in a position not to tolerate such a disrespectful gesture, Horner decided to take the higher ground. He called Cermak back several times until he finally got through. Eager to repair the damaged bridge, Horner discussed the matter with his usual amicable, rational logic. He assured Cermak that he was only trying to match the best man to each job. The scrupulous honesty that Cermak had laughed at when Horner was his campaign treasurer had become a thorn in his side. However, he was convinced that Horner's appointment choices were the result of naïveté. The governor did not intend a personal affront to him, nor did he mean to send a message to the Chicago machine that he was giving them the slip. Horner ended by inviting Cermak and Pat Nash, chairman of the Cook County Democratic Party, to the governor's mansion, a clear message that they were still very much in the loop in Springfield. It is said that Cermak and Nash were so unsure of the kind of hospitality that might be offered by the bachelor governor that they arrived at the mansion with a basket of food in tow.[4] But Horner's entertaining skills were apparently sufficient to smooth over the early rift between himself and Chicago.

Having completed the difficult task of making his appointments as quickly as he could, Horner cleared his mind for the storm to come. He began to realize that this was not going to be a typical legislative term. The economy was not merely weakened by the Depression; the whole system was on the verge of collapse. A key location of the U.S. transportation network, Chicago had become a major gathering place for transients streaming in from all over the country. These were economically displaced people searching for temporary employment or simply hoping to take advantage of the city's breadlines. The edge of the Loop District on Randolph Street had by now been completely transformed by the burgeoning homeless population. Shacks made of cardboard, the permanent residences of transients, formed communities nicknamed "Hoovervilles" in honor of the former president who seemed so divorced from the reality of Depression agonies. Chicago's most affluent society could no longer be sheltered from the desperate and ragged who spilled out of the crowded tent cities and collapsed under and on top of park benches, slept beneath bridges, and queued in breadlines. They sold apples or pencils on the streets; they begged for nickels in every neighborhood. The whole city winced in pain and anticipation. Relief agencies were depleted, and the underworld economy of the city, hardened as it was to suffering, now funded much of the food relief in the city. It seemed as if it couldn't get any worse. But it did. To make matters much worse, the city was ill-equipped to handle its financial emergency because of the tax-revenue crisis that state government had been bungling for many years.

In 1927, the state's notoriously inequitable property tax system had gone under review. It was decided that the real estate tax assessments had to be restructured. During the restructuring, which took two long years, the state suspended all tax collection. During that time, the coffers were bled without being refilled. When taxes were finally reassessed, Chicago's properties were greatly devalued from their former taxable status. The result was a massive deficit that left the city unable to effectively deal with the economic depression that followed soon after. To compound matters, a large number of property owners, disgruntled with the outcome of the restructuring, launched a property tax strike. In 1930, 50 percent of the property taxes went unpaid. The result was that the city of Chicago had little relief money and was not even able to pay its municipal employees. Policemen and firefighters were laid off. Schoolteachers continued to work without pay. In Anton Cermak's first year as mayor, Chicago schoolteachers had only received three months' worth of pay.[5] In 1933, the University of Illinois found that it could not meet its payroll. All state employees were persuaded to take a 10 percent pay cut.

Elsewhere in the state, conditions were just as bad. The coal mining industry was on its knees, and violent skirmishes dotted the ruins. Farmers across the state, and indeed the country, were facing foreclosure. Horner knew the state was in a grave condition, but he only fully realized the gravity of the situation when he received his first report from the Illinois National Guard. The state militia was trying to keep its finger on a proliferating number of sites of potential violence in the state. According to the report, the city of Chicago was nearing a boiling point. The coal strike, which expressed the miners' anger with both the Peabody Coal Mine Company and John L. Lewis, seemed destined to turn into a violent struggle. Nobody knew what would happen if the banks gobbled up all the indebted farms. And now, two more factories were closing in Quincy. As the resources of the state and city were depleted, eyes began to turn toward Washington for assistance. Cermak paid a visit to the nation's capital in June 1932. With the Hoover administration still in office, Cermak addressed the House of Representative's Banking and Currency Committee to communicate the gravity of the situation in Chicago. He once again argued that "It would be cheaper for Congress to provide a loan of $152,000,000 to the City of Chicago, than to pay for the services of Federal Troops at a future date."[6] The national legislature was hearing similar threatening rhetoric from leaders around the country. A month later, Hoover reluctantly signed a bill enabling the Reconstruction Finance Corporation to provide $300 million in loans to the states. Illinois received a $3 million loan, the first of many federal loans that the state would gratefully accept.

When Roosevelt and Horner took office in 1933, it was clear that both would have to plan massive action. While Cermak dealt with the fiscal crisis in Chicago by plunging the city into austerity spending, Horner picked his first major battle: the coal mine wars that were heating up across downstate Illinois. Although he had experience in arbitrating labor disputes in Chicago, he soon learned just how different the stage of state government was from the courthouse. His first attempt to intervene in the conflict used a technique that had been successfully employed by Big Bill Thompson in Chicago. On the first Sunday after his inauguration, Horner gathered together the disputing sides in the coal mining debacle—fifty men in all, representing the Peabody Coal Mine Company, the United Mine Workers and the Progressive Miners of America—and hosted them at the Executive Mansion. He also invited mayors of many of the affected towns. Horner trusted in his ability to read people and to communicate with subtle effectiveness to assuage anger and encourage reconciliation. Biographer Thomas Littlewood notes that when Horner saw that finger sandwiches were being wheeled in, he read his rough-and-tumble audience and requested more appropriate, sizable roast beef sandwiches be served instead.[7] Such efforts to accommodate others indicate just how much stock Horner put in a friendly, social environment. He truly believed in the power of goodwill; however, such niceties could not soothe the deep hostility in that room. Horner announced that no one was going to bed until a peaceful agreement was reached. The sun rose, and no such agreement was in sight. Trying another strategy, Horner attempted to forestall the violence by issuing a general disarmament order in the affected counties. As might be expected, people in those regions strongly protested having to turn their weapons over to National Guard troops.

On January 25, 1933, 200 PMA protestors were thrown out of the Illinois House of Representatives when they attempted to force legal redress for their mistreatment at the hands of Peabody and the UMW. Their anger and rebelliousness intensified by this treatment, they then stormed the statehouse. They were a rough, brawling bunch, more ready to fight than to negotiate. Horner emerged from his office when he heard the uproar, and he immediately offered to meet with five of their leaders. They responded with shouts of "We voted for you, we'll tell you what to do!"[8] Unused to such a reaction to his honorable overtures, an indignant Horner ordered the state police to disperse the crowd. The situation grew chaotic. Horner was shocked to witness a physical clash in his new workplace that produced injuries, arrests, and some damage to the statehouse. The scene offended him. He believed that things should be accomplished amicably, with civility and respect, just as they had been in his probate court; he strongly voiced his refusal to deal with angry mobs. His first priority in the matter became law enforcement. He still sympathized with the cause of the PMA protestors, however. They were the underdogs and had been unfairly treated, and Horner knew that poverty and hunger fueled their desperation. Still, their tactics in pursuing their cause seemed ineffective and offended his sensibilities. His first major battle, the coal mine wars, creaked on without a definitive resolution.[9]

The attention of the beleaguered new governor next turned to the epidemic of farms that were dangling over the precipice of foreclosure. More and more families that had once been respectable property owners were reduced to the status of vagabond wanderers. The collapse of the farming sector was threatening to snap the most integral thread in the fabric of American industry. Farmers had long labored in poverty; they did not enjoy the rollicking good times of the 1920s. And were they now to lose all that they had built? The thought was too much for the country and the governor to bear. Many advisers urged Horner to issue an emergency moratorium on farm foreclosures. He considered this option but was concerned about the impact on the banking industry, which was also on its knees. He stopped short of that level of government interference in banking affairs, instead offering a personal appeal to mortgage holders to exercise restraint on foreclosures during the trying economic times. Many responded to his call.

As Roosevelt was beginning to line up his appointments after the 1932 election, Anton Cermak stewed uneasily. The mayor was not used to a feeling of powerlessness, but after being a latecomer to the Roosevelt camp, he was not in a position to assert great influence on the new president. Casting an insider's light on the relationship between Roosevelt and Cermak, the colorful alderman of the Forty-third Ward, Paddy Bauler, had this to say of the fateful meeting between the two men: "Cermak didn't like the son of a bitch, this Roosevelt, and he didn't want to go see the son of a bitch. I says, 'Listen, for Christ's sake, you ain't got money for the Chicago Schoolteachers and this Roosevelt is the only one who can get it for you. You better get over there and kiss his ass or whatever you got to do. Only you better get the goddam money for the teachers, or we ain't gonna have a city that's worth runnin'."[10] Roosevelt and Cermak were certainly from different backgrounds and had contrasting political styles. Roosevelt came from a wealthy and refined family, and his power over the rough mayor from Braidwood differed greatly from any power differential between Cermak and Horner. Roosevelt had a quiet and genteel leadership style, while Cermak was an unapologetic table pounder. Roosevelt was just the kind of man Cermak didn't like to have to approach with his hat in his hand.

Although Bauler's characterization of Cermak's attitude may not be completely accurate, the tenuous relationship between Cermak and Roosevelt had the potential of disastrously impacting the material conditions of Chicago in upcoming years. In addition to the need for federal aid for the ailing city, Cermak was concerned about issues of patronage. Always worried about his own position in the Democratic Party, he viewed the empty federal posts and the available Illinois statesmen lining up to fill them as a threat to his throttlehold on the state. Already, men outside the machine, reformers like Harold Ickes and Carter Harrison, were rumored to be considering significant federal positions. Cermak knew that he had to get some of his men into the picture.

Thus, it was with no small degree of trepidation that he traveled to Florida in February 1933 to meet with the new president-elect. That fateful evening, Cermak waited with the restless crowd for Roosevelt to arrive in Miami at the end of a yachting trip and make his appearance at a reception in the park. Handlers placed Cermak, as the representative of a major American city, in a prominent location with other special dignitaries ready to receive the president. Roosevelt arrived by open car. According to Cermak's biographer, Alex Gottfried, Roosevelt spotted Cermak immediately upon his arrival and gestured to him that he would receive him at the car. Perhaps not properly reading the sign or hesitant to step to the fore, Cermak did not approach the car at that moment. Roosevelt instead delivered a few remarks to the crowd from the car. After the speech, Cermak joined a group of special guests to be the first to approach the car and greet the president. He shook hands with Roosevelt, and they exchanged pleasantries. Roosevelt's driver started the ignition, intending to deliver Roosevelt to the reception. At nearly the same moment, shots rang out.

Some accounts indicate that the instant Cermak took a bullet, he cried out, "The President: get him away!"[11] Other accounts less generously suggest that Cermak said, "They got me!"[12] Cermak's character continues to remain a matter of debate.

The assassin was Giuseppe Zangara, a bricklayer from New Jersey and an anarchist who believed himself to be terminally ill, who was described as an "undersized, strange gnome-like creature."[13] He had crept up through the crowd and sent a scattering of bullets at the gentlemen huddled about the car. He injured five individuals, including Chicago's mayor. It remains uncertain which man he really meant to assassinate. Most historians assume that Zangara was after a symbolic big fish, namely Roosevelt, and argue that he hoped to go down in a triumphant act of glory by assassinating the president. Others speculate that the real target of the assassination attempt was Cermak and that gangland complications in Chicago were relevant to what took place. However, these latter speculations, while interesting in theory, have generally not been supported by facts. Whether accidentally or intentionally, the assassin killed Anton Cermak. After struggling to recover and then enduring the setback of a secondary infection, he died in a hospital in Florida on March 6, 1933. He would not be the "World's Fair Mayor" after all.

9

The Crux of the Crisis

At a crucial time in American history, three important players in this piece of the story stepped into office. It was the year of the Democrats. The Republican Party had developed a reputation for insensitivity and inaction that simply could not be tolerated by the suffering populace. And so, on a wave of energy that demanded change, Henry Horner had sailed easily into office as governor of the pivotal state of Illinois. Franklin Delano Roosevelt, a Democrat with striking similarities to Horner in philosophy and even background, left the governorship of New York and moved into the White House. In his inaugural address, he promised a "new deal" for Americans. Both had to hit the ground running. When Cermak died, a temporary vacuum was created in the city of Chicago, now a tinderbox of poverty and unrest. Soon, however, a new mayor, Ed Kelly, took the seat. Each of these figures confronted the hurricane of panic that descended on their office doors in different ways. Their strategies, policies, and agendas intertwined, sometimes causing frustrating knots. Still, they were in the same fight—the fight to save the democratic, capitalist system from itself.

America in 1932 and 1933 was at a crossroads. The collapse of the stock market and the banking industry and the suffering that resulted made people question whether the great capitalist experiment was a failure. They craved a guarantee against future economic catastrophes. Society seemed to be falling apart, and everyone was searching for a new blueprint. Everywhere one looked, there was chaos, controversy, and emergency conditions. Many people who had quietly accepted their lot and expected little more than to subsist were now unable to do even that, and they were enraged. As the industrial magnates failed and became embroiled in controversy, Americans read in the papers about their egregious evasion of taxes and the graft and favoritism that occasioned their rise to power. Jobs were so scarce and precious that business owners could expect prospective workers to fight over jobs that were ridiculously low-paying and arduous. Workers across the nation were laboring unpaid, like the Chicago schoolteachers, and pensions and promises had run out.

In the summer of 1932, while Herbert Hoover was in his last year as president, 15,000 people formed the Bonus Expeditionary Force. They were World War I veterans, now destitute, who traveled to Washington to demand that their veteran bonuses, approved by Congress in 1924, be paid early. Although the House agreed, the Senate did not. Most of the veterans returned home, but those who stayed built a shantytown at Anacostia Flats, within view of the nation's capitol. After District of Columbia police panicked and shot into the crowd, killing two veterans, Hoover ordered in July that the army remove the protestors. General Douglas MacArthur, along with young officers Dwight D. Eisenhower and George S. Patton, accomplished the task. With 700 troops, they destroyed Anacostia Flats and dispersed the veterans and their families. Although many were injured in the melee, only one death occurred. An eleven–week-old boy, who had been born in the Flats, died from tear gas. This incident fueled the anger of many Americans at Hoover's insensitivity to the common people. Gathering, picketing, protesting, even storming government buildings in angry mobs became the order of the day. The protest activities of the American people at this time were so numerous and so noisy that they make the activism of the American 1960s seem like a quiet blip on the radar screen of U.S. history. During the Depression, people invented new ways to make the many heard by the few. They followed the model of the labor activists who had agitated on behalf of workers in urban centers like Chicago and in coal mines and rural industries across the country. But now, the angry crowds represented the whole American working-class population—men, women, and children rose to assert their basic right to survival and even happiness.

Henry Horner had always felt that his role in life was to assure such rights. But now he was on one side of the door, while the angry mobs clamored on the other side. Horner had never responded well to threats and intimidation. He favored the orderly, rational dialogue that typified operations in probate court. He had to figure out how to enter into this new, unruly arena, and how to problem solve and make inroads back toward order. Roosevelt, too, had to invent a new way of governing in extraordinary circumstances. His strategy was to gather together a group of intellectuals and professionals, what came to be known as "the Brain Trust," to rapidly problem solve and reinvent government, which needed reinventing at the time. Everyone sensed that the system, as it now stood, simply was not working. People hit hard by the Depression craved order and prosperity. Eyes turned abroad for answers. American capitalism was in crisis. The question seemed to be, can we fix it, or should we abandon it and try something else?

It was at this time that a number of radical, alternative political movements experienced rapid growth because they seemed to offer economic models that would protect America from future collapses. A number of prominent figures came out publicly as communists and, for a time, seriously considered this mode of government as a legitimate alternative to capitalism. People began to see their situations reflected in the writings of Karl Marx and were moved by the principles of shared wealth promised in the model set forth there. Socialists set themselves up against right-wing industrialists. The common people often found themselves on the same side of the fence as the socialists, even if they didn't always know what economic system they themselves favored. People also looked to the new governments being forged by then-obscure leaders such as Mussolini and Hitler, whose names hadn't yet become synonymous with tyranny and evil. They saw how Italy and Germany seemed to be making inroads into social and economic reconstruction. Although their modes of government seemed radically different from the ideals of the Founding Fathers of America, perhaps those were what was needed here as well as in Europe. Perhaps the people would be better protected under such strong-armed systems of leadership.

During Horner's first term in office, the state was no longer just teetering on the edge of bankruptcy; it was hovering on the verge of a full-scale revolution. Everywhere there were picketers and protestors, establishing an uneasy and fragile boundary between political expression and violence. Historian T. H. Watkins notes, "There probably had never been so many eruptions of public unrest in such a short time over so wide a spectrum of geography and population in the nation's history as those that punctuated the months between the winter of 1930 and the winter of 1933."[1] Horner's field advisers informed him regularly about revolutionary sentiment in the state. They apprised him of the protest activity that was going on, the degree of "redness" of the protest, and the proximity of that activity to revolution. Horner and other leaders across the country considered a second American revolution to be a legitimate threat, a possibility that the general public of today, for whom revolution is an abstract, academic concept, would find difficult to understand. However, in the 1930s, the Bolshevik Revolution of 1917 was still fresh in the public's mind. The revolutionary scenario seemed to fit the times that Americans were experiencing. People could envision the social order being toppled, the rich being driven from their homes by mobs of the desperate and angry poor who looted their possessions and perhaps even murdered them. As leaders looked at the hungry faces filled with resentment, they felt that the revolutionary potential of the times was very real. Quelling it was urgent. It was under this kind of pressure that Governor Horner and President Roosevelt attacked the problems of abject poverty, hunger, and joblessness.

Desperate Americans toyed with communism, fascism, and even Nazism during those vulnerable times. While the Nazi Party in Germany used the Jewish people as scapegoats for the economic travails in their country, similar ideas were taking root, to some degree, in America. In fact, the American Nazi Party had its roots in central Illinois, where the party's founder, George Lincoln Rockwell, was born in 1918. This rising global anti-Semitism must certainly have exerted pressure on the first elected Jewish governor of Illinois. With his deep convictions concerning the rectitude of the plan of the Founding Fathers and the sanctity of the Declaration of Independence, Horner probably felt the threat to these principles very keenly when he saw Americans consider turning over their power to dictators, the state, and even deterministic racial theories of social hierarchy. Horner's philosophy would be tested in the difficult years leading up to World War II. He had long believed that those in public life should represent the people as a whole and stay away from ethnic politics. Personally, he valued his faith, his heritage, and his community highly, but he hesitated to make himself a figurehead for Jews or to use his influence to further Jewish causes. Each time he was called into service because of his Jewish background, he hesitated. He had vowed to be the people's governor, a position that transcended ethnic considerations. Unlike many of his Jewish peers, he did not believe that people's religion meant very much in differentiating them from one another. He found religion to be largely a matter of chance, determined by the happenstance of birth, and did not see any great value in drawing political boundaries based on the circumstances of birth. He took very seriously the rhetoric of the Founding Fathers about the equality of all people, also prevalent in the thought of Lincoln, and believed that ethnic politics ran counter to that philosophy. But still he valued friendships, allegiances, and family, and he was concerned with the position of Jews in American society.

Torn as he was, his activity on behalf of Jews was somewhat ambivalent. For example, he attended a meeting of the Jews of Chicago to discuss the rise of anti-Semitism in Europe, but was criticized for giving one of the shorter addresses of the evening. Horner also inflamed Jewish opinion when he did not commute the sentence of a Jewish man who was scheduled to be executed on Yom Kippur. Now and then, he declined to appear or speak at a Jewish function. Horner was, in some ways, a typical member of the Standard Club, which was made up of German Jews who were not particularly consumed with their Jewish identity. Some critics praised Horner's handling of the matter, lauding his refusal to be a "professional Jew," but many Jewish citizens were disappointed that their moment of triumph, a Jew in the statehouse, had not produced the transformative results they expected. One rabbi, for example, accused Horner of not being a "real Jew," saying, "A real Jew is one who is first and last for his people, not one who avoids mentioning his ancestry as though it were something of which to be ashamed."[2] While there is little evidence that Horner was ashamed of his religious identity, and he certainly never hid his heritage, the rabbi does point out a philosophical difference. Horner did not seem to be "first and last" for *his* people and probably would have rejected such an attitude. He felt that his job was to be "first and last" for *the* people. It was this value that was consistently reflected in his actions. He did, however, receive a good deal of political fallout for his decision not to be a "professional Jew."

While Horner and Roosevelt were preparing to take office, the national emergency greatly worsened. Suddenly, the banking system seemed about to collapse. The nation watched this situation in horror, but Hoover refused to take heroic action. Thus, both Horner and Roosevelt had to make preventing the collapse of the banking system their first priority when they took office. The instability of the banks cut so close to the heart of the now diseased American dream that their failure would be a national emergency. Decades of common wisdom proved worthless in an instant. Americans had been promised that if they were wise and hardworking, if they carefully saved and put away their earnings, they could achieve the good life. They trusted the national institutions, and most could not even comprehend that their savings were vulnerable to the Great Depression. After all, they had not been gambling in the stock market; they had taken the safe route. But it was becoming clear that no one's financial position was secure any longer, least of all that of the modest, hardworking people who most deserved security. A newspaper reporter profiled a small town in the Midwest that was one of the first to see a bank go under. He told the story to give the rest of the country a sense of the human tragedy of the banking collapse, giving the bank in question the name "First National Bank of Melrose" to conceal its real identity:

> There was no warning; in the middle of the banking day examiners closed the doors. It was one of the oldest banks in the state, regarded as a branch of the United States Treasury. Within two or three hours everyone knew of the disaster. Depositors, stunned and disbelieving, gathered in small groups to read the notice on the door. . . .
>
> There was little public lamentation. The most shocking example was old Mrs. Gearman. She beat with her fists upon the closed plate-glass doors and screamed and sobbed without restraint. She had in a savings account the $2,000 from her husband's insurance and $963 she had saved over a period of twenty-five years from making rag rugs. Nothing was left but charity.[3]

Faith in the capitalist system, of which the bank was the central symbol, was already at a breaking point, and national and state leaders feared that a full-scale collapse of the banking system might arouse public sentiment into a revolutionary fervor. The bank had long since replaced the underside of the mattress as the hiding place of choice for Americans' money. Losing the money kept there for safekeeping would be a grievous personal violation, akin to a stranger ransacking one's bedroom.

Some states closed banks in a desperate attempt to reinstitute stability and prevent collapse, while cheerfully referring to these closures as "banking holidays." Fearful depositors stood in long lines, trying to get into the banks to withdraw their funds, which only weakened the system further. A group of bankers from Chicago waylaid Governor Horner, who held train tickets in his hands, on his way to the presidential inauguration in Washington. They begged him to implement a moratorium on withdrawals from banks to prevent the institutions from going under. Horner did not attend the inauguration; he had to attend to the banking crisis in Springfield.

Roosevelt was inaugurated president of the United States on March 4, 1933. He had let the lame-duck Hoover twist uncomfortably without his help or support during the banking crisis. On the day of Roosevelt's inauguration, Horner closed all the banks of Illinois; after a telephone conversation, his New York counterpart, Herbert Lehmen, took the same action on the same day. Illinois banks were supposed to be closed for ten days. But just days after his inauguration, Roosevelt made this span of time redundant, closing all banks in the nation in an effort to prevent them from going under and wreaking devastation on all of their depositors.

This national banking holiday provided extra time for legislators to hammer out ameliorative banking legislation. Many called for Roosevelt to nationalize the entire banking system. If he had been the socialist that he is often characterized as being, he might have done so. However, he took a more conservative approach. The Emergency Banking Relief Act was pushed through Congress in one day without most of the legislators having even read it. It gave the secretary of the treasury the power to reopen fiscally sound institutions, while others would remain under federal review until sound again. Roosevelt presented his plan confidently to the public through one of his ingenious public relations tools, the radio broadcast "Fireside Chat." His presentation was so reassuring and convincing that it led people, in mass, to redeposit funds in the nation's banks.

Horner and Roosevelt had the same task: to quickly stabilize a critical condition. However, their strategies for doing so differed. Horner rolled up his sleeves and took on problems one by one, starting with the coal-mining crisis. He addressed problems head on with all the energy he could muster. He was confident that if his heart was in the right place and he gave it all he had, he could resolve the issue. Accustomed to the Republican strategy of waiting for the system to correct itself, the public seemed to appreciate Horner's direct style. Gathering together the sides of the coal-mining dispute and insisting that they hammer out a resolution was typical of his straightforward governing style. When reason and action failed to produce results, he reluctantly moved on, giving all his attention to the issue of tax revenue and relief. Accustomed as he was to the case-by-case style of the courts in which matters got settled one after another in an orderly fashion, he was not used to integrating his efforts strategically into a larger system, something that machine politicians had long been accustomed to doing.

Roosevelt, on the other hand, favored a shotgun approach. Any measure that might cut into the Depression was worth trying, as far as he was concerned. He had no overarching political philosophy other than to defeat the Depression. Roosevelt put together his Brain Trust and sent everyone into a flurry of activity that came to be known as "the Hundred Days" (March 9–June 16, 1933). During those early days, Congress passed the Emergency Banking Relief Act, which was essential in dealing with the banking crisis; the Civilian Conservation Corps Reforestation Relief Act, to create jobs; and the Economy in Government Act, which cut 22,000 jobs from the federal government. Another piece of legislation, the Federal Emergency Relief Act, would have a major impact on economically depressed states throughout the country. Two other key acts that passed were the Agricultural Adjustment Act, to control crop and livestock production, among other measures; and the Tennessee Valley Authority (TVA) Act, to produce electricity and determine its cost so that charges by private electrical firms could be measured against the cost of government-produced electricity, a comparison that was called the "yardstick principle." When President Eisenhower complained in the 1950s about New Deal socialist measures, the only example that he could cite to the press was the TVA. On the other side of the political spectrum, the National Industrial Recovery Act (NIRA) created the National Recovery Administration (NRA), with General Hugh S. Johnson as its director. The NRA was as close to fascism as the TVA was to socialism. Fortunately, the Supreme Court declared the NRA unconstitutional in 1935 and saved Roosevelt the task of scrapping the NRA. Title 2 of the NIRA established the Public Works Administration (PWA), with a fund of $3.3 billion. Harold Ickes, the head of the PWA, ended up spending $4.35 billion on 34, 000 public projects. In November 1933, Congress established the Civil Works Administration under Harry Hopkins, a social worker from Iowa who had run the relief program in New York for Governor Roosevelt. Then, in 1935, Hopkins was put in charge of the Works Progress Administration (WPA), undoubtedly the largest organization in

U.S. history. There were so many new agencies that they became known by their initials rather than their names and were referred to collectively as Roosevelt's "Alphabet Soup." During this time, Roosevelt's field agents spread out about the country, establishing and enhancing a web of political connections with state leaders that would be a platform for the feverish creation and implementation of new emergency programs.[4]

It was during this period of frenzied government offensives on the national and state stages that Cermak died and left Chicago without a leader. Pat Nash immediately stepped up in the city council and proposed that Alderman Francis Corr of the Seventeenth Ward be appointed temporary mayor of Chicago. Corr was not a charismatic figure on the local political scene, and he was not known for his ambition for advancement. Nash believed that Corr would be unlikely to seize the opportunity to try to ensconce himself in the temporary position. Although chaos ensued briefly, the voting was completed, and Corr became the mayor pro tem, the plug that would hold back the flood until a new mayor could be selected. With the death of Cermak, there were two positions to fill: Democratic Party chair and mayor. City leaders were temporarily in a state of disarray as they tried to determine what to do. There were two years left in Cermak's term. Could the city withstand another election? The process seemed too costly for the besieged city to undertake. Nash argued that launching a new election would be an insult to the schoolteachers and police officers who could not collect their rightful pay. The Democratic Party needed leadership and guidance, and it turned to Horner.

A typical Chicago politician would probably have seized on this opportunity to take control of the party. There was nothing preventing Horner from acting both as governor and as party chair. After all, there was some precedent for the practice. This opening could have allowed Horner to expand his power greatly and to assure that, as governor, he would experience little interference from Chicago. He could have strategically selected candidates, and he had plenty of friends who would have served him with loyalty. However, there is no evidence that Horner even considered taking control of the party. Instead, he quickly signed a bill that would delegate the task of selecting a new mayor to the Chicago

City Council. In this manner, Pat Nash was placed in the unique position to handpick the next mayor. Ed Kelly, having been at Cermak's side during his lingering demise in Florida, had been privy to the discussions regarding Cermak's replacement. Kelly had been one of the many who were disgruntled with Cermak's leadership style, and like many of his compatriots, he was eager to see an Irishman back at the top of the party. However, he had wisely kept silent.

Kelly, the chief sanitation engineer for the city of Chicago, was the prototypical Chicago Democrat. He had working-class, Irish roots. His father was a police officer, and Kelly himself had worked up from a blue-collar job in the Sanitation District. Like many men of his day, he had begun his career at a young age, having quit school at the age of twelve to do odd jobs and landing at the Sanitation District at the age of eighteen. He began by cutting trees and shrubs to make way for sanitation infrastructure and gained a solid reputation as a hard worker. Step by step, he worked his way up to the chief engineering position in a career with the district that spanned more than forty years. He showed a proclivity toward politics when he was elected president of the Brighton Park Athletic Club as a young man. Local Democrats noticed him in that position and recruited him, and he became active in the street-level workings of the party. His story was similar to that of other Irish young men who chose to hang their hats with the Democrats. From almost the outset, he was very much an insider in the party.

Some critics charged that Kelly wasn't qualified for the position of chief engineer. After all, he had no formal training in engineering and only attended school until the age of twelve. But at this time in history, the bootstraps mode of advancement was well established and fairly well respected. When he became chief engineer in his forties, the 1920s were in full swing. City officials prided themselves on bending the rules, and business became just another form of the "whoopee" that the whole city was joyously embracing. Throughout his career at the helm of the Sanitation District, Ed Kelly weathered a steady stream of scandals and accusations of corruption and waste. It was said that he awarded bloated contracts to friends and that the Sanitation District was one of the Chicago organizations with the worst record of kickbacks and corrupt bidding procedures. He was also continually dodging charges of personal tax fraud. However, this was business as usual in Chicago city government, and Kelly enjoyed a solid reputation as a competent manager, a hard worker, and a powerful and well-respected player in the Democratic Party organization.

Kelly's ability to emerge from scandal relatively unscathed may have had something to do with his professional dress and demeanor. He simply looked and acted the part of the respectable political leader. He had none of the vulgar showmanship of Big Bill Thompson or the rough-around-the-edges, tough-guy persona of Anton Cermak. Despite his humble beginnings and his toughness, he was polished and professional. He was also helped along by a random meeting that turned into a fortuitous friendship. As a foreman at the Sanitary District, he had come to the notice of Robert Rutherford McCormick, the unconventional owner of the *Chicago Tribune*. McCormick is most notable for being a proponent of phonetic spelling, and his newspaper was "spelling words like *tho* and *thru* and *frate* in the 1960's."[5] At the time, McCormick was president of the Sanitary District board. His philosophy was that merit should decide advancement in business, as opposed to political connections, the prevailing mode of social mobility in the city. He thought he had found a kindred spirit in the young foreman when he witnessed the man punch a politically connected underling to the floor for talking back. He liked the direct he-man approach and determined that he would keep an eye out for this young Ed Kelly. Despite McCormick's being a Republican, he and Kelly became fast friends. It is said that McCormick was socially awkward, especially when it came to meeting women, and Kelly made some fortuitous introductions for him that cemented their friendship. This friendship would prove especially handy when Kelly was later investigated for tax evasion and fraud involving Sanitary District contracts. During Kelly's troublesome periods, McCormick made a point of being seen with him at high-profile events, lending his good name to the chief. And more important, readers of the *Tribune* would never read of Kelly's travails in their favorite newspaper.

When Kelly aggressively campaigned for Henry Horner under the direction of Cermak, he gained visibility, and he and Horner developed an amicable political relationship. However, this relationship was not to last. Governor Horner soon found a knife in his back bearing the prints of the man who had once spoken so highly of him on the radio.

Given the opportunity to recommend a mayor, subject to approval by the city council, Pat Nash surprised many by selecting a man who had never held public office. It is said that Ed Kelly was reluctant to serve when his name came up and agreed to be suggested to the council as Cermak's successor only if it was made clear that, should he become the mayor, he would expect to have independent authority. He wasn't going to be a party puppet. That seemed to suit Nash just fine. He had horses to breed, and the spotlight didn't suit him. However, the story of Kelly's surprise at the offer is not entirely believable. After all, he had Cermak's ear before his death, and Nash's family had been awarded millions of dollars in sewer contracts by the Sanitation District. Kelly had made Nash a rich man, and now Nash would make him mayor.

Horner was surprised when Nash called him and proposed Kelly for mayor. Although Horner had his eye on a prominent attorney in the city, he decided that it should be a Chicago issue and supported Nash's decision. There was another name thrown about in city hall for the position: Jacob (Jake) Arvey, the alderman of the pivotal Twenty-fourth Ward. The issue of Arvey's ethnicity eventually undermined his candidacy. He was a Russian Jew, and as such, he wasn't part of the German Jewish set to which Horner belonged. However, as the council hashed it out, it became clear that such distinctions were too fine for the larger population. The council decided that having a Jewish governor and a Jewish mayor would simply be too much. The Irish in the Democratic Party would balk at the shift in the ethnic power balance, and the election of Horner had already placed the state in an unusual light on the national stage. It was best that this situation not be exacerbated by the appointment of a Jewish mayor following closely on Horner's heels. The proposition that Ed Kelly succeed Anton Cermak passed with forty-seven affirmative votes in the city council. Many in the Democratic Party were pleased to see the city back in the hands of the Irish. The famous Kelly-Nash machine was born.

Like Horner and Roosevelt, Ed Kelly had to hit the ground running as Chicago's new mayor. Before he was cut down by a madman's bullet, Cermak had instituted emergency measures and scraped together temporary relief funds that were just about used up by the time Kelly took office. Kelly was immediately besieged by desperate people converging angrily on his office. While Horner had rough coal miners on his hands, Kelly hosted outraged schoolteachers who had reached their limit and were storming city hall and disrupting government functioning all over the city. He realized that his first job would have to be securing the funds to repay the debts that the city owed to its employees. He scrambled together funds for unpaid salaries but could only repay a fraction of what was owed. Still, it soothed the savage beast of the city for a time. Kelly also followed up Cermak's emergency measures by aggressively cutting city costs down to the bare bones. When no more could be cut, he had to concentrate on the accumulation of more revenue.

During his campaign for governor, Horner had promised to sharply curtail the state's dependence on property taxes, which disproportionately targeted landowning but cash-destitute farmers. He intended to fulfill his promise, but he first had to pass a new taxation bill that would make up for the losses. Even though much of the incoming property tax revenue was in arrears because of the devastating financial situation of the farming industry, the state was highly dependent on the property tax system. A state income tax had been deemed unconstitutional by the Illinois Supreme Court. Therefore, all hope rested on a sales tax. Governor Horner introduced a bill into the legislature calling for a 3 percent tax on retail sales. The bill exempted farm products and motor fuel in an attempt to shield farmers from any further economic damage. The Democratic majority in both houses approved the 3 percent sales tax, to begin April 1, 1933, but the Illinois Supreme Court ruled it unconstitutional on May 10 because of the exemptions. As a compromise, Horner proposed a 2 percent sales tax with no exemptions, and the measure passed. The sales tax was to go into effect on July 1, 1933, with the revenues to be distributed by the Illinois Emergency Relief Commission instead of the counties. Since the six-month life of this tax was set to expire in 1934, additional legislation would be needed.[6] Although Horner fulfilled his promise to lower property taxes, the new sales tax did little more than offset that loss. Still, Horner felt that the new system was more equitable and that alleviating the inequitable burden on the farmers had to be the top priority. He had made an unpopular decision in adherence to his principles. It was not the first time, and it would not be the last.

Already economically deprived consumers resented the extra expense added to their purchases. Many residents of Illinois began to use a common colloquial expression that revealed the link between deprivation and racial scapegoating. When totaling up accounts, merchants were known to remark, "and two pennies for the Jew," referring to the two cents on the dollar that represented Horner's sales tax. Horner would absorb a great deal of tension and hostility on the subject of taxation. There was no way to become a hero when it came to raising taxes to feed the destitute.

The issue of taxation also became a fly in the soup of the new Chicago mayor. No stranger to scandal, Kelly found himself under investigation for tax evasion. The public, disgruntled by the new sales tax, was deeply offended by the blithe arrogance of the wealthy who acted like only the "little guy" ought to pay taxes. The press fed off the public sentiment to sell newspapers, and the Hearst papers began to dig assiduously into the financial histories of prominent men. The Kelly-Nash machine players were among those under the microscope. They especially targeted Kelly himself, raising questions about the discrepancies between his net worth and his official salary as a public figure. Kelly was evasive and defensive. The papers charged that his wealth resulted from the massive amount of graft he had received while working for the Sanitary District. But investigators, while privately suspecting the same, decided it would be too difficult to prove and focused on the inadequate amount of federal income tax paid by both Kelly and his cronies. Kelly and the rest were ordered to repay the back taxes. Nash had the highest bill from the government. The scandal was noisy and public, but the machine weathered it. Chicago was more interested in relief than in having the city's leaders crippled for past wrongdoings.

Despite the grave state of the nation and of Illinois, there were also some developments that caused the angry public to cheer for a time. Early in 1933, a lame-duck Congress passed the Twenty-first Amendment, which would repeal the Eighteenth Amendment and strike down the Volstead Act. The amendment was ratified by the states on December 5, 1933. The measure was buoyed by the support of the popular President Roosevelt as well as the public, which was possibly in search of a source of comfort in those trying times. With the repeal of Prohibition came great jubilation. Governor Horner himself joined in the national celebration. While others were simply cheering the opportunity to have a drink, Horner was thinking about the larger meaning of the repeal. He proclaimed that the Twenty-first Amendment "is declaring the strong opposition of our people to any amendment of our national constitution that denies to the several states the control of the habits, customs and privileges of its own citizens."[7] Horner's statement is telling because of its emphasis on the state's independence from federal control. The statement may also shed light on his ambivalence about the massive buildup of federal programs in the early reign of the Roosevelt administration.

The repeal of Prohibition also became the first of many opportunities for Governor Horner and the new mayor of Chicago to bump heads. Having liquor reinstated in Illinois meant that new regulatory procedures had to be determined. People were worried that the legalization of alcohol would usher in a return to the riotous saloon days captured in the specter of the First Ward Ball. The issue of liquor regulation presented a perfect opportunity to resurrect the old home-rule disputes. Horner was under a great deal of pressure from the press and influential associates to push through legislation that would assure that Chicago did not reinstitute the old saloon culture to its political advantage. Reformers suggested that corrupt politicians were salivating over the new opportunities for kickbacks and graft that the renewed industry would present. Horner was also committed to making sure that the saloons and politics remained separate. But he received a great deal of criticism in the press for not being particularly outspoken on the issue. Speculation about his course of action was rampant, and the city of Chicago seemed poised to defiantly dare the governor to interfere in its business, especially when it came to the people's precious drinking habits. The situation became a microcosm of the home-rule battles. Horner insisted that liquor regulation was a state concern, while Mayor Kelly argued that, since the liquor trade affected Chicago in a strikingly different manner from the rest of the state, local controls made sense. Kelly also was determined that the licensing fees for the newly legitimized establishments stay in Chicago. These were his official arguments, but surely he also saw that the saloon was a pivotal piece of the machine that had been crippled when the Volstead Act handed over the industry to the gangsters.

Both sides refused to budge on liquor regulation, and the issue dragged on for many months. Horner and Kelly began to express a mutual irritation with one another. The mayor was beginning to perceive that Horner was not going to let him implement his agenda for Chicago smoothly and easily. Horner's critics began to argue that he stubbornly focused on each isolated situation at hand, refusing to make concessions toward a broader goal. Whether this approach to governing was a strength or a weakness on Horner's part is debatable. He did seem to puzzle the politicians around him. One moment, he would be their ally, signing a bill or approving an appointment, and shortly afterward, he would seem to be an obstructionist, doggedly refusing to budge on a pet issue of his former ally. It seemed almost like naïveté on his part. Did Horner not know how to play the game? Or did he play up his jovial and blithe proclivity to focus on the issue at hand, *nothing personal, you understand,* in order to forward his own larger vision? Regardless, he found himself ruffling feathers, and Kelly seemed to be moving toward a state of permanent disdain for the governor.

Finally, on the issue of the regulation of liquor, a compromise bill was hammered out in the legislature. Regulatory powers would be shared by the city and a state agency. However, the state agency was stocked with appointees representing Chicago interests, and so it seemed to both parties that the bill was a victory for Kelly and home rule. However, the symbolic effect of this dispute was perhaps more significant than its practical outcome. It was now clear to Kelly that Horner was not "an organization man" anymore. As an independent, he was not the man Cermak had put in office in service of the machine. He would bear close watching.

In addition to the repeal of Prohibition, there was another bright spot in Illinois in 1933. The Century of Progress Exposition finally became a reality, with Kelly as the World's Fair mayor. The fair was an enormous success. It brought millions of dollars of revenue into the city as a steady stream of fascinated people entered the gates to view the spectacle, immerse themselves once again in the grand dreams of their suffering nation, and simply have a bit of fun. The exposition was such a success that Kelly ordered that it be continued for a second year. The prosperity of such an event highlights the central role of escapism during hard times. At that time, the movie industry too was siphoning off a good number of the precious pennies of indigent America. The images on the screen were "eye candy"—light and inconsequential. Will Rogers and Shirley Temple were big stars during the Depression. People were not interested in seeing the seriousness of their material conditions played out on the silver screen. Most industries were crumbling at the time, but those offering hope and diversion did well. People became obsessed with trivial, sensationalistic journalism, and fortune-tellers, astrologers, and charm sellers did a brisk business.

In Illinois, Henry Horner was busy prioritizing the myriad emergencies that cried out for attention on his desk. He still had the coal-mining wars to contend with—and by that time, they had indeed become wars. There was gunfire passing between the PMA and the owners, and police were getting involved, clubbing, tear-gassing, and shooting. The death toll was rising. When the situation was deemed to be on the verge of a statewide explosion, Horner ordered all the mines in Illinois closed. He believed that before any conciliatory talks began, law and order had to be established first. The coal mining industry came grinding to a halt. During that time, Horner, with the backing of a federal mediator, called for a reorganization of the industry, with one new union for all employees and with wages and positions equitably distributed among all employees. However, the key figure, the UMW's John L. Lewis, refused to budge on any issue. He was gaining prominence as a national union leader, and he could not afford to look weak in the face of state government. When the mines reopened, Horner was frustrated to find that no progress seemed to have been made; the violence resumed. Still sympathetic to the PMA, but fearful of their vulnerability to communist sentiment, he finally called in National Guard troops, who would wrestle with the problem for the remainder of his time in office. Similar violent labor disputes simmered across the nation. Politicians were called on to decide whether they were with the owners or with the workers. The union fracture in Illinois made this decision more complicated.

Other emergency issues presented themselves to the new governor. Just as the banking industry needed to be frozen for a time to assure that depositors would not abscond with all of their money, Horner worked to freeze mortgage foreclosures until relief could be provided to property owners teetering on the edge of disaster. And finally, he had to do something about the disastrous state of education in Illinois. He ordered the diversion of half the motor fuel taxes to education—half of which would go to Chicago. The city desperately needed to pay its schoolteachers, who seemed about to exchange their rulers for bayonets. He also tried, unsuccessfully, to consolidate the schools in the rural parts of the state. One-room schools dotted the landscape, some only serving a small handful of students. However, the rural culture was such that the locals resisted the centralization of their cherished institutions. Horner was gaining a brisk education in frustration and failure, but he gamely swung at the incoming pitches and earned a reputation for assertive action and tireless activity in the statehouse.

10

Horner, History, and the New Deal

To counter the criticism that he was nothing more than a puppet for Anton Cermak, Henry Horner proved early on that nothing could be further from the truth. When he made his appointments, he emphasized that he would exercise his own logic at all times but still wished to have collegial relationships and was willing to negotiate in some areas. Ironically, he then became the subject of criticism for his refusal to rubber-stamp edicts from Chicago and Washington. Indeed, he was so independent that sometimes it seemed to his colleagues that he was a bit of a troublemaker, or at the very least, an obstructionist. But Horner was always able to offer a convivial pat on the back and a reasonable argument to make the critic realize that, with Horner, it wasn't personal. He was simply trying to make the best decision in each case that came along.

Another criticism of Horner concerns his stance toward the New Deal, an issue about which historians disagree.[1] The policies and programs of Roosevelt's New Deal dominated Horner's first term as governor of Illinois. However, his ideological commitment to the New Deal is a matter of speculation and debate. Horner's biographer, Thomas Littlewood, portrays the governor as a loyal New Dealer and cites as evidence Horner's early statement of support for Roosevelt when he addressed a group of nervous business interests: "I have full confidence in the leadership of President Roosevelt, and so have a vast majority of this state and nation. It is my sincere desire to follow his masterful guidance, his integrity and his genius of statecraft."[2] Clearly, Horner was not a vocal critic of the New Deal, and he was highly motivated to treat, in some fashion, the economic disease that was sickening the nation. But his relationship to the New Deal is much more complicated than those words would indicate. In contrast to Littlewood, historian Roger Biles, biographer of Ed Kelly, presents Horner as generally uncooperative with and critical of the New Deal. The truth is that it was difficult to form a thorough theory of Depression reform while living through it. Horner did hope that the New Deal would help Illinois, and it did, but he also had deep-seated reservations, some of which were reflected in his interactions with Washington. Of course, he favored relief for the poor. The issue dominated his thinking and probably took a few years off his life. However, he showed some level of discomfort with the methods of the Roosevelt administration in dealing with the economic emergency. For a variety of reasons, the implementation of the New Deal in Illinois was rocky. There were disagreements, delays, and incompleteness.

An examination of Horner's relationship to New Deal politics gives further evidence of his willingness to go against the tide. As a machine politician, Ed Kelly valued a political network in which participants greased the system to make a larger agenda go forward smoothly. Although sometimes characterized as a politician who chose to "go along," Horner was clearly not a politician who took the easy route when it came to policy. His principled independence held true not only in Chicago machine politics but also in national politics, and it distinguished him from many other politicians of the time. He was faced with enormous pressure to act quickly to implement the New Deal in Illinois. But bowing to the pressure of public opinion is the way of the politician, not the intellectual statesman. What, Horner might have asked himself, would Lincoln do?

On the surface, there were many similarities between Roosevelt and Horner, but there were also key differences that made them uneasy allies. Both of them indisputably had been good-government candidates. Roosevelt took on Tammany Hall, vowing to clean it up, while Horner occupied a space at the periphery of corruption, not engaging in it but not fighting it aggressively as a reformer might do. He simply refused to "go along" with it. It can be argued that Horner was a good-government candidate, while Roosevelt was an architect of the good-government movement. But Roosevelt proved more amenable than Horner to turning a blind eye to corruption and "going along" for the sake of the national Democratic Party. Roosevelt worked with the big-city bosses to make local political machines work for the New Deal. Although he was uneasy with the tactics of Nash and Kelly, he could work with the corrupt Chicago machine, while, ironically enough, the square-dealing Horner confounded him. This situation sheds light on the difference between the practical and theoretical dimensions of good government, while Horner's political fate testifies to the problematic nature of realizing it.

Both Horner and Roosevelt were statesmen very much oriented toward the people. They shared a common humanitarian vision, even if they did not always agree on how to bring that vision to life. Both had vulnerabilities that perhaps made them more sensitive to the common people. Horner had a fatherless childhood, while Roosevelt had his illness. Both men had doting mothers who had a tendency to smother, and both had chafed at one time or another under the characterization of being a "mama's boy." The key difference between Roosevelt and Horner, it can be argued, was their political vision. Roosevelt was a big-picture person. During his first hundred days, he passed a great abundance of legislation and started numerous agencies—some of which were not very well thought out or planned in detail. However, he believed that he must make the broad strokes of re-creating a government in crisis and was able to overlook various problems or ideological inconsistencies that might slow down rapid forward progress. Horner, on the other hand, was a master of detail, and sometimes the immediate, larger picture seemed to elude him. He carefully plotted out the ramifications of each decision he made. He found importance in the minutiae, and using principle and common sense, he would argue over a minor policy or appointment, alienating those around him and sometimes obstructing a larger agenda. He personally kept tabs on the accounts of the state and let no detail elude his scrutiny. In order to get all the things done that were demanded of his office and still maintain such a level of vigilance, he simply had to work night and day.

Horner and Roosevelt did agree on the necessity of a balanced budget for the state and the nation. Roosevelt's commitment to this principle can be seen in his 1932 election campaign, as well as in his support of the Economy of Government Act of 1933. Horner committed himself to a similar position before his election: "The first thing I intend to do as governor of the state is to reduce the costs of government and thereby reduce taxes." He pointed out that during one four-year term of a Republican governor, government expenses increased four and a half times.[3] Horner represented a sort of populist fiscal conservatism. His propensity for thinking things out led him to be nervous about the hasty changes issuing out of the New Deal. He was concerned about the larger social ramifications of such heavy federal involvement in the economic life of the people. However, he always weighed the immediate need of the public against his intellectual analysis of political and social policy. He didn't believe that a welfare state was necessarily the best thing for the poor, but his first priority was always to feed the hungry; he could worry about their economic independence after they were fed. Eventually, his reluctance to "play along" with wholesale agendas persuaded those around him to begin to plot his downfall. But clearly, the core humanitarian values and the gentle political demeanor of Horner made Roosevelt uneasy about siding with Horner's strong-armed political rivals. However, the triangle of power in Illinois—Roosevelt, Kelly, and Horner—was becoming unsteady. Kelly and Roosevelt would soon try to cut Horner out of the triangle.

Roosevelt and Kelly were unlikely allies. Kelly's corrupt machine represented everything Roosevelt despised about Tammany Hall, but Horner's particular brand of good government was creating a ripple in the Democratic Party. Roosevelt needed the Illinois Democrats to be united behind him in any future elections. He could not right the ship if he was no longer at the helm.

When Roosevelt established the Federal Emergency Relief Administration (FERA), he naturally appointed as its head Harry Hopkins, the former head of the Temporary Emergency Relief Administration that then Governor Roosevelt had established in New York. Hopkins, who was from the Midwest, had experienced the grinding poverty of the New York City slums when he moved there to take a job in one of that city's notorious settlement houses. As a social worker, he moved through the ranks of the various relief agencies in the city. He garnered an exceptional amount of power under the Roosevelt administration, where he held the purse strings of relief money for the states. Then he also was placed in charge of the Civil Works Administration (CWA) when it was created in November 1933. In order to obtain federal assistance during the trying times, everyone had to go through Hopkins, who was known to be an aggressive advocate for the poor. As an administrator, he was impatient and informal, caring little for bureaucracy or delay. His office was almost bare of any decoration, with only a wooden desk and a few chairs. Henry Horner's meticulous and thoughtful style of doing government business no doubt grated on Hopkins, and Hopkins's personality was probably equally abhorrent to Horner, who valued congeniality, or at least civility, in his colleagues. Accustomed to the drab squalor of the New York slums, Hopkins had perhaps developed a personality to match. He was sarcastic, abrupt, and even at times sour. But his commitment to the poor was sincere, and he labored hard for the Roosevelt administration. Although both Horner and Hopkins believed in hard work and commitment, their different personalities resulted in a very bad relationship almost from the outset.

The first year after Horner took office, federal money constituted over 99 percent of the relief funds in Illinois. After that, Hopkins held federal funds hostage pending the accumulation of matching funds on the part of the state government. Since funds were so scarce in the state, Horner requested leniency on the matching requirement, but Hopkins retorted sternly, adopting a patronizing tone that would characterize all of his interactions with the Illinois governor: "Matching requirements will be continued and I expect the Illinois Legislature to meet its own needs so far as they are in excess of matching arrangements for Illinois approved by me."[4] Having no alternative, Horner and Kelly got together in the fall of 1933 to pass a $30 million bond issue that would provide the matching funds through much of 1934, since the state's share was $3 million per month. . For Horner, appropriating such a large sum of money was a very serious step, one that he did not take lightly. He was a firm believer in fiscal responsibility and thought that it was his sacred duty to keep the state solvent. He also believed strongly that work relief was preferable to direct relief. However, he lobbied hard for the bond issue that would assure federal relief funds. He drew a vivid and passionate portrait of the suffering and even deaths that would be averted if the bond issue passed and funds were secured. He argued that if the bond were not passed, "The results would be too frightful, too disastrous, too inhumane to contemplate."[5] Horner worked from June to November 1933 to pass the bond issue so that it would go immediately into effect, rather than become effective on July 1, 1934. The measure passed the General Assembly, but with much political sniping and conflict and only by one vote. But passage of the bond issue meant that Illinois would have the match required by Hopkins and that relief for Illinois was assured through the first nine months of 1934.[6] Horner was exhausted and disillusioned by the process. He could not comprehend how such a clear-cut cause as feeding the hungry could attract so much petty political posturing.

When work relief did come to Illinois, it came in the form of the Civil Works Administration (CWA). Problems with the CWA seemed a natural outcome of Hopkins's (and implicitly, Roosevelt's) frenetic style. The CWA was sweeping and rapid in its scope, but problematic and short-lived. The unfolding of programs like the CWA illustrates well the contrast between the administrative styles represented by Harry Hopkins and Henry Horner. Roger Biles, in *A New Deal for the American People*, appraises the CWA in this way:

> The haste with which the CWA took shape caused logistical problems. Assigning too many workers to a project site left some men leaning on their shovels with nothing to do. Some projects lacked adequate supervision; others, poorly conceived, were of questionable value. Although Hopkins policed the projects avidly, some graft and corruption crept into CWA affairs. Suppliers of materials and equipment sometimes charged exorbitant rates, and local politicians attempted to use CWA labor as patronage.[7]

As might be expected, when it came to "policing" the CWA projects to reduce corruption, the Chicago CWA was suspect number one, and there *were* various irregularities. The aggressive and impatient Hopkins responded to the investigative findings by assigning an army engineer to head up the CWA projects in Chicago. This angered the independent Horner, who felt that the engineers at the helm of the project should be Chicagoans. It was a minor disagreement, and the CWA project rolled on, but it would set the stage for a contentious relationship between Hopkins and Horner.

When the $30 million bond for 1934 ran out, Hopkins began to pressure Horner for a second time to come up with matching funds or expect the federal relief to cease. It was Hopkins's unyielding policy that state matching funds were required for federal relief funds that finally forced Horner to take the unpopular step of advocating an increase in the sales tax to 3 percent. Hopkins said that Illinois needed to continue coming up with $3 million per month starting in 1935 and that the penalty, if the state failed to make this match, was no more federal funds. Meanwhile, Horner used a $9 million surplus from the state treasury for the early part of 1935 and tried to persuade the General Assembly to pass a 3 percent sales tax with 1 percent specifically earmarked for relief. He also wanted the legislature to pass an emergency clause so that the tax would begin immediately upon passage; this provision required a two-thirds majority in each house. Such a majority would also imply that the tax increase was bipartisan, an impression that the governor certainly preferred. Even though Kelly lobbied just as hard for the tax increase as Horner, it was the governor who took the public relations hit. When Kelly was elected mayor in April 1935, he received 76 percent of the vote. His advocacy for increasing the sales tax had not hurt him. After Kelly's election, the General Assembly finally passed the 1 percent sales tax increase, but without the emergency clause that Horner had hoped for. It was signed into law on May 23, 1935.[8]

Horner became known as "High Tax Henry" and garnered criticism for being insensitive to the poor. But he also heard from friends and supporters who realized the unfairness of the situation. Public criticism was something that wore significantly on the amiable governor who valued relationships over power. The fight to pass the 3 percent tax had not been an easy one. It had not passed until the sixth roll call. The bill had been held up, in part, because of a controversy over whether or not it would be implemented as an "emergency bill" and go into effect immediately upon passage. Republicans in the legislature had helped to obstruct the bill's passage, but Horner's insistence on the bill's emergency status was probably the chief reason for the bottleneck. The slow process irritated the impatient Hopkins. "In the meantime," writes historian Dwayne Cole, "Hopkins, in an effort to hasten legislative compliance, cut off federal funds in May and the end of June causing a cancellation of relief throughout the state." Hopkins also criticized Horner's handling of the legislature, "causing an estrangement between the two men."[9] Sensing the disapproval from Washington, Kelly proclaimed support for either form of the bill. It is unclear whether Horner suffered material consequences from losing the fight over the "emergency" clause, but it is clear that his standing on principle did not do his reputation any good. Hopkins felt that Horner had bungled the matter and attributed the final passage to Kelly's political savvy. From this time on, Hopkins developed a very congenial working relationship with Kelly. He favored a brusque and efficient political style, and Kelly had impressed him as being just such a man. In the end, any business having to do with relief funds in Illinois would be handled between Hopkins and Kelly, and they came to revel in making Horner feel out of the loop.. Horner complained that he could not even get Hopkins on the telephone.

The final break between Illinois and the New Deal came when the Works Progress Administration (WPA), again headed up by Harry Hopkins, geared up in Illinois. The WPA, which was created as part of the Emergency Relief Appropriations Act, took effect on April 8, 1935. Eighty-five percent of WPA funds were expected to go to wages and salaries. When the WPA officially ended on June 30, 1943, it had employed 8.5 million people on 1.41 million projects and had spent about $11 billion. Hopkins again demanded that the state of Illinois bear a large responsibility in the financing of such relief. Protective of his state's treasury, Governor Horner drew a line, refusing to go along with Hopkins's spendthrift philosophy. Hopkins was infuriated. He argued that the Illinois relief fund might be empty, but there were surpluses in other areas that could be tapped. Horner again refused, asserting that in Illinois the WPA should be funded by the federal government, as the previous work program (CWA) had been. Refusing to accede to Governor Horner, Hopkins declared that, without local financing, there would be no more federal grants to Illinois. Horner was prepared for such a break. He ordered that federal relief stations be dismantled and declared that relief would henceforth be handled by local communities in Illinois. Horner was now persona non grata in Washington. He had grown tired of dealing with Hopkins and his particular form of bullying. Now everyone began to predict Horner's involuntary retirement from public service.

Horner's difficulties in dealing with the Roosevelt administration go beyond a personality dispute with one man. His uneasiness with the administration can be traced back to the presidential election, when he was pressured into being a Roosevelt supporter. Cermak's initial rejection of the Roosevelt ticket had to do with his preference for Roosevelt's Republican opponent, Al Smith, who was standing as a "dripping wet." However, Horner's ambivalence about Roosevelt was more substantive. Although it was unfashionable at that time for a politician to associate himself with business interests—the Insulls and Mellons were the monsters of the day—Horner was never comfortable with the antibusiness orientation of Roosevelt's politics. After all, Horner was a member of a social network rife with business interests, and he genuinely seemed to feel that an economic policy that did not energize business was shortsighted. He was arguably more fiscally conservative than the Democratic Party mainstream at the time. He expressed his concern over "the dole" and its long-term effects, seeing direct social welfare only as a necessary evil in the height of the Depression. He felt much more comfortable with purposeful work-relief programs.

With the transmission and implementation of New Deal programs not going smoothly between Washington and Illinois, Horner developed a reputation as a troublemaker among some Washington politicians. The more generous interpretation of Horner from Washington was that he was naive. But Washington's interpretation arguably represented a superficial understanding of Horner's relationship to the New Deal. The whole debacle, however, played very nicely into Kelly's long-range plans. Whatever problems Horner had with Roosevelt were mostly expressed through his contentious relationship with Harry Hopkins. As men, Roosevelt and Horner were probably quite compatible. Both were genteel, civil, warm, and thoughtful. But Horner's difficulties with the New Deal caused Roosevelt to hold him at arm's length. Horner, however, did seem to develop a sincere friendship with Eleanor Roosevelt. Both were very drawn to individual cases of hardship. After receiving a letter from an Illinois family undergoing hardship, Eleanor Roosevelt often wrote to Horner asking if he would pay the matter some personal attention. Horner almost always did. They seemed to see each other as allies in defense of the poor. Both of them saw their work not in terms of abstract policy, but in terms of people and material conditions. Other politicians could not be bothered with one name, one case. But Henry Horner could, and this endeared him to Eleanor Roosevelt. A compelling portrait of the Great Depression can be drawn from reading the desperate letters of individuals seeking help from politicians. Horner and Mrs. Roosevelt passed such letters between them in a sort of secret alliance.[10]

Horner may at times have obstructed the New Deal in Illinois or slowed its implementation, but he was not alone in feeling that such a delay was justified to permit time for consideration. He found a Washington ally, at least ideologically, in the secretary of the interior, Harold Ickes, a

Chicagoan who had long been associated with the Progressive Party. Ickes had spent the 1920s railing over the power of the industrial magnates in Chicago. Since he was of a more fiscally conservative mind than many in the administration, he and Horner tended to think alike. Hopkins and Roosevelt shared a habit of taking hasty and aggressive action in common. But Ickes was uncomfortable with the sometimes ill-conceived, fiscally reckless, and shortsighted vision of some of the New Deal legislation. When questioned about the long-term efficacy of a New Deal solution, Hopkins would counter that when people were hungry, discussions of the long term were irrelevant. Both Ickes and Horner would probably have disagreed. Like Horner, Ickes was more careful with funds than Roosevelt or Hopkins.

While Hopkins headed up the FERA, the CWA, and later the WPA, Ickes was in charge of the Public Works Administration (PWA), which was responsible for expanding federal public works projects in an effort to stimulate the economy. Unlike Hopkins, who was known to have spent $5 million in his first two hours on the job, Ickes was more cautious with his budget and had a long-term vision for the PWA. He was determined that the agency would accomplish more than just immediate palliative effects on the country. PWA projects would be ones that expanded the American infrastructure, not just provide busy-work for the destitute. Each PWA project would employ the best of everything—architects, engineers, planners, materials—to ensure that the end result was of some enduring value. Determined that the money would not simply be thrown into the relief wind, Ickes did, indeed, ensure that the country emerged from the PWA with an array of infrastructural improvements.

When it came time to choose the director for the new agency (WPA) that would replace the CWA, Roosevelt's decision revealed much about his philosophy of the best way to operate work relief. The choice was between Hopkins and Ickes to head up the new program. Ickes had spent a good deal of his budget on experts and materials, while Hopkins had spent most of his budget on wages, emphasizing the immediate but temporary relief aspect of the program. Roosevelt considered both approaches, but in the end he went with Hopkins.

Roosevelt was understandably in a hurry to lay food on the tables of hungry families, but it is arguable that Ickes's projects brought about more long-lasting relief. The choice of Hopkins rather than Ickes to head the WPA highlights the different political visions of Roosevelt and Hopkins, on the one hand, and Horner and Ickes, on the other. Horner admired Ickes, while Ickes and Hopkins were generally considered enemies within the administration. It was Ickes and Mrs. Roosevelt who would stand by Horner in his hour of need and urge the president not to withdraw support from him. However, even Ickes misjudged Horner's tenacity. When considering Horner's chances for reelection, he wrote in his diary, "Horner is an honorable man and an able man, but he is a poor politician and he certainly lacks guts."[11]

This persistent impression of "a gutless" Horner begs reassessment after his showing in the 1936 election, but it still raises an important question: Can an official who is perceived as *not a politician* but rather as a *public servant* also convey to the public the impression that he has "guts"? Is it hardball political gamesmanship that mesmerizes and inspires confidence in the public? Certainly, because he refused to play the political game by the machine's rules, Horner had to withstand serious pressure from his own party, and he showed exceptional internal fortitude in doing so. That he seems not to get credit for such strength suggests something about American values and attitudes toward public service. The political bullies who ran the Chicago where Horner grew up did not seem to have the same public relations dilemma, despite their proclivity for "going along" with the political machine. This is a fact of some significance that should be considered when tracing the historical legacy of Henry Horner.

While Horner's problems with Washington were somewhat complicated, Kelly's problems with Horner had simply to do with Horner's independence and his principles. Under pressure from Hopkins, both Horner and Kelly had tried to secure votes to raise the state sales tax to 3 percent, a measure desperately needed to provide relief. Here, the mayor and the governor were united; they both recognized the unfortunate necessity of the tax increase. However, when the governor approached legislators about supporting this legislation, he refused to pay for the votes with state government positions. Trading jobs for votes was something that he could not do, *on principle*, even if this way of doing things was "business as usual" in politics at the time. When those who had been rebuffed by Horner called Kelly to complain, he did not hesitate for a moment. "Will they take city jobs?" he asked immediately. He didn't have any principles about the matter that needed bending. He believed in greasing the process.

A similar, but more damaging, breach between Horner and Kelly over issues of principle occurred in 1935. Kelly was, at the time, trying to reconcile a budget shortfall that would make it difficult to meet his obligations to the schoolteachers and the police once again. To produce the necessary revenue, he seized on the idea of regulating gambling on horse races, already a widely recognized industry in local taverns. Under this new legislation, the number of gambling institutions would be limited to 2,500 and made subject to licensing fees and regulations. The measure would only apply to Chicago, not to downstate. One-half of the licensing fees would be used for the schools and the other half for general expenses. Because Kelly knew that the bill would be a hard sell downstate, he and his representative lobbied hard and made deals with downstate legislators. Kelly was confident he had the vote, but cold water was splashed on the mayor's plan from an unexpected pail. Horner informed the mayor that he didn't think he could ever support a bill that legalized gambling; his moral reservations on the subject were simply too strong. Kelly, aghast, railed on about how much revenue could be generated from such a measure and how badly the city of Chicago needed it. Clearly torn on the matter, Horner told him he would consider it. When both the House (89–53) and the Senate (31–14) passed the bill, Horner was visibly distressed. He had hoped that the final decision wouldn't come to him. If Horner approved the bill, it would become law on July 11, 1935.[12]

Kelly looked to the statehouse in rancorous anticipation. "If Horner vetoes the bookie bill, I'll sign his death warrant," he snarled. Horner vetoed it. In his veto statement, he explained that there were significant and troubling moral ramifications of a legal sanction of gambling. His move was lauded in the newspapers, which said that he had courageously bucked enormous political pressure and made a principled decision. Even the pretense of a cordial relationship was now set aside. Weeks later, Kelly said to Pat Nash, "We're going to take that son-of-a-bitch out of the mansion. We're going to drop him down the chute, and there's nothing he can do about it."[13]

11

The Governor Gives Himself Away

Henry Horner received the following letter amid a pile of other correspondence offering the governor unsolicited advice:[1]

Dear Governor:

After you have read this letter you can throw it in the wastebasket or do otherwise with it as you please, and it doesn't demand any reply. My observation of the way that you are working is that you are trying to do altogether too much yourself and I think it is about time for you to let up and turn some of your responsibilities over to others. You certainly started out right with your administration and everybody is pulling for you to make a real success, but I don't believe it is physically within your power to continue giving yourself so completely to the job. I am afraid that perhaps your training as a Judge, where you naturally would do everything yourself, may

> have formed habit which you have been unable to throw off. You have surrounded yourself with some very capable men and undoubtedly they are working to the limit. If they can't turn out the work why don't you get some more fellows to help you out—if need be draft them, if there is no provision in law for employing them. Maybe you will think all of this is none of my business, but I will disagree with you. I wish you could see your way clear to get some recreation such as you were accustomed to in days gone by without devoting every minute of your time, day and night, to the job.
>
> Sincerely yours, B. P. Alschuler

Horner wrote politely back to his friend and supporter in Chicago, as was his practice, indicating that Alschuler was undoubtedly correct and that he would try to take his advice. Alschuler probably gave him the single most valuable piece of advice that he received during his political career, and yet it was the one of which he was least mindful. Henry Horner would give everything he had to the state of Illinois during a time when she needed him most.

Sunday is habitually considered a day of rest in American culture for even the hardest of laborers. Horner too saw the possibilities of a Sunday—a bit of free time stretched in front of him. The phone was often blissfully silent on that day, and of course, he had no appointments. On a typical Sunday, Horner was known to load into the Buick that he had picked up at his brother James's dealership and hit the road with his personal secretary. It was time for a "Sunday Tour." They may have headed down a sunny dirt road, but their destination was not the picnic grounds. Instead, a typical destination might be a mental hospital a few hours distant from Springfield. The staff at such an institution, unaccustomed to such personal attention by the governor of the state, would undoubtedly be thrown into a frenzy of anxiety about what they viewed as an impromptu inspection. However, in such instances, the governor's demeanor was disarming and cordial, as if his visit were nothing more than social. His secretary, however, dispelled that impression by carrying a briefcase full of paperwork and preparing to take thorough notes about what was found.

As soon as he arrived, Horner usually took a leisurely tour through the building and might go into a patient's room to check the windows and the radiators. He was also known to go through cabinets in kitchens. It was reported that on one occasion he discovered that some rats had gnawed into a bag of flour that was sitting on the floor of a pantry in a government institution. Rather than dress down the attendant, Horner rolled up his sleeves and squatted down to demonstrate the proper way to stack bags of flour—something he had learned in his days in the grocery business. Much to the chagrin of many a bureaucrat, Horner was known to enter a storage room, pull out a ream of vouchers, and begin checking the supplies against the paperwork that had been submitted. When he noted an excessive expenditure or a discrepancy, he made quite an issue of it and followed up to see that the situation was corrected, no matter how trifling the sum at issue.

On his impromptu "tours," people were put at ease by his grandfatherly demeanor. It was clear that his mission was not personal. He shook hands and took a great interest in their well-being or in the job that they were assigned to do. He wanted to know all that he could about what went on in the state that he had been elected to govern. He was known to stop and talk to patients in state institutions and was not above personally granting their requests, whether it was contacting a relative or having a personal need met. On a single Sunday, it was not unusual for Horner to visit a mental institution, a fish hatchery, and a teacher's college and then stop to visit the home of a Democratic colleague to discuss policy. On Monday, he would follow up on any necessary business that his Sunday tour had unearthed. Such is a typical account of one of Governor Henry Horner's "days of rest."[2]

Horner's story is compelling in part for its connections with the larger state and national story. He lived through the industrialization of Chicago; he learned politics at an unusual and formative time in urban political history; and of course, he rose to the rank of governor just as the nation seemed on the verge of apocalypse. However, Horner is also a notable figure for his unique personality. His remarkably kind nature and his unusual work habits made him arguably one of the most singular figures ever to grace a state executive mansion. As one might glean from his "Sunday Tour," Horner's governing style was highly unusual. Being a micromanager and a perfectionist caused his already overwhelming workload to be greatly increased. Delegating responsibility was difficult for him. How was he to assure that things were done right if he didn't do them himself? He felt that "doing the right thing" was important, down to the smallest detail. If a working family could not afford twenty-five cents for a solid meal, then his administration was certainly not going to overlook a twenty-five-cent discrepancy in spending on a rotary fan in the basement of a state office. His frugality was based in a deep respect for the poor.

His scrutiny of accounts at every level of state government also served as a clear message that graft was not going to be "business as usual" under his administration. Not having hammered this issue home during his campaign, he surprised everyone with his demand that government be on the up-and-up. In Chicago, he had coexisted affably next door to the crooked machine and had scarcely raised a public eyebrow about the spoils system. He was not one to accuse and point fingers; however, he expected members of his administration to be honest in the extreme. He would encourage good government throughout the state, not through rhetoric, but through example. He shocked more than one former colleague with a friendly refusal to do anything that would compromise his integrity. A state office would be ill-advised to pad a budget during his administration since he might personally go over the account books line-by-line. When he caught a discrepancy, he was stern but usually still managed to maintain a positive working relationship with the offender.

Horner used an air of political naïveté to his advantage. "Why, naturally, we all want the best man for the job, don't we?" he would inquire when a shady patronage arrangement was suggested to him. "Why take a higher bid when we can get good work done with the other guy for less?" he might say when an inflated bid landed on his desk. His inability to read a wink or take a hint was most likely a studied way of salvaging a relationship while at the same time rejecting dishonesty. While he brought good government to Illinois, he did not do so with a sword and a volley of accusations. He simply acted, when necessary, as if he were not aware that corruption was de rigueur. It was a strategy that would cause him to be labeled politically naive, but on closer inspection, this apparent naïveté might have been a very practical approach. It saved him many a battle and let him move on to the next item on his agenda.

Horner was a "hands-on" governor to the extreme. He visited every state office, feeling that it was his duty to gather a detailed sense of the issues and operations that went on there. However, rather than "throwing his weight around," he exhibited to the state employees a very keen interest in their work and a recognition of the importance of every job. He might be stern about discrepancies and hand out suggestions for improvements, but his general purpose was constructive, and his warm and affable demeanor made him a popular visitor around the state. In the process of "nosing around," he made a lot of friends and created a strong impression of being a sincere and people-centered governor. But all this hands-on activity did not come without a cost. When he returned from the statehouse to the mansion in the evening, Horner went right to work, poring over paperwork, reading legislative bills, and penning correspondence. He almost always worked until after midnight, and his butler often entered his room at three in the morning to find him finally asleep, surrounded in his bed by sheaves of paper, his pen having fallen out of his hand as he dropped off to sleep. The butler would clear the mess from his pillows and switch off the light.

Horner found life in Springfield less comforting than his existence had been in Chicago. In Chicago, he had felt cozy in the confines of his bachelor apartment with his Lincoln artifacts around him. There he belonged to clubs and organizations that were filled with good friends who were always available for dinner or a drink and a good conversation. In Springfield, Horner lived alone, except for his butler Clarence, in the immense, echoing mansion. He confined himself to just a handful of rooms and often took to conducting his affairs from bed. He made friends wherever he went, but as governor, he always found himself surrounded by people who wanted to influence him in some way. Even old friends from Chicago now took advantage of their long-term relationship to suggest a relative for a state position or to try to influence policy.

Now Horner valued his true friendships more than ever. In Springfield, his two closest friends were the Roman Catholic bishop, James A. Griffin, and the poet Carl Sandburg. Horner's friendly relationship with the clergy in Springfield demonstrates that, despite his loyalty to his religious heritage, he did not make unnecessary distinctions between people. Although he had been criticized by members of his faith for not sufficiently emphasizing his Jewish identity, it was not in his nature to play identity politics. Like Lincoln, he truly felt that people's differences were mainly superficial. He saw no conflict of interest when he had dinner with Roman Catholic clergy, and he regularly sent Christmas poinsettias to the church at holiday time. His friendship with Carl Sandburg also deepened during this period of his life. He was beginning to realize that he was simply not compatible with politicians and preferred the company of intellectuals and artists. He enjoyed Sandburg's disarming humor and his left-of-center, independent persona.

During this time, Horner's physician, Dr. Nathan Rosen, was growing increasingly concerned about him. After the struggle over the 3 percent sales tax, Horner was absolutely depleted and had to take himself to bed for several days. Rosen grew alarmed when he listened to the governor's heart; the sound told him that all was not what it should be. He had a serious talk with Horner about taking care of himself. Horner's eating habits were unhealthy, he smoked cigars, and he did not take the time to rest or rejuvenate. Horner, however, was never amenable to being fussed over by doctors and nurses. He dismissed Dr. Rosen's warning with a scoff and went on with his bourbon consumption, his cigar smoking, his late-night eating habits, and his relentless work schedule. Rosen was also concerned that the governor was showing signs of depression. Indeed, the governor's seat, especially at this time, was not a healthy location for someone who craved harmony and disliked conflict. When Horner was criticized, especially by someone representing the voice of the common people, he took it to heart.

He found himself continually caught between difficult alternatives in implementing policy under emergency conditions. He had to take many unpopular steps as a Depression governor, and much of his constituency was aggrieved and suffering. If he was walking down the street and a disgruntled citizen yelled something at him in anger, it could plunge him into a depression. This was in keeping with the general bent of his personality. Small things mattered to him, and what mattered most was the approval and happiness of those around him. He was people-centered, an unusual trait among politicians who generally developed the practical habit of being system-centered.

Politicians receive thousands of letters a year; few politicians read more than a fraction of these letters. Henry Horner read all of them, and he personally answered a good many of them. Often he found himself unable to sleep, and not wanting to remain in the empty mansion, he would walk the streets of Springfield late at night, peering into the shop windows and thinking: He could have taken a different path in life. He could still have been living a comfortable life in probate court, well regarded by all, married, perhaps even a grandfather by this time. Instead, he was at the eye of the storm, living alone, carrying the weight of a sea of voiceless faces on his back.

But just as he would not let a faulty receipt pass him by, Horner would never shirk his duty to the people of Illinois. This duty weighed hard on him in Springfield. He had always enjoyed the company of women, and he had been free to pursue social and romantic relationships when he was a probate court judge. However, he relinquished even that natural right in Springfield after the sensation-hungry press made an issue of his having well-known singers stay overnight in the Executive Mansion on two occasions. Horner decided that the luxury of female companionship was something that he could not afford. Because he was a bachelor governor, the public scrutinized his every relationship. He soon learned that he would have to live very circumspectly.

In office, Horner exhibited a great concern for vulnerable people, just as he had in the probate courts. Rather than spending his time courting the power players, he took up the cause of the people least likely to be able to marshal political pressure for themselves—another indication that he lacked a typical political personality. Long before the deinstitutionalization movement of the 1960s, he was an advocate for institutionalized people, and he was known to intervene personally when a tragic story was related to him. When he read in the newspaper that a widow with two children had lost in a fire the dilapidated shack they called home, he invited the family to the Executive Mansion and gave the woman a state job. It is unclear whether she was the best "man" for the job, but it shows that Horner was not above bending the rules in the interest of humanitarian relief, while he rejected such practices in the interest of his own or others' political advantage. He continued to assist Eleanor Roosevelt with various "secret projects" that involved "doing a little something" for specific people undergoing hardship. Busy as he was, he couldn't shrug off a request from someone who was suffering and alone.

Despite the political pressure he was under, his instinct was to aid the ordinary citizen rather than the demanding politician. A good example was his response to the notorious "Eyedrop Bill," which provided for all infants in the state to be treated with a drop of silver nitrate to the eyes at birth to prevent gonorrheal blindness. Many powerful interests were against the measure, arguing that it opened a door toward state interference in personal medical issues. It also ran counter to some religious traditions that opposed medical intervention for church members. When the Eyedrop Bill was introduced, Horner received an avalanche of mail from powerful sources warning about the political fallout of setting such a precedent. The papers speculated that he would veto the bill. When Dr. Louis Mann, a rabbi from Chicago and an old friend of Horner's, heard the news, he raced off to Springfield. Rabbi Mann remonstrated with Horner and fully informed him about the suffering of blind babies—suffering that could easily be prevented. He ended by saying, "I doubt if you could sleep another night if by your veto you thrust even one baby into perpetual darkness."[3] Horner had a litany of intellectual retorts to the argument—the dangers of state interference in individual lives, in religious matters, and so on—but Rabbi Mann knew him well. The image of a blind newborn *would* plunge Horner into lasting sleeplessness. In fact, he did not sleep well that very night. Shortly afterward, amid much political invective, he signed the so-called Eyedrop Bill into law. Gonorrheal blindness among infants virtually disappeared after its implementation.

Horner was famous for his fondness of children. When children visited the Executive Mansion, he personally gave them tours, made sure their favorite treats were at the ready, and sent them away with picture books to keep them entertained on their way home. He was known for attending Boy Scout functions, and whenever the circus came to town, he made it known that children who could not afford tickets should meet him at the gate at a certain hour. It was astonishing enough for a governor to buy tickets for indigent children, but Horner would go with them to enjoy the sights and amusements through their hungry eyes. Far from being an ivory tower intellectual or a closed-door politician, Horner enjoyed the sights and sounds of American culture. Just as he found an excuse to get himself to the circus, he also enjoyed going to the movie theater to indulge himself in an occasional Hollywood melodrama.

Coming of age when an enterprising young man could make an astonishing fortune and still pursue a political career, Horner was unusual for his disinterest in material wealth. He did not invest in business and did not make money through graft, as so many of his colleagues did. And he did throw around what money he made as if it meant very little to him. Money appealed to him only as a means of expressing his lifelong theme of "friendly interest." He was a lavish gift giver who never delegated his gift buying to his assistant, Ella Cornwall. If he overheard a friend admire or express an interest in a particular item, Horner would secretly purchase whatever perfectly matched the desires of the recipient and would include a cheerful personal note with the gift. Amazingly, he managed to keep up with such personal correspondence despite his crushing official work burden. He managed to find time to comment to the newspapers about stories in the news; he reviewed politics and history with his Lincoln correspondents; and he discussed philosophy and literature with old friends from the Standard Club, the Skeeters, and the Bandarlogs. When he read of a notable achievement by an acquaintance, he never failed to send a congratulatory note, perhaps in tandem with a gift. He even wrote a fan letter to a Hollywood notable now and again. He probably would have liked dabbling in more literary writing, building on his *Restless Ashes* experiment when he was a judge, but there were only twenty-four hours in each day. If he had ever enjoyed the privilege of being a retired gentleman, he might have gone on to be a novelist or an essayist.

Horner was keenly interested in the work of philanthropic and people-centered institutions in Illinois and visited the lonely halls of prisons, mental institutions, orphanages, hospitals, and juvenile advancement agencies. In the process, he met many leaders in the human sciences and kept abreast of developments in ongoing efforts to elevate the vulnerable. The story of Helen Keller was now famous, and children who were once packed away in institutions and forgotten now enjoyed a glimmer of hope. Horner was interested in such advancements and had long lobbied on behalf of juvenile research. From his web of acquaintances in public welfare, he learned of a particular case that reminded him of Helen Keller. A little girl had lived for all of her four years in the back ward of a hospital, curled up on a bed, doing little else than tearing at her clothes and groaning. She had almost no connection with the world around her, and everyone had given up on her, which was often the case with severely disabled people in that day—they were simply institutionalized and forgotten. Horner inquired about the little girl and learned her story.

It seems that in late February of 1932, a newborn infant was abandoned outside the Cook County Hospital. The child, who became known as Carol Sanders, was afflicted with an eye infection and chronic ear infections that left her blind and partially deaf. Because of these disabilities, she did not develop speech. This triple disability left her unable to communicate, and she failed to develop normally. Blind, deaf, and mostly mute, she could do nothing for herself and was considered a hopeless case for four years. But then Dr. Robert Gault from the American Institute for the Deaf and Blind, who was a psychology professor at Northwestern University, heard of her case. He had developed the theory that deaf and blind individuals could compensate through their sense of touch.

When Horner learned of the little girl's situation, he hastily brought Dr. Gault and Carol Sanders together. He allocated $5,000 a year from the Department of Public Welfare's contingency fund to support Carol in foster care in Evanston while she worked with Dr. Gault. And Horner did not forget her; she became the closest thing to a daughter that he would have in his life. Rather than shrinking from the severely disabled little girl, Horner delighted in her, showered her with affection, played games with her, and bought her gifts, especially ones that might help with her treatment, and he conferred frequently with Dr. Gault. He visited her frequently in her foster home in Evanston, and she was also a frequent guest at the Executive Mansion. She made remarkable progress in Dr. Gault's program and emerged a warm, well-mannered young woman who seemed fully capable of enjoying life. One of the last duties that Horner feverishly attended to on his deathbed was making arrangements for lifelong, state-funded care for her. He didn't want to leave the earth without having provided for Carol.

His concern for Carol Sanders was typical of the way that Horner liked to use his political power. He had willingly given up marriage, fatherhood, and grandparenthood, but that only meant that from his position in Springfield he could now look out for all the needy children of Illinois. Horner's combination of humanitarian interests and selfless characteristics made him an odd political figure for the times. Such a portrait might suggest that his political career would not be long-lasting. After all, the common wisdom of the time dictated that a politician had to cultivate a hard exterior and learn to play the game. A successful politician was a frontrunner and needed to cultivate imposing personal power over others and did not have time for all the groundwork. Real politicians shook hands and kissed babies while campaigning and let the pencil pushers do the accounting.

12

A Stab in the Back

While Horner's hardworking, gentle, and friendly persona was singular for a politician, he soon found that being the governor of Illinois during the Great Depression was a thankless job. There was nowhere to hide from the onslaught of discontent, criticism, and anger. It seemed that his job was to absorb the angst of his troubled state. His sensitivity to suffering made him a rigorous defender of the underdog, but it also made it difficult for him both to be the eye of the storm of public discontent and to weather that storm as well. It seemed he could do nothing right in the opinion of his critics.

In the hard times of the Depression, it seemed like everybody had one reason or another to appeal for help to the governor. From the high-ranking official to the lowly laborer, people were desperate for employment. Previously prosperous men had lost everything in the crash of the stock market and now were seeking some way to survive. A former university professor, who had lost his job when budgets were tightened, appealed to

Horner for a letter recommending him for a job as an attendant in a mental hospital. Proud matriarchs, whose sons were once assured of a prosperous future, now frantically sought ways to save their sons, and hence their families, from the disgrace of a penniless fate. Thomas Littlewood reports that it became an accepted habit for mothers at state functions to request a position for their sons when they arrived at the governor in the receiving line. With steely determination, they breached the rules of etiquette they had long subscribed to and stubbornly refused to budge until the governor promised their sons a position. One can only imagine the awkwardness that this behavior caused for both sides of the receiving line. Old friends and acquaintances sent letters to the governor reminding him of past favors and requesting help, but often with an undertone of veiled hostility. Letters from the destitute, begging for a special favor, pulled at his conscience.

These requests for favors were especially difficult for Horner, who did not endorse the philosophy of patronage and spoils. He believed in lining up the candidates for a job and selecting them on their merits so that each public service position would be filled with the most qualified person. But there were teary-eyed mothers, panic-stricken old acquaintances, and suffering strangers pulling aggressively at his coattails, constantly begging, cajoling, and even threatening. Horner might have saved himself from this the agony if he had delegated his correspondence to someone else. Determined not to use his personal secretary to send out form letters dismissing these requests, Horner held fast to his practice of answering all of his correspondence himself and personalizing each response. And so, he received each dagger and agonized over each principled decision, until he fell into a restless and uneasy sleep at night.

Although he had won the election with strong support from all across the state, Horner did not fare so well in the court of public opinion during his first term. It is questionable whether anyone could have fared better as governor during those dreary times. He faced especially harsh criticism about the sales tax required to secure federal relief funds to address the emergency of human suffering in the state. The tax had been successful in stabilizing the state's budget and providing emergency relief, and without it, the state might have faced civil disorder, and a mobilization of federal troops could have been necessary. On the other hand, had he left the property tax in place, many farmers would doubtless have gone under. But it was difficult for the besieged citizenry to see the whole picture, so consumed were they with their own desperate straits. Consumers whose pennies were already stretched to their limit grumbled at each retail transaction across the state, and their discontent was aimed at the figurehead in Springfield. Even though Mayor Kelly had lobbied for the sales tax side by side with the governor, it was Horner who bore the brunt of the criticism when the measure passed. The papers began to launch a relentless diatribe against him. Not one to simply brush off public criticism as inevitable, he engaged in back and forth communication with members of the press, pointing out their inaccuracies or unfairness. However, many of them were in the service of a larger social agenda and cared little for subtle matters of accuracy, being more inclined to inflame the public or mobilize the state on behalf of a specific policy issue.

The press's criticism of Horner after the repeal of Prohibition demonstrates how this brand of journalism worked. Reformers and downstate interests expected Horner to take definitive action to ensure that saloons and politics would not have the close relationship that they had once enjoyed. Taking up the same cry, the papers accused Horner of taking a lackadaisical approach to the issue of liquor regulation and speculated that he was in league with Kelly. All this furor in the press took place at the same time that Horner was putting together the liquor control bill package that he would present to the legislature. The criticism in the papers ignored the content of his proposed legislation, which aggressively sought to separate saloon interests and political interests. Horner was angered by what he viewed as sloppy journalism. He dashed off a letter to one of his critics requesting that he read the legislation and asking what he meant by the "Horner-Kelly Program." "Do you know of such a program and are you familiar with the Horner program?" he asked. The editorialist responded to Horner in a private letter acknowledging that the presentation of facts in the piece was somewhat distorted, but claiming that his aim had been to arouse Horner's emotions on the issue in order to prod him into taking dramatic action. Even though he was aware of Horner's balanced and fair approach to matters of policy, he had decided to use a little showmanship to ensure that the matter of liquor control was handled correctly.

It is easy to imagine Horner's disillusionment with such dishonest tactics. What's more, the editorial writer in this instance was none other than Dick Finnegan, the man who had kindly finished Horner's election speech when Horner drifted off to sleep during the rigors of the campaign. Throughout Horner's career, Finnegan would continue to use the press to prod and manipulate him.[1] It was only one of many such betrayals by old friends that Horner would experience. The press continued to harangue him with accusations. As the nation became more aware of the sinister happenings in Germany, Horner, as a Jew of outstanding reputation and visibility, was called on to issue public statements and support policy measures related to Germany. He made it known publicly that he felt the emerging German state was based on hate and tyranny, but privately he felt hesitant to make addressing that issue a priority among his duties. That hesitation became a subject of much public controversy.

Horner took a beating in the press. He even was assaulted in print with scandalous suggestions about a woman in his life. Perhaps this was business as usual for a politician, but Horner, who had never envisioned himself a politician and didn't even like political types very much, found it a slap in the face. He felt that he was a public servant—a public servant who worked seven days a week, seventeen hours a day, most of the time. He had been given much approbation in probate court, but now it seemed that his labors went unappreciated. He began to feel depressed, disillusioned, and cranky. His usual jovial demeanor was punctuated at times by a gruffness that was uncharacteristic of him. The changes in him seemed a testament to how the vagaries of political life could wear away at a good and honest man. Again, his singularity as a political figure and the severity of his difficulties in office beg the question: Is there room for a genuinely good man in political office?

While Horner suffered under the burden of Depression-era politics, the Kelly-Nash machine seemed to prosper from it. Although Anton Cermak had chosen Pat Nash to be *his* sidekick, the same arrangement worked equally well, if not better, for the new mayor, Ed Kelly. As fellow Irishmen who had long economic and political connections, Kelly and Nash functioned as an impeccable unit, probably more smoothly than Cermak and Nash would have. Nash turned out to be the charismatic and beloved figure who focused his political wisdom on long-term party strategy and left the aggressive, detail-oriented Kelly to mind the store on his own. Although Kelly's appointment had once been seen as an odd stopgap measure for the city after the death of its elected mayor, he was now emerging into the public consciousness as a legitimate leader. Throughout his career, he had successfully weathered a series of scandals. The public allowed him to "push the envelope" of propriety a bit. It was a level of corruption that the populace found tolerable then. When it came time for Kelly to be reaffirmed in his position by the ballot, he was in a solid position to succeed. Moreover, the corruption woven into the fabric of Chicago politics was a condition that Washington was well aware of.

The reformer from Chicago, Harold Ickes, who now held the position of secretary of the interior, had the ear of the president and whispered a steady stream of warnings about doing business with the city. When the Civil Works Administration (CWA) got started in Chicago, Washington leaned over watchfully, holding its breath, expecting that the city machine would seize on the program as a resource ripe for the spoils and patronage system. But Kelly dealt authoritatively and professionally with Washington, setting the apprehensions of program administrators to rest to some degree. Although his long-standing actions were in perfect step with corrupt city practices, somehow Mayor Kelly always seemed to create doubt in the mind of critics as to his real political nature. After all, he cut such a professional and imposing figure—a very tall man, perfectly dressed, with a straightforward, businesslike demeanor—that he seemed the very image of a mayoral presence. Kelly's presence alone seemed sufficient to indicate that the circus had ended and something more legitimate had taken its place. But the crooked system didn't fade away under Kelly. It simply got more organized and professional in its operation. The Chicago political machine was, if anything, strengthened under his guidance. While the desperation of the people made Henry Horner a scapegoat, that same desperation had the power to make Ed Kelly a hero. The public was eager to accept an organization that might offer some protection. Bill and Lori Granger describe the relationship between the Depression and the Kelly-Nash machine this way:

> These were desperate years when people doubled and tripled up on apartments and dodged the landlord while looking hopelessly for work. Welfare was an invention of the future. Government relief was direct—mostly food—and was for today alone. The struggle to survive made people appreciate the favors of the Machine, which were delivered by the precinct worker, the lowliest and most important cog in the Machine. There were three thousand precincts in Chicago, mini-neighborhoods inside neighborhoods, and they were all manned by loyal Machine hands who, in addition to recommending people for jobs, brought food, relief and friendship up the back stairs of the tenements. They gave valuable favors and expected votes in return.[2]

This description is a reminder of the fundamental relationship between hard times and the underworld. Just as the saloon syndicate of Hinky Dink Kenna and Bathhouse John Coughlin did favors for the working class in return for votes, the Kelly-Nash machine filled needs that the legitimate system could not or would not.

Kelly and Nash also did an excellent job of updating and professionalizing the political machine. Roger Biles describes how a system that had relied on currying advantageous political relationships, creating a political "in-crowd," and swapping favors got an infusion of capitalistic practices that increased its efficiency under Kelly and Nash: "They established clear-cut standards of performance, whereby party workers advanced or were demoted according to successes or failures within their own fiefdoms. Given a certain latitude and hope for advancement within the hierarchy, the party faithful, from ward committeemen down to precinct workers, had a reason to work hard." Biles attributes Kelly's success in operating the machine to his ability to combine a "system of incentives" with his own leadership style of "stern discipline."[3] Nash, on the other hand, acted as a bridge linking the tradition of the old organization with its new infrastructure. In this way, the Chicago political machine began to resemble a corporation more than a mob organization or a circus. Its more colorful days were behind it, but the machine was alive and well. Kelly was even beginning to convince Washington that his administration just might be legitimate, or at least it was convenient for the federal government to believe that it was.

The CWA brought 30,000 jobs to Chicago, and the work projects necessitated buying materials, issuing contracts, and a legion of other opportunities for Chicago. The beneficiaries lined up hungrily. Suspicious from the start, federal officials chased rumors of CWA jobs being filled with men clutching letters from ward bosses. Scandals regularly sprouted up concerning the purse strings of the CWA and political influence. Harry Hopkins investigated and appointed a federal administrator for the local problem, but he couldn't stop graft from gripping the CWA. There was a struggle back and forth between the federal administrator and the Chicago grafters, but before they could reach an understanding, the temporary program came to an end. Still, it had brought relief and some economic revitalization to the city, and it had also given the Kelly-Nash machine some spoils to manipulate for its own benefit.

The Roosevelt administration was riding high on a wave of positive public sentiment. The New Deal was a public relations success. Hundreds of thousands of people were finding sporadic employment in work relief programs. Many families would not have made it through the winter without federal relief, and more programs were continually being introduced, bringing hope to a population that had grown desperately angry with the "wait and see" attitude of the prior administration. Realizing that a close relationship with the federal administration was key to his continued power, Kelly made it priority number one in his administration to woo Washington. With the approach of the 1934 state primaries, Kelly saw an opportunity to prove to Roosevelt that his machine could mobilize voters. He knew that the Roosevelt administration would not forget such a display of power when it came time for their own reelection efforts in the upcoming national race in 1936. Kelly and Nash exhibited an advantageous solidarity with Washington when they adopted the Democratic campaign slogan "Forward with Roosevelt and Recovery!"[4] As usual, charges of election fraud accompanied the Democratic victory by Kelly and Nash's slate of candidates. Evidence suggests that the usual questionable election practices were at work but were not the decisive factor in these elections. As recovery inched along, it was inconceivable that the general public would try to reverse this course and vote with the Republicans. Kelly felt sure of support from Washington when it came time for him to prove himself in an election. However, such support was not quick in coming. Roosevelt was a longtime political reformer who had fought determinedly against Tammany Hall in New York.

Roosevelt was comfortable with Kelly and considered him a fairly professional administrator who might be able to steer Chicago away from the Tammany model, but he also knew Kelly's history. The president was apprehensive because Harold Ickes, a Chicago reformer, had continually warned him that Kelly was corrupt. His advisers told him that Thompson was gearing up to run again for mayor of Chicago, and Big Bill was certainly no antidote for political corruption. But the influence of respected power players like Ickes and Chicago reformer Charles Merriam persuaded Roosevelt to take the steps necessary to block Kelly's nomination for reelection. However, his advisers reported back that the Democratic political machine in Chicago would wholeheartedly embrace Kelly, with or without Washington's approval. Trying to buck the machine in Chicago could spell trouble for Roosevelt in Illinois when he stood for reelection two years later. Also, causing a schism in the Democratic Party in Illinois might create an opening for Thompson to sneak back into public office. The horror of that thought sealed the deal. Roosevelt went ahead and backed Kelly for mayor, but he made it secretly known that if Charles Merriam were to launch any opposition, he could expect covert support from Washington.[5]

When Ed Kelly ran for reelection, his Republican opponent was not Big Bill Thompson but attorney Emil Wetten. Despite being a very weak candidate, Wetten was still more vigorous than his opponents in his desire to face Kelly. Although Thompson was not a contender, he did run a candidate. And once again, he had a surprise in store. The once professional bigot now championed women's rights activist Mrs. John Wesley Grace for mayor. Wetten ran a very lackluster campaign, making few public appearances and operating with insufficient campaign funds. There was speculation that he must have been handpicked by the Democrats, since Kelly defeated him by the largest majority in a mayoral race in the city's history.

After Horner's veto of the so-called Bookie Bill in the summer of 1935, his relationship with Mayor Kelly was beyond repair. Horner knew that this schism was a liability, but not how serious a liability. The relationship between the two became prickly. When Kelly sent Horner a request for an appointment, he would bristle when Horner did not approve it on the spot but only promised to "review it." His irritation would grow into a rage if Horner informed him later that he had found someone better qualified than the mayor's choice. When Horner insisted on the autonomy of his role, he broke a long-standing tradition in Illinois politics that considered the positions of Illinois governor and Chicago mayor of equal status. There had been struggles between the two sites of power in the past, and the current situation was no exception. Although Horner realized that he had originally been nominated by his party to play a subservient role to the Chicago mayor, he intently refused to do so. Kelly was continually annoyed by Horner's lack of deference. He believed that whenever Horner had business in Chicago, he should first phone in to the mayor's office to keep city hall in the loop. When an aide expressed Kelly's discontent at not being contacted during one of Horner's trips to Chicago, Horner reportedly responded, "'Why should I call him? I've got nothing to say to him. I'm the Governor of this State.'"[6]

Once a master of conciliation and preserving cordial relationships, Horner now seemed to have almost given up trying to get along with other politicians. Instead of working to smooth over disagreements, the tired and disillusioned governor now often uttered bitter and cynical responses in the direction of his political critics. Kelly was certainly the most critical, and Horner resigned himself to the reality that his and Kelly's friendship was a thing of the past. Still, he believed that he had a strong relationship with Washington. Despite what he considered his personality conflict with Hopkins and some internal reservations about the direction of the Roosevelt administration, he believed that he had been a loyal New Dealer. In all of his public statements, he continued to support the president.

Horner also felt confident about his record in the state. In his first term, he had miraculously pulled the state out of debt. There had been some rankling about the sales tax, but it was evident to Horner that if the sales tax not been instituted, the state would have collapsed financially. The fomenting revolution had been dispelled, relief programs had saved thousands from starving, farmers facing foreclosures had held on to their farms, and banks had been stabilized. There was still a great deal of hardship in the state, but the worst appeared to be over, and he had been at the helm of the turnaround. Surely the people of Illinois would recognize how he had worked long and hard on their behalf.

But Horner was overlooking some ominous signs in the air. In his Governor's Day speech at the state fair in 1935, he triumphantly announced that he would proudly represent the Democratic Party in a bid for reelection. However, the other politicians who spoke that day ignored his announcement in their speeches; the traditional statements of support were conspicuously absent. It was not a surprise to Horner that Kelly had not graced the affair with his attendance, but he was unaware of the impact of Kelly's way of thinking on others in the party. There were other signs that followed. A painful reality was beginning to emerge, as Horner noted in dismay that the Young Jewish Lawyers' Association did not endorse his candidacy, citing as their reason Horner's refusal to grant the stay of execution for the Jewish inmate who had been executed on Yom Kippur. Clearly, Horner was beginning to feel the brunt of his decision to distance himself from ethnic politics.

He also began to receive letters urging him not to run for reelection. He was warned that his unpopularity would hurt the chances of the Democratic Party. Criticism seemed to come at him from every direction. Every difficult decision that he had had to make during his first term was destined to come back to haunt him. However, if he had made the opposite decisions, they would almost certainly have also become reasons for his loss of the public's high regard. Horner was becoming proof positive that if "they" don't want you, there is nothing you can do right. And he was becoming increasingly convinced that "they" was none other than Ed Kelly. Still, Horner had some devoted supporters. His true friends began to show themselves. Bishop Griffin and Carl Sandburg kept in close touch with him. They continually reminded him of the difficulty of his position and predicted that his grace and performance under such conditions would surely be recognized by voters in the 1936 elections.

Most notably though, Horner found himself with a surprising *contingent* of friends he was not even aware that he had. While the Chicago political machine and even Horner's formerly loyal network from Chicago began to turn from him, many downstate residents who admired the governor's forthright, people-centered honesty rose up to assert that *they* still admired it. During this period, a new organization called the "Southern Illinois Horner Club" was born. It boasted over eleven thousand members who wanted to see the Jewish governor from Chicago reelected. This surprising show of support seems to shed light on the strange position of a nonpolitical figure in a political seat. Even when—perhaps especially when—the independent-minded individual is made a victim of the changing tides of political fortune, that person may find admirers from among the legions who distrust politics. This is the surprise that Horner had in store for Chicago.

In the meantime, Kelly officially began the stratagem to oust Horner. Nash was reluctant. He felt it would damage the party to institute a break with state government, and he didn't have quite the personal distaste for Horner that Kelly had. After all, it wasn't *his* authority that had been challenged by the governor, and Nash wasn't obsessed with his own authority anyway. But Kelly was dead set on it. He began to argue that Horner was so unpopular that they risked the return of a Republican governor if they kept him on the ticket. The 3 percent sales tax had set public opinion against Horner, Kelly insisted, ironically seizing on the sales tax as the deciding issue, although he had stood beside Horner (or perhaps slightly behind his shoulder) when the governor instituted and subsequently raised the sales tax. Kelly was not about to connect himself with the unpopular measure he once supported if it could be used against Horner. Moreover, the mayor needed a "Kelly man" in Springfield as much as Cermak had needed a "Cermak man." If Cermak had lived, he would have realized that he didn't get his wish, and neither had Kelly. The governor of Illinois, for the time being, was to be *his own man*. Kelly realized that eliminating Horner was a risk. If Horner decided to put up a fight, it could get ugly and divisive for the party. The trick would be to get him to bow out gracefully by bribing him with some other alternate position. At this critical juncture, someone whispered into Kelly's ear that indeed Horner *would* bow under the pressure. He *would* step down if leaned on. According to biographer Thomas Littlewood's research into the matter, that whisperer was Ben Lindheimer, a member of the family that had given Horner a start in politics.[7]

On December 9, 1935, Horner rested in the back of his limousine on his way to a Democratic Party luncheon honoring President Roosevelt. When the limousine pulled up at the front of the Stockyards Inn, Horner was surprised to have visitors join him in the backseat. They were Kelly and Nash. They got straight to the point and informed him that because of the taxation issue, he didn't have a chance for reelection and should step aside for the party's sake. Horner was said to have responded as firmly as possible but with a shaky voice, "I'll beat the hell out of both of you. I've got more friends over the state of Illinois than you realize. You'll find out."[8] Nash seemed chagrined during the awkward conversation, but Kelly was all business.

Kelly and Nash dashed out of the car and flanked Roosevelt on either side as he entered the luncheon on crutches. Horner looked out the window, still in shock. Normal protocol demanded that the governor and the mayor share the duty of escorting the president, but all normal hierarchies were suddenly turned on their head. Horner took a deep breath and got out of the car. He entered the luncheon on his own and found a seat at the far end of the head table, now indistinguishable from the regular rabble of party men. Everyone in attendance knew what this meant. The governor had been thrown aside by his own party. It only remained to be seen what Roosevelt would make of all this. Although Horner still hoped that Roosevelt would disapprove of the move made by Kelly and Nash, the governor had enough political savvy to assume that the decision had already been run by Roosevelt, since Kelly and Nash were so set on currying the approval of the White House. His only hope would be to talk to Roosevelt one on one.

Horner's opportunity came the next day, when he, Nash, and Kelly took a train ride with Roosevelt to South Bend, Indiana, where the president was to receive an honorary degree from the University of Notre Dame. When Horner and Roosevelt met, Horner's worst fears were realized. Roosevelt offered him a plum federal judgeship and led him to believe that a position on the Supreme Court was a plausible aspiration for the distinguished former judge. Horner probably would have been wise to take the offer. After all, the happiest times of his life had been on the bench. A job in the courts made use of his intellect, his attention to detail, his objectivity, and his principled decision making, attributes that only seemed to arouse suspicion and criticism in his current occupation.

Horner was not cynical or hard-hearted enough to easily endure the position of lightning rod in the state capital. His first term as governor was killing him. He had had doubts about his desire to be governor before he ran for it the first time, and surely he had even greater doubts about whether he wanted to continue. But now his sense of duty was inflamed and fed by an anger unlike any he had ever felt. The procession of bullies that he had encountered during his career in public life now must have paraded before his eyes. Perhaps Lincoln was in his thoughts at this time. Having made a fateful decision, Horner turned up his nose at the beguiling federal judgeship. Already half worn out, he was determined to give his remaining half to stopping Kelly in his tracks. He had no wife or mother to beg him to do otherwise.

13

Into the Snake Pit

As a symbolic gesture of their united front, Ed Kelly and Pat Nash triumphantly escorted President Roosevelt back to the White House. Meanwhile, Henry Horner limped dejectedly back to the Congress Hotel in Chicago, his head undoubtedly spinning from the unexpected reversal of his political fortunes. He had tried to do the right thing at every turn. He had not expected the torrent of criticism and the lack of appreciation that he received for his efforts, but he had chalked it up to the unfortunate condition of his office. But what had just happened to him was not the run-of-the-mill turmoil of political life. He had just fallen victim to a betrayal of epic proportions. The blow sapped his vitality, and he sank into a temporary depression. He sank deeper as he received a procession of calls from former political allies and even friends who wished to express their regret on the occasion of his political demise. They had to go along with the party, they sadly explained. Horner mumbled his way through these awkward farewells. When Nash returned from Washington, he paid a personal visit to Horner. Nash had not fully supported his partner's decision to oppose Horner's nomination; this breach of loyalty within the party troubled him. It was with warmth and sincerity that he told Horner that, despite their political parting of the ways, he considered him a friend and hoped he would remain so.

By the time Horner returned to Springfield, he was vacillating between depression and defiant rage. His friends were troubled to see signs that the stress was wearing on the governor's sanity. He wavered unsteadily between frenetic activity and anger and a depressed inertia that suggested that he might just throw in the towel after all. It was during one of his more active phases that he made some telephone calls and fired some of the Kelly-Nash appointees that he had approved over the years. He was, after all, still the governor of Illinois.

Roosevelt was also facing a reelection bid in 1936, and although Illinois politicians felt that riding his coattails would be advantageous, Roosevelt was less sanguine. His New Deal had brought him a lot of acclaim from the bottom of the social order, but he still faced increasing opposition from the top. He felt that he must keep a strong grip on the power coalitions that he had already formed if he were to defeat the burgeoning movement against him. After the legislation of the first hundred days, wealthy business leaders began to grumble about the increased regulation that was being applied to their endeavors. The preceding decade had been a time of enormous freedom and opportunity for big business, and business interests increasingly saw their latitude being circumscribed. At first, Roosevelt had directed some New Deal funds and energy to strengthen the business sector and shore up collapsing industries, but when he continued to receive criticism from business interests and the wealthy, he grew more and more antibusiness in his orientation.

In reaction to the president and his New Deal policies, a group of wealthy business leaders who usually voted Republican formed the American Liberty League in 1934. The DuPont family led this group, and its membership included conservative Republican Alfred P. Sloan, longtime president of General Motors, some conservative Democrats such as Al

Smith and John W. Davis, both former Democratic presidential candidates in the 1920s, and former president Herbert Hoover. According to Roger Biles, the league's "principle aim was to restore to business the freedom it had enjoyed before excessive government regulation despoiled the nation."[1] Although this group continued to lobby against Roosevelt's legislation until the eve of the 1936 elections, the organization had a terrible public image because of its association with the richest individuals in America. Most of the nation saw Roosevelt as the defender of the poor and saw the American Liberty League as the incarnation of their hero's villainous rival. When Alf Landon, the popular Republican governor from Kansas, went up against Roosevelt in 1936, the endorsement and support of the American Liberty League hurt Landon's campaign. However, Roosevelt found himself continually swimming upstream during his first term in office. The initial spate of legislation had provided relief to millions, but it had not provided any long-term stabilizing effects. Once the relief funds had been used up, circumstances seemed as dire, if not worse, than they had before.

In the spring of 1935, the Roosevelt administration decided to undertake a second aggressive offensive against Depression-era conditions and began hammering out new legislation to extend the revision of America's political and economic structure. While the first wave of the New Deal had been aimed at relief and recovery, the second was aimed at reform, targeting wealthy business interests and trying to create a more equitable distribution of wealth in the country. Pressured on the right and on the left, Roosevelt decided to take additional action. In his annual message to Congress on January 4, 1935, he stated that his new program would provide not only security of livelihood but also security against old age, unemployment, and ill health; in addition, it would focus on better housing and slum clearance.

The first measure to be passed in the so-called Second New Deal was the Emergency Relief Appropriations Act that created the Works Progress Administration (WPA), with an allocation of $4.8 billion. Critics balked at the outlandish price tag, but the strategy of work relief enjoyed widespread popular success. Work relief programs had touched nearly every community across the country, and nearly every working-class family had a member who, at one time or another, was part of a WPA program. Historian Edward Robb Ellis explains that the WPA's impact was so broad because it "built 651,087 miles of highways, roads and streets; constructed, repaired or improved 124,031 bridges; erected 125,110 public buildings; created 8,192 public parks; [and] built or improved 853 airports."[2] The WPA did receive some criticism for not paying workers as much as they would have received in the private sector, but many American citizens knew that they would not have survived without the modest WPA wages.

Amid charges of socialism, the Second New Deal instituted the Social Security Act as a long-term protection for the vulnerable. Roosevelt proved that he was not currying the favor of the wealthy by introducing "soak the rich" taxes intended to create a more equitable distribution of wealth in the country. But when Congress had finished with it, the Revenue Act of 1935 (the Wealth Tax Act) did little more than target an extremely select group of America's wealthiest citizens. Nonetheless, it achieved a symbolic effect. The Wealth Tax Act increased taxes on all annual incomes above $50,000, with those of $1 million or more being taxed up to 75 percent.

The days of the carefree giants were over; Roosevelt had firmly positioned himself as an advocate of the common person. Having come from blue-blood ancestry, he was called a traitor to his own class, but such comments did not move him. His political orientation was self-chosen. His choice to take care of one side rather than try to please the whole nation was a gamble, especially when he made enemies of those who had the public voice and the greatest resources in the nation. The opposition to the New Deal was splashed all over the media. In 1934 and 1935, Roosevelt had much to fear as the reelection campaign of 1936 approached. He and the New Deal were now being attacked from both the political left and right.

Providing opposition from the left was the Farmer-Labor Political Federation, which was formed in 1933 and soon had membership in twenty-six states. Its greatest achievement was establishing the Wisconsin Progressive Party under the leadership of two brothers, Bob LaFollette Jr. and Philip LaFollette. Bob was elected to the U.S. Senate, and brother Phil was elected governor of Wisconsin, both in 1934. The same year, Floyd Olson, another supporter of the Farmer-Labor organization, was reelected governor of Minnesota. At that point, it seemed that there might be a Farmer-Labor convention in Chicago in 1936 to form a third political party and nominate a presidential candidate to run against and possibly defeat Roosevelt. Still another leftist group, the American Commonwealth Political Federation (ACPF) was formed at a conference held in Chicago in July 1935. This organization favored cooperatives for all producers and consumers and advocated public ownership of industries, transportation, and utilities. In 1936, the ACPF tried to gain support from Dr. Francis E. Townsend, organizer of the Townsend Old Age Pension Plan in 1934.[3] However, he refused to join them and moved instead to the far right and allied himself with the Union Party. Although Townsend had testified at congressional hearings about Social Security, he was greatly dissatisfied with the act that resulted in 1935. To counter the opposition of the DuPonts and the Liberty League to Roosevelt's candidacy, the newly formed (April 1936) Labor's Non-Partisan League endorsed him. Then on May 5, 1936, the fiery Milo Reno, head of the Farm Holiday Association, died. Reno had been the strongest link between the agrarian movement and the third-party movement, but with his death, there was little chance that an opposition party on the left could or would be formed. Governor Olson urged members of the Farmer-Labor movement to stay away from the Chicago convention if they intended to nominate a national ticket. The opposition to Roosevelt from the left had failed to develop, and he had nothing more to fear from it by midsummer 1936.

The opposition to Roosevelt from the right was equally threatening in 1934–35. Father Charles E. Coughlin, the CBS radio Catholic priest from the Detroit area, was originally a supporter but had become disillusioned with Roosevelt by 1934 and formed an opposition organization, the National Union for Social Justice. Coughlin claimed that this right-wing group had 8 million followers. Then an even more threatening personality than Coughlin, Huey Long, the "Kingfish" from Louisiana, threatened Roosevelt's candidacy. In 1933, Senator Long offered his "Share-Our-Wealth" program and won many supporters throughout the country.

The following year, Long broke with Roosevelt and talked about capturing the Democratic Party's presidential nomination in 1936 or, if he couldn't manage that, forming a third party. James A. Farley, Roosevelt's campaign manager, was concerned about the threat of a third party after a private poll indicated that Long might draw 3–4 million votes away from the Democratic Party and assure a Republican victory in the election. Fortunately for Roosevelt, Long was assassinated in September 1935 on the steps of the Louisiana capitol. The next year, Long's right-hand man, the Reverend Gerald L. K. Smith, joined Father Coughlin and Dr. Townsend to form the Union Party, which nominated Congressman William Lemke as its presidential candidate. Lemke let the Union Party dub him "Liberty Bell" Bill. This proved to be an unfortunate choice of a nickname since the opposition pointed out in the campaign that the chief distinguishing feature of the Liberty Bell was that it was "cracked" and, obviously, "so was Bill!" When the 1936 presidential election was over, Lemke had received less than 2 percent of the vote, and Alf Landon, the Republican candidate, had carried only two states. Although Roosevelt had appeared to face serious threats to his reelection hopes in 1936, he actually won by a landslide victory. However, his precarious position in 1935 and the first half of 1936 affected his dealings with the political situation in Illinois.[4]

It was this perilous political atmosphere that surrounded Roosevelt when he beheld the discontent in the Democratic Party in Illinois. He knew that an improvident move on his part could incite a wing of the party against him. He didn't know whether siding with the Chicago political machine was in keeping with his "people politics," but he had seen Kelly's ability to mobilize voters. He had also discovered that where Kelly went, so went the machine. He couldn't cross Kelly. And yet, he didn't want to associate himself with the political fracas that was so out of keeping with his larger vision. He hoped that the problem would be smoothed over with a minimum of disruption. If Horner would only step aside quietly, the situation would not escalate and would not attract national attention. Roosevelt dispatched a Washington official to approach Horner again with the offer of a federal judgeship, emphasizing the promising career he would enjoy. Roosevelt could not have been comfortable with the brutal tactics of the Democratic Party in Illinois. After all, he had worked long and hard against similar machine politics when he took on Tammany, and now he was turning his back while Ed Kelly attempted to take down the governor.

Roosevelt may not have gotten the most positive impression of Horner's capabilities through intermediaries like Harry Hopkins and Senator William Dieterich (D-Ill.), but he knew that he and Horner had some things in common. They were both for the common folks, and they weren't bullies like many machine politicians. They both knew what it was like to be a gentleman in a sea of crude power players. Roosevelt had done what was most politically expedient for him to do, but he could not have relished seeing a man, in whose face he must have seen many features of a character similar to his own, dragged through the mud to slaughter. He would have felt much more comfortable if Horner had gracefully withdrawn to a comfortable and dignified position on the judiciary. Wasn't it the ambition of every judge to occupy a seat on the Supreme Court? Eleanor Roosevelt agreed with Harold Ickes on the matter; both of them disapproved of what Kelly and Nash were doing to the honorable Governor Horner. Roosevelt probably agreed with them. Regardless of whether they supported Horner or not, none of them thought he could withstand the test.

Throughout the Illinois campaign, Roosevelt studiously tried to look the other way and adopted an official stance of neutrality. Kelly and Nash assured him that other than the ousting of Horner, there would be no other shake-up of the Democratic political positions. Roosevelt was concerned that the machine would punish Horner loyalists after the governor's defeat and create negative political ramifications for the president and his reelection bid. With the assurance that a shake-up in the Democratic Party would not follow the unseating of Horner, Roosevelt gave Kelly and Nash his tacit consent and did not interfere with them. Still, he distanced himself from the ugliness in case some of it should come back to haunt him at an inopportune moment. Most of all, he hoped to avoid the confrontation altogether by having Horner comfortably settled in a federal judgeship.

Roosevelt's wish for a quiet resolution would not be fulfilled. In Horner's letters as well as in his conduct, he demonstrated that he was not one to give up on a commitment or to shirk a duty; but submerged in melancholy in the empty governor's mansion, he must have seriously considered Roosevelt's offer. Horner's shortness of breath and his heart irregularities were growing worse. His exhaustion made it more and more difficult for him to withstand the marathon work sessions that were demanded of him. All that he had enjoyed in earlier years seemed to have been taken from him: the satisfaction of having his efforts appreciated, as they had been in probate court; a thoughtful conversation over bourbon and a cigar at the Standard Club; a relaxed evening of sorting through his Lincoln letters; friendship, warmth, conviviality. There were so few of these pleasures left in his life now. When he looked ahead toward the election, he was surely locked in a dilemma that Shakespeare's Hamlet might relate to. Certainly, there would be an element of suicide involved in the decision to fight. It would be the fight of his life.

Some Republicans had told Lincoln that he should step aside in 1864 and not run for reelection because he couldn't win. Lincoln had ignored them and won the election. Both Lincoln and Horner, in their own ways, had struggled through their first terms and might be expected to welcome leaving office. But Horner and Lincoln both felt they had missions to finish and did not shirk that responsibility. Such idealistic comparisons surely motivated Horner, but he was also so incensed by the behavior of the Chicago machine that he was resolved that, no matter what, Ed Kelly would not win the battle.

Meanwhile, back in Chicago, Kelly and Nash were dealing with the consequences of their decision, busily strategizing the next move in their plan to oust the governor. When Kelly had first made his intentions known to party leaders, he suggested that his replacement candidate would be Bruce Campbell, the most visible political figure from downstate. This choice would have been a logical one. Assurances were given that the Chicago machine could bring in the Cook County vote; therefore, selecting a downstate candidate should lock up that end of the state for the Kelly-Nash agenda as well. And so, it shocked everybody, including Campbell, when Kelly announced instead that his candidate would be Dr. Herman Bundeson, the health commissioner of Cook County. Dr. Bundeson was a very visible public figure in Chicago at the time and an energetic and flamboyant spokesman for health issues in the state. After he had proved himself successful at the polls when he ran for county coroner, there was some serious discussion of his entering the mayor's race against Cermak. But the party had convinced him to accept the helm at the city's Health Commission instead. He had achieved some notable goals for the city as health commissioner, having successfully dealt with diphtheria and smallpox outbreaks in the city and instituted a measure requiring the pasteurization of milk. Although dairy farmers objected to the pasteurization requirement as interference in their industry, claiming that it was both an expense and an inconvenience, Bundeson was generally known for improving health conditions in the tattered city. He was outspoken about matters that most people of the day were reticent to discuss. He acted as if the prevention of venereal disease were a subject suitable for the dinner table and was known to proclaim proudly that under his administration Chicago was the safest city in the world in which to have sexual intercourse.

Bundeson's pet cause was also uncharacteristic fodder for a Chicago politician. He was an outspoken advocate for babies and felt that the general public needed a solid education in the proper methods of caring for them. He wrote several books on the matter and emerged as the "Dr. Spock" of his time. Utilizing the birth records of local hospitals, he instituted a program that provided one of his books to every new mother in the city, lending his name a great deal of positive visibility in the city. When he proposed expanding this program statewide, he bumped heads with Governor Horner. Horner didn't like programs from Chicago being shoved down his throat in Springfield, and he remembered that Bundeson had once had his eye on the mayor's seat. Under advisement from the state health director, Dr. Jirka, who was also Cermak's son-in-law, Horner decided not to feed that particular political interest. Instead, he commissioned an alternate, state-approved baby book for distribution. Bundeson still succeeded in making the care of babies a major priority in Chicago, and under his leadership there was a drop in the rate of infant mortality.

But Bundeson did seem to be an odd candidate for such a pivotal expression of Kelly's power. Shortly before his death, John Stelle, the lieutenant governor in Horner's second term, provided an interesting explanation of Kelly's choice of Bundeson in an interview with Thomas Littlewood. Stelle suggested that Kelly selected Bundeson fully expecting that he would defeat Horner in the primary, because, Kelly believed, Horner didn't have the strength to launch an effective defense without the support of the state or national party. But Kelly expected the Republican candidate to defeat Bundeson. According to Stelle, Kelly no longer wanted to have a Democrat in the governor's seat because it would pose too great a threat to his supremacy in the party. He was tired of his rivalry with Horner and thought it more politically expedient to be the only Democrat occupying a high elective office in the state. As it turned out, the dispute within the Democratic Party about who should run as Horner's successor in 1940 paved the way for the victory of Republican Dwight Green. Whether or not Kelly had ulterior motives, his selection of Bundeson is generally considered a fatal error in his 1936 Democratic campaign strategy.

When Horner found out that Herman Bundeson was going to oppose him for the Democratic Party nomination, his decision to remain in the race was sealed. He felt sure that he could defeat such an ill-conceived candidate. Shortly thereafter, Horner presented Cook County with an ultimatum. It would not be granted additional relief funds if it did not begin allocating more relief revenue from its own budget. Cook County, he declared, needed to shoulder more of the burden of relief. As he leaned on Cook County, Horner was pleased to think of Kelly scrambling to raise the funds, just as Horner himself had scrambled when Harry Hopkins had issued the same ultimatum. Horner also proposed a levy on Chicago property taxes that became known as the "Soak Chicago Tax." The governor had decided to fight with all the tricks that he had learned from the masters. Kelly's house would be brought down with his own tools. From then on, the state saw a different Henry Horner. He now employed many of the political tactics that he had once despised and let loose of principles and gentility. Finally, he became a politician who would beat them at their own game. It was either play hardball or let the bullies win.

History may never conclusively decide whether Horner still fought on behalf of the people, or whether he had given himself over to personal retribution and the settling of a grudge against Ed Kelly. He now brought out the campaign slogans, the catchy attacks, the airing of dirty laundry. He would need every weapon in a politician's arsenal.

"Bossism" became his theme. He had never taken the noisy route of the reformer, but he would do so now. He presented himself as the little guy against "Boss Kelly." He reminded the public of Kelly's tax-evasion scandal and exaggerated things a bit for good measure, proclaiming that Kelly had been on the doorstep of the jailhouse. He now decided to break the hush-hush policy regarding Cook County's legendary election-fraud habits. He proposed a system of permanent registration to combat voter fraud. Under this system, voters would have to register, and their signatures would be kept on file for comparison with signatures at the polls. This change of policy would have prevented a myriad of fraudulent practices: multiple votes cast by one voter, voting under the names of deceased persons, and buying votes from transients at multiple voting places with food or money. When the legislature failed to pass the permanent voter registration measure, Horner used the bill's defeat to his political advantage, claiming that "Boss Kelly" had persuaded the legislators to keep corruption alive in the election process.

Notoriously uncharacteristic of the governor was his demand for support from a Jewish colleague, Judge Harry Fisher. If this prominent Jewish Chicago politician switched allegiance, such a surprising political twist would set the tone for the Jewish vote in Chicago. Horner knew that the appointment of Fisher's son David as an attorney in the Cook County Office of Public Administration was hanging in the balance. Horner decided to take advantage of this situation and phoned the judge, requesting a letter of endorsement immediately. Horner made it clear that if the judge did not send his endorsement, his son would not receive the appointment. Fisher was against the course that the party had taken and had discussed his position with Kelly, but formally endorsing Horner would mean committing political suicide. Fisher expressed his outrage at being blackmailed into choosing either his son or himself for exile. He found the move so out of character for his former friend that he called it "an irrational blow struck during the madness of a violent political struggle."[5]

Whether Horner's tactics were studied and rational or wild and irrational is a matter of interpretation. Certainly, Horner made many decisions that suggest he had finally decided he would "play the game" and make moves that he had hitherto steadfastly rejected. His first campaign for governor strikes a startling contrast to his second. Was it madness that drove him to finally become the politician that so many had condemned him for not being, or was it Carter Harrison's example of realpolitik taken to an extreme? Some observers believe it was madness. They point to his deteriorating health and document his mood swings—melancholy rapidly giving way to a manic determination and aggressive actions directed at his reelection effort. But another interpretation reads this period as an exercise in analysis and strategy. This was not a typical political battle and therefore could not be fought with conventional weaponry. Horner could serve the people of Illinois only if he stayed in office. Running his campaign in his normal, "friendly" fashion would be tantamount to handing the keys to the statehouse over to Cook County. Horner had worked among corrupt bullies all of his life. Perhaps he had consciously determined that he would not give in to them in the end. Perhaps it was a mix of reason, madness, and anger that dictated his actions during this period. Regardless of why he chose them, his aggressive tactics paid off. However, the Henry Horner of old would have been saddened to see David Fisher withdraw his bid for a position in the Cook County Office of Public Administration in order to protect his father. But Horner wasn't alone in his hard-nosed tactics. It was to be a dirty fight all around.

During Horner's first campaign for governor, the fact of his being Jewish had not caused a great deal of conflict. Only a hushed whisper on the matter had met the candidate on his rounds about the state, and he had admirably brought those rumors out into the open, dispelling the issue from the campaign. However, now that Horner was not the powerful frontrunner and the seeds of World War II were beginning to sprout, the issue became more contentious and unavoidable. Horner was clearly a governor who was being strong-armed out of office by his party, and people began to speculate about how his ethnicity bore on the matter. Julius Klein, for example, a prominent Chicagoan working for RKO Studios in Hollywood, became alarmed when he heard that the Jewish governor was being placed on the chopping block. He wrote letters to prominent Jews of the city to warn them of the danger in such a move during a time in which Hitler was rising in Europe. The fact that Horner's rival for the nomination, Bundeson, was born in Berlin made the contest take on an even greater symbolic significance. While views were mixed among the rabbinical order, the meaning behind the recent treatment of Horner alarmed many.

Kelly actively campaigned to get Chicago Jews on his side, urging them not to vote along ethnic lines. In order to show that the challenge to Horner was more than just a local political issue, Kelly gathered together two of his Jewish allies, Jake Arvey and now Harry Fisher, and scheduled them to meet with the Jewish precinct captains of the city. Arvey and Fisher worked to convince the Jewish wing of the Democratic Party that it was more important to vote with the organization than to vote according to ethnic and religious identification. Horner was stunned to lose much Jewish support during this period. Even the Lindheimer family, which had been like a second family to him and instrumental in his career, now supported the party and deserted the governor. A rift had clearly occurred between Horner and Ben Lindheimer, the son of Jacob Lindheimer. Harry Fisher was willing to speak out as a party loyalist since his recent exchange with the governor. He posed the question to an assembly of Jews, "Shall we endanger the jobs of thousands of Jews in public life in this state just to go in and support an irresponsible bachelor?"[6] Although Horner's bachelorhood could be attributed, at least in part, to his overly keen sense of responsibility, it was often used against him during the 1936 campaign. Surely seeing old friends turn on him must have been painful. It was a muckraking election; nobody was pretending to take the higher ground.

The general tone of the campaign was ugly and vindictive. Bundeson seemed out of step with the larger campaign that was being run on his behalf. His style was not political invective; in fact, it was not very political at all. The monocled Bundeson seemed more a flamboyant salesman, jaunting around the state demonstrating his superior energy and urging everyone to follow his example. He did not choose to step very far outside the role of health purveyor to portray himself as a candidate who could handle the array of issues that present themselves to a governor. And his top issue didn't seem to be party loyalty. In fact, one could argue that his chief preoccupation was milk. He was an avid milk drinker and believed that this beverage was the key to good health. When he conducted a meeting, he plopped a glass of milk down in front of every perplexed attendee, while most of them were probably thirsting for something a bit stronger. During campaign speeches, he never failed to urge the audience to take up the practice of drinking milk. On the campaign trail, he found opportunities to demonstrate his good health by veering off the normal routes and dragging campaign staffers on vigorous walks down country roads. On these side trips, he stopped to talk to farmers along the way. He usually lost valuable time because he couldn't resist picking up a pitchfork and helping the farmer with his work as another testament to his fitness. He did present quite a contrast to Horner, who was in poor health by this time. Horner was tired and increasingly suffered from a weakness of the circulatory system; he was overweight and also somewhat bitter and despondent. Bundeson was filled with good cheer and enjoyed public displays of thumping on his stomach with his fist to demonstrate his toughness. Also, he was a married man with six children, another contrast to the bachelor governor. However, in the battle for the governorship, it seemed like Bundeson was superfluous—the real combatants were Horner and Kelly.

Horner did not mince any words when he criticized his political foe. He portrayed Kelly as the malevolent boss of a crooked machine. Kelly, on the other hand, presented his cause as that of the average-Joe Chicagoan. He accused Horner of being a hypocritical reformer who wanted to interfere with a person's right to have a drink and bet on a race. He hearkened back to their disputes about liquor regulation and the Bookie Bill to portray Horner as a meddling snob. No matter what position Horner took on an issue, Kelly put an unfavorable spin on it so that Horner came out looking like a judgmental aristocrat who was against the common people. Kelly praised the defeat of the permanent voter registration bill and claimed that it would not have been a means of stopping voter fraud but a means of stopping the common folks from voting. After all, what would become of the poor folks who came to cast their votes and were turned away because they couldn't sign their name? Horner and Kelly hurled insults at each other and developed caricatures with which to taunt each other. Kelly encouraged Bundeson to set aside his milk lectures for a time and go after Horner. Horner authorized his backers to pull no punches when it came to Kelly. However, he did urge them to stay away from attacks on Nash. He still recalled the sincerity with which Nash had expressed regret at the turn of political events. It was clearly a Horner-Kelly match.

Through his old network of contacts and his aggressive fund-raising strategies, Horner amassed a campaign fund that far outpaced his rival. He mobilized an army on his behalf, and he didn't seem to care if they were voluntarily on his side or not. Workers on the state payroll were pressed into service on behalf of the governor's reelection campaign. Businesses that received state contracts were approached for campaign contributions, and the consequences of refusal were understood. Similarly, in Chicago, Kelly was busy making use of the WPA for his own political objectives. Washington squirmed when it heard reports of staffers campaigning for Bundeson during work hours on WPA projects. Various WPA directors used their power to drive home the Democratic Party line and to "encourage" the workers under them to throw their support to Bundeson and to contribute to his campaign. Hopkins was infuriated to see the WPA used for political purposes, but chasing down the offenders was a little like trying to nail smoke to a wall. The ripples of political activity would dissipate just as they were about to be pinned down.

Kelly believed that he had Chicago tied up for Bundeson, but the situation downstate was more tenuous. The "anti-Bossism" theme that Horner was running played into the perceptions that downstaters had already formed about Chicago politics. Ironically, when Horner, who had always tried to be straightforward and honest, tried his hand at political "spin," something close to the truth actually emerged. Littlewood notes that

"In small towns all over the state the voters were somehow getting the message that the sinister big city bosses in that penthouse were trying to do in a fellow who was honest and had done the best job he could for the whole state."[7] In Chicago, the party's dilemma was murky and confused, but when viewed from the distance afforded downstate, the forest seemed to emerge from the trees. Oddly enough, Horner somehow recovered his reputation by his willingness to be a little bit disreputable for once in his life—a sad testament to the realities of political life. His position was solid downstate not only because his message played well there but also because he had made a good impression in the rural parts of the state during his earlier campaign and his first term as governor. He had made a habit of visiting all over the state in person and so was able to present himself as a man and not simply a figurehead. He had exhibited a personal investment in the doings of the whole state. Because he was a "people person," he had a way of winning over even his harshest critics. However, he did have a couple of pivotal enemies downstate. Senator William H. Dieterich, who had continually poisoned Roosevelt against Horner in Washington, now made it his business to campaign aggressively for Bundeson in the southern part of the state. Dieterich and Horner had a contentious relationship dating back to their days as judges. Dieterich was a downstate judge, but he had spent a great deal of his time in Chicago as a visiting jurist. Cermak had slated him for senator at the same time that he backed Horner for governor. After Cermak's death, Dieterich, a loyal party man, worked closely with Kelly, and Kelly's problems became his. As Kelly and Horner clashed, Dieterich's disdain for the governor grew. Dieterich, while a downstater, had the temperament and political style of a city machine politician.

Another rival that figured largely in Horner's later political life was John Stelle. When Kelly put Bundeson up for governor, he also put Stelle on the ticket for lieutenant governor. Stelle's nomination was a way to assuage downstate voters who were angry because Kelly had abandoned the candidacy of downstater Bruce Campbell. Stelle, who was a formidable figure in southern Illinois, had been a coordinator of Horner's original downstate campaign. He came from a prominent landowning family in

McLeansboro and was a World War I veteran who played professional baseball before going to law school. He managed to juggle a legal career with farming as well as several large-scale entrepreneurial ventures. He had gained political prominence as a founding member of the American Legion, a powerful political organization at the time. After Horner's first election, Stelle grew disenchanted with the governor over issues of patronage. He was upset that Horner distributed power outside of the Democratic Party. When Kelly decided to break with Horner, Stelle went along with him, and he had been the loudest critic of Horner's sales tax proposal, capitalizing politically on the governor's difficult position. Stelle and Dieterich became the downstate arm of the Kelly-Nash machine.

But in the end, downstate belonged to Horner. This surprised no one. What did surprise everyone was Horner's strong showing in Cook County. Most of his Jewish allies had deserted him, and Kelly and the machine had already been writing his political eulogy. But Henry Horner fought to the end. His final and most effective weapon was the five attorneys he sent to Chicago to oversee the ballot counting and the detectives he sent to the precincts to watch out for the anticipated "creative" voting procedures. Horner used his knowledge of established practices in Chicago elections to launch a defense against fraud. In particular, Horner's team anticipated the practice of holding back returns from various precincts until downstate returns had indicated just how many votes had to be stolen to assure that the desired candidate came out on top. Horner's people countered this tactic by suppressing the announcement of downstate returns and sending detectives out to monitor things at those precincts that were a little slow in their ballot counting.

Both sides gritted their teeth over the numbers coming out of Cook County. Horner was winning handily in the south, but a wide margin of victory for Bundeson in Chicago could eclipse his lead in the rest of the state. However, Horner's security force beat back the vote stealing, and the margin between Horner and Bundeson in the city remained about half of what the machine had anticipated. Bundeson won Cook County by only 156,013 votes, and Horner took the rest of the state by 317,105. The besieged governor had narrowly accomplished the impossible. With the backing of neither his party nor Washington, he had defended his position as the Democratic candidate for governor.

The ugly primary campaign took everything out of the governor, who was overworked and exhausted before it even began. Littlewood describes Horner's transformation: "Through it all the governor drove himself until he nearly collapsed from exhaustion. In the latter weeks he was bothered by a persistent hacking cough and a noticeable diminution of his vitality, until he seemed like an automated creature spewing out a mechanical barrage of charges at his adversaries."[8] There was some speculation about his mental health when he began the campaign, and then he had driven himself even further into exhaustion while fighting for his political survival. If he won the campaign, those who knew him well wondered if there would be anything left of him. Ironically, he had to give up nearly everything that made him the comeback sensation in order to triumph in the end. In order for the nonpolitician to win, he had to become a politician. An exhausted, weakened, but triumphant Henry Horner returned to Springfield to gear up for the general election. Horner might have lost nearly everything else in the process, but the bully had lost the election.

Kelly saved face by being stoic about the loss, but inwardly he must have been reeling. He would not have attempted such a risky coup if he did not expect that he could win, and yet, underestimating Horner's popularity, he had chosen a weak candidate. If he had indeed made the unorthodox choice of Bundeson so that the Republican candidate would win, he must have had a very low opinion of Horner's chances to beat even the weakest of candidates. Realizing that Horner's victory jeopardized the party's chances of winning the general election, Nash immediately moved toward reconciliation, and Horner graciously accepted his overtures. At the end of September, Horner signed several bills dealing with relief, and one, which went into effect immediately, allowing Chicago to sell warrants for relief funds.[9] Nash strove to establish the public perception that the party was now reunited. Horner, however, could not bring himself to reconcile with Kelly, despite the pressure from members of the Democratic Party. He publicly denied that he and Kelly were on speaking terms again. Any profession of amicability toward the mayor would have seemed hypocritical after the mudslinging of the campaign. Kelly was reluctant to extend an olive branch, but he was more circumspect than Horner out of concern for the party. Finally, Kelly made his position clear when he suppressed his distaste for Horner and came out in favor of party unity: "I'm for every man on the Democratic ticket from top to bottom. Personalities have no part in this campaign."[10]

The Republican Party had chosen prosecutor C. Wayland Brooks as its nominee. (Among the candidates he had defeated in the primary was none other than the irrepressible Len Small, who had been governor from 1921 to 1929.) Brooks hit the campaign trail on an obvious note: his theme was taxation. He promised to lower the sales tax and eliminate any taxation on foodstuffs. At the same time, however, he promised new government programs that, Horner charged, would double the overall operating costs of state government. In response to Brooks's "have your cake and eat it too" strategy, once reluctant support for Horner now grew more fervent. But on November 1, 1936, the *Illinois State Journal* published an article reporting a rumor that Horner would be double-crossed by Kelly and sold out in Cook County. In the election, Horner defeated Brooks 2,015, 390 to 1, 630, 505, a margin of over 384,000.[11] Horner was returned to the governor's seat in a landslide. The *Illinois State Journal* reported, "The much talked of Cook County machine defection from Governor Horner failed to materialize." The editorial continued, "Horner's re-election makes him the actual as well as titular head of the Democratic Party in Illinois—in Chicago, as well as downstate. His dominance will not again be challenged by the politicians of that party, either in Washington or Chicago."[12] The editorial writer had no idea how wrong he would be. It is true that on November 6, 1936, Governor Horner received a Western Union telegram from James A. Farley congratulating him on his reelection. Farley concluded, "The people of your state and the members of our party have ratified your official course and we all look forward to cooperation with you for the good of America and the welfare of the people of your state."[13]

Roosevelt had also surprised the powers that be with the extent of his reelection triumph. The quiet masses had marched to the polls in droves to register their support for the man who had proclaimed himself, in word and deed, their defender. Everyone had thought that his victory would be a narrow one. Some sources had even predicted a narrow victory for Alf Landon. There is no question that the collapse of the opposition from both the left and the right was extremely helpful to Roosevelt in his reelection in 1936. But it must be pointed out that key legislation passed by the Congress and supported by the president was also a major point in his favor. Significant legislation passed in 1935 included the National Youth Administration, the National Labor Relations Act (the Wagner-Connery Act), the Social Security Act, the Banking Act of 1935, and the Public Utility Holding Company Act. When the returns came in, it was evident that Roosevelt's detractors, while noisy, signified very little. He had won with 523 electoral votes, compared to Landon's 8. Democrats across the country, following Roosevelt's lead, marched into office. The Democratic majority was 77–19 in the Senate and 328–107 in the House.[14] The second half of the 1930s would be driven by the efforts of a fairly unified Democratic government that would not be able to rest on its laurels. The next term would present both the continuation of old challenges and a spate of ominous new ones.

14

The Horner Ticket

Henry Horner had poured every last ounce of energy into his reelection campaign, but he was not able to sit back and enjoy his triumph. There was no interruption in his duties as governor, and much was still left to do. In addition, now that he had broken with Ed Kelly, he found himself with a new set of responsibilities as the leader of one wing of the splintered Democratic Party. Horner went to his second inauguration with less idealism and verve than he had felt at his first, and his audience was probably grateful. He cut his intended speech short, revealing that he may have become better at reading audiences than he was the first time around, but he was also less fervent in his desire to "get the job done" regardless of the pressure around him. Horner seemed, in many respects, to be a different man than he was in 1932. On the one hand, he was tired, disillusioned, and diminished from his trip through the mud of an ugly campaign. But on the other, he was much stronger than he had been in 1932, when he was bristling under the thumb of Anton

Cermak. This time around, he had not run on anyone else's ticket. He had entered the race his own man and had won the race through his own gritty determination and effort. Now he had earned the right to flex his new political muscles. In his shortened inaugural address, he reminded his listeners of the myriad problems that the state still faced and made clear his intention to get back to the business of solving those. He called for an amendment to the Illinois Constitution to permit an income tax so that the state would no longer have to rely overwhelmingly on the unpopular sales tax. Also, in a stab at Kelly and his power, he argued that control of state relief should not be turned over to local agencies, because this was an invitation to corruption. There was little doubt about which locality Horner meant. He knew that much of Kelly's power in the Depression era resulted from his control over relief funds. Kelly had handed out the prizes while Horner took the heat for the taxation that paid for them. Horner was not going to make it so easy on Kelly in the future.

The governor had not changed his larger vision for the state. He had learned some things during his first term, and the bullies would not be dealing with the man that they thought could be so easily bumped aside. No one would ever consider him an easy target again. He did not conceal the fact that he intended Kelly and the Chicago machine to take a political blow for their betrayal. Kelly's split from Horner had been a huge debacle for the party, and Horner was not going to forgive and forget and let party politics go on as usual. The Democratic Party in Illinois would have to be remade in a new image. First, however, the party lineup controlled by Kelly would have to undergo some chipping from the statehouse. Even before Horner had completed the general election, he picked up the ax. First, he intended to move against the election-fraud system in Chicago whose tentacles his reelection had narrowly eluded. In that spirit, he resurrected the political battle over permanent registration of voters. He had lost on this one before, but he was prepared not to lose on it again. Controlling the city's election process was key to Kelly's grip over the party in Chicago, and he could generally manipulate enough votes in Cook County to edge out contenders with a base of support downstate. If he lost this power, Kelly knew that he could not keep his favorites in office, radically destabilizing the machine. To make such manipulation less possible, Horner brought the issue of permanent registration in front of the legislature again. He pointed to the shenanigans of the last primary election that his team had so effectively fought as clear evidence that voter fraud in Cook County was a problem that needed to be addressed. There were protests from those in the Democratic Party who argued that the counties with high transient and out-of-work populations would be most affected by this measure, and they were Democratic strongholds. But the measure ended up passing anyway. The act that was defeated before the 1936 primaries applied only to Chicago and other municipal governments that had boards of election. This time around, the Permanent Voter Registration Act would affect voting practices throughout the entire state.[1] Commenting on Horner's overall legislative accomplishments, one historian stated, "In Illinois, Governor Henry Horner, a professed supporter of the New Deal, was too busy fighting the Democratic machine in Chicago to accomplish much on the legislative front."[2]

Through careful political spin during the election, Horner had sharpened his hitherto hazy image as a reform-minded politician, and on the tail of his triumphant underdog reelection, this reform rhetoric was playing well. Horner was seen in many circles as the victimized "good guy" who had beaten the corrupt traitors, the lone figure who opposed the machine. Before his election, he had indeed been a good guy, but now he realized that his refusal to play tough had almost cost him his career. He now presented himself differently. Instead of shoring up a relationship threatened by a political dispute, as he had done with Cermak and Nash after his first election, he now dismissed his critics with harsh language. He resisted the urging of Democratic Party leaders to make peace with Kelly. Also, he adopted a sprinkling of mannerisms and ways of speaking that seemed more in keeping with the persona of a "boss" than the intellectual public servant of former years. He now pounded the table with the side of his hand to emphasize a point and even threw in a swear word now and again for good measure. It is a matter of debate whether his new, more abrasive political demeanor resulted from his good spirit simply being worn away through hardship, disillusionment, and failing health or whether he had finally accepted the prevailing view that being a politician required a certain amount of ruthless bullying. Again, the truth probably lay somewhere in the middle. But it is clear that Horner had not abandoned his Lincolnian principles about honesty in government. He was not now going to become a "party player." In fact, he now saw himself even more intensely as an independent politician. More than ever, he emphasized his determination to keep government honest; he seemed to be bringing his new toughness to bear on his long-standing role of defending honesty in the state. He cautioned new employees to resist political pressures in decision making and issued a pledge that would later take on an eerie significance: "I am going to make sure that however else the Horner administration may fail it's not going to have any scandals that I can stop."[3] He also made it clear that Kelly and his loyalists would have to pay the price when the time came to reassess appointments in the state government. Ben Lindheimer was one of the first to go. James Slattery replaced him on the Commerce Commission. Other reprisals followed against appointees that Horner now viewed as traitors. However, he forgave and left alone many of those in lower-order positions that he had turned over to Kelly. He surmised that pressure from the party had won them over and that their show of loyalty to the machine could easily be transferred back to himself. He reasoned that removing all or most of them from their positions and replacing them with employees who were not yet trained in the same capacity would have a destabilizing effect on the state.

Horner acknowledged that many of the people who worked for the state were still the best people for the job, regardless of which candidate they supported during the turbulent campaign. However, the often surprising loyalties that surfaced during the campaign did affect Horner's sense of his own team. In the primary, Horner's running mate, John Cassidy, had been defeated for the position of lieutenant governor by the machine candidate, John Stelle. Stelle and Kelly had been in lockstep in their desire to see Horner forced out of the statehouse. Now Horner found himself in the uncomfortable position of having to work closely with one of the architects of the attempt to unseat him, and he readily expressed his desire that Stelle be deposed. Early in Horner's second term, a number of vacancies opened up in the state supreme court, and his name was mentioned for one of the coveted positions. The possibility must again have pulled at the weary governor for whom such a seat would have been a magnificent opportunity; but having Stelle sitting beside him in the lieutenant governor's chair was the deciding factor in his refusal. He would not leave control of the state to Stelle, since he knew that such an action would lead to the dismissal of all of his staff and his supporters from their positions. He would not be responsible for doing that to his friends.

Having taken up a very vocal anti-Horner position during the campaign, Senator William Dieterich now found his political power somewhat diminished by the unexpected turn of events. He still was a Washington insider, but his reputation in the state was now questionable. There was speculation about whether he had sufficient popularity to be selected the party candidate when it came time for his reelection. Both Horner and Kelly viewed the opportunity to handpick a candidate to occupy Dieterich's seat as a test of which wing of the fractured Democratic Party would prevail. Despite their mutual exhaustion with the last campaign, they both knew that the war was not over. Now they were locked in battle as opposing party bosses. Both knew that the outcome would greatly impact future party politics and the survival of the Chicago organization. Horner, once a product of that machine, was now pitted against it; the born and bred Chicagoan was now essentially a downstate politician.

Because Roosevelt had not explicitly come out against Horner during the campaign, he was able to repair his minor rift with Horner with some ease. He simply sent a note of congratulations, as if he had never turned his back on the governor. Cordial relations between the governor and the president resumed without a hitch. Horner retained his position as a loyal supporter of the New Deal and continued to speak out in favor of Roosevelt's legislation and to urge business interests to cease their protests and see the larger picture. However, his new political savvy did not induce him to become a rubber stamp in order to fulfill his own political ambitions. He demonstrated this continued independence when Roosevelt sought to expand the Supreme Court with new appointees of his own choosing.

During Roosevelt's presidency, the decisions of the circumspect Supreme Court were not motivated by human suffering so much as by the future legal implications of hasty government action, and the justices had repeatedly obstructed the implementation of New Deal legislation. The Court first reviewed a New Deal statute in January 1935. In the next sixteen months, it decided ten major cases or groups of cases involving New Deal legislation, the "nine old men" declaring eight of those statutes unconstitutional. Roosevelt was the first U.S. president to serve a full term without having the opportunity to appoint someone to the Supreme Court. After his overwhelming reelection in 1936, he had the Judiciary Reform Bill introduced in Congress in 1937. Roosevelt's idea was to increase the number of justices on the Court, adding additional members who, it was generally assumed, would be handpicked, loyal New Dealers. This idea was labeled by critics as a "court packing scheme." Roosevelt turned to his friends to support the expansion of the Court, including William Dieterich, one of his most ardent and vocal supporters. However, the practical benefits of this plan seemed overshadowed by its questionable ethics, and it met with a great deal of protest. Roosevelt went on a public relations tour to meet the opposition head on. He invited Horner to one such meeting at the Chicago Stadium. Horner responded that although he would be happy to attend the event, he would have to make public his stance on the matter, which, to Roosevelt's great surprise, was that he staunchly opposed it. Once again, the cordial relations between Horner and the White House cooled. Horner's position clearly suggests that although his exterior demeanor might have seemed a bit more typical of a politician, his overall political practice was the same. He might have supported the New Deal agenda in total, but he believed that "court packing" was an objectionable way to achieve that agenda. Supporting Roosevelt in this instance could have been an excellent chance for him to curry the favor of the White House and further his political standing, ahead of Kelly and the rest of the party. However, once again, Horner was willing to be the burr under the saddle of the larger agenda when it came to matters of principle.

As it turned out, the Supreme Court, in *National Labor Relations Board v. Jones & Laughlin Steel Corporation* in 1937, upheld the Wagner Act of 1935 that mandated collective bargaining after certain procedures had taken place. The vote was 5–4 with Chief Justice Charles Evans Hughes writing the majority opinion. This decision, which essentially endorsed a key element of the Roosevelt administration's agenda, has become known as "the switch in time that saved nine." Later, on August 24, 1937, a mild, face-saving Judiciary Reform Act was passed that did not add justices to the Court.

The simple interpretation that Horner did not change in principle but simply became more of a lion in defending his good and noble causes appears more complicated when his second term election policy toward relief is considered, especially in relation to Chicago. He had come to accept the reality that issues of relief and revenue came down to the proverbial "between a rock and a hard place," and he refused to soften the presentation of that dilemma to shore up anyone's political image, even his own. To spend money, one had to raise money. Public sentiment had smacked this fact in Horner's face many times, and now he seemed willing to smack such reality back into the face of the public. When he heard a cry for relief, he responded curtly by asking which form of tax increase was the preferred method to achieve that end. Politicians and citizens alike could not bring themselves to howl for additional taxes as much as they were willing to howl for state funds. Horner revealed that he was not in a mood to soft-pedal reality to save anyone's feelings any longer. When it came to his new "real" stance on relief, he was especially hard on Chicago. During this time, the Depression raged on. The jobless rolls, ameliorated sporadically by work relief, remained enormous, the applications for welfare assistance ballooned, and the numbers of hungry and homeless had not significantly diminished. Relief was funneled into the stomachs of people who would grow hungry again the very next day. During the primary election, Ben Adamowski, the charismatic Chicagoan who in 1931 was elected a member of the Illinois House of Representatives, sponsored a bill at Kelly's behest that would increase the revenue available for relief in response to the increased economic crisis in Chicago. Kelly proposed that one-half of the state sales tax, rather than one-third, be devoted to relief in Cook County. Although the bill passed in both the House and the Senate, Horner vetoed it, arguing that he could not jeopardize the state's fiscal stability to bail out Chicago. He leaned on Kelly to raise the necessary funds locally. Kelly steadfastly refused to impose an additional tax burden on his suffering city. Horner had been put in the position of imposing unpopular tax measures on disgruntled citizens many times; he had also borne the consequences while Kelly played the benevolent lord of the machine who would bend the rules and help out the "little guy." Horner was no longer willing to play the whipping boy for Kelly's benefit. Of course, Horner maintained his decision was made for fiscal reasons. The governor had always been vocal about his commitment to a balanced budget, but Kelly was convinced that his veto was motivated by revenge. The animosity between the mayor and the governor sizzled on.

Perhaps still steaming over the second-round success of the permanent voter registration bill, Kelly decided to revive the corpse of the "Bookie Bill." However, this time it would bypass Springfield entirely. Kelly presented the measure as a city ordinance, and it readily passed through the city council. Horner was furious, calling the ploy a nullification of the state's previous decision. Realizing that he had shaky legal grounds on which to stand, Kelly withdrew the measure. Still, Horner had Kelly in a corner, desperately searching for revenue.

In the meantime, the international crisis was escalating, and it was beginning to play a part even in local politics. Senator William Dieterich's already tenuous popularity was further destabilized when he was accused of harboring pro-German sentiment. He had reportedly used anti-Semitic rhetoric against Horner during the 1936 campaign, and Horner was not about to let that fact settle into the dust of yesterday's news. Kelly distanced himself further from the increasingly untenable candidate.

Horner's new position as the party's strategist and leader only added to his overwhelming workload. The men who had stayed loyal to him during the attempted coup now looked to him for guidance, and many more were flocking to his side, preferring to hang their hats on the side of power. It was clear that in the upcoming elections, he would have to put forth a "Horner Ticket," exercising the same kind of power over political careers that Cermak had. Two figures who seemed destined to benefit from this turn of events were Horner's steadfast loyalists Tom Courtney and Scott W. Lucas. When Cermak had created the ticket that had put Horner in the statehouse, Courtney had been on the ticket as the candidate for state's attorney. As an ironic side note, Harry Fisher, who was pressured by Horner to support him or have his son David passed over for a position, had been Cermak's first choice for the state's attorney position. However, the party had argued that having more than one Jew on the ticket would be too much, and so Cermak had replaced Fisher with Courtney. Whether he knew it or not, Horner was more than once a thorn in Fisher's side.

Courtney, an Irishman from the southwest side of Chicago, had been a political ally of both Horner and Kelly before the split between the two. Courtney and Kelly had similar interests and socialized together at local prizefights and horse races. However, Courtney was said to have a personality similar to Horner's; he was fiercely independent and resented taking orders from party leaders. Horner, however, was more circumspect and understated in his displays of independence. In 1935, Courtney was nearly killed in an assassination attempt that was chalked up to an underworld reprisal for a crackdown on vice issuing from the state's attorney's office. Courtney was offended when Kelly not only refused to take the matter seriously but even suggested that Courtney may have had the attack staged to gain notoriety that would be useful in his future political life. When Kelly and Nash chose not to endorse Horner, Courtney stayed mysteriously neutral. He did not come out to campaign in Horner's defense, but he also refused to endorse Bundeson. Following the primary election, however, it was Courtney who stood up at the state fair and delivered a speech articulating what many around the state were feeling—that Horner was a good man and an admirable leader, whose benevolent guidance of the state was continually being thwarted by dishonest interests. The term *dishonest* was clearly aimed at Kelly and intensified the irritation Kelly felt toward his erstwhile friend after his refusal to go along with the party line and the Bundeson campaign. After Horner's reelection, Courtney became a part of his inner circle, and Horner's favor was worth a lot more than it had been, now that there was such a thing as the "Horner Ticket" to consider. It was widely speculated that when the time came for Horner to take down Ed Kelly, Tom Courtney would be his candidate.

The other steadfast Horner loyalist, Scott W. Lucas, came to Horner's mind when he cast his eye downstate to the Senate seat of William Dieterich. Dieterich had long tried to undermine Horner in Washington and had eagerly jumped on the Kelly bandwagon, campaigning long and hard for Bundeson. Horner thought Lucas would be the perfect candidate to run against him in the primary. Lucas, who had previously lost the Democratic nomination to the Senate seat occupied by Dieterich, later served in the U.S. House of Representatives. Horner had cemented his relationship with Lucas during the appointment process after his first election when he appointed Lucas chairman of the State Tax Commission. Lucas had been a coordinator of Horner's downstate campaign in 1932, and he would remain loyal to Horner until the end. Placing Lucas on the ticket to replace Dieterich would be another convenient way for Horner to drive home a point to those who had abandoned him in 1936. Lucas had a conservative voting record in the House, had been a vocal opponent of Roosevelt's strategy to expand the Supreme Court with more New Deal supporters, and had voted against many of the New Deal programs. Roosevelt was already disenchanted with Horner because of his refusal to go along with "court packing" and became decidedly unhappy with the choice of Lucas. Horner was clearly feeling his oats, demonstrating that he needed neither Chicago's nor Washington's approval for any of his actions. When it was finally determined that William Dieterich was too problematic a candidate to run, Kelly replaced him with Mike Igoe. Washington supported Igoe, but this didn't faze Horner. He was running on the heady elation of his surprising upset of the Kelly-Nash machine, and he hungered to give it another blow. As he campaigned vigorously for Scott Lucas, he looked like a party boss who was as interested in elections as he was in governance.

In 1937, the Depression further deepened, thrusting the already imperiled Chicago into near chaos. The WPA was slowing down, and welfare applications tripled in the city.[4] Although thousands of people went without relief during this period, Horner remained uncharacteristically unsympathetic to the plight of Chicago. He continued to turn a deaf ear on Kelly's cries for more aid. Critics argued that Illinois was in a sufficiently solid economic position to provide relief, but Horner steadfastly refused to allow the state treasury to be the mode of rescue for the city. The war between Kelly and Horner was playing itself out on multiple fronts. Kelly and his allies began to close ranks, and Horner loyalists in Chicago were now at risk.

Kelly's first target was Edmund Jarecki. Jarecki, as county judge, was in charge of the election infrastructure, and his friendship had been pivotal in helping Horner to police the polls in the 1936 primary, an act that Kelly saw as traitorous to the party. The temporary straightening of the crooked voting culture had cost Bundeson the election. Jarecki also had endorsed Horner's permanent registration bill. Kelly and Nash leaned on him to retire, but he would not. And so, Kelly and Nash ran another candidate against him, seizing on the convenient excuse of blaming Jarecki for the tax debacles of the early 1930s. They also turned election-fraud reform into another one of their favorite "white-glove-bashing" issues, arguing that the crackdown on violators was a cruel display of power against the poor unfortunates who inadvertently, through their own naïveté and diminished circumstances, had cast their ballots incorrectly. The argument was laughable to anyone who understood how election fraud *really* operated, but the class-inflected spin had worked well for Kelly in the past, and he tried to adapt it to fit a myriad of convenient circumstances. The break with Kelly now freed Jarecki to be explicitly part of the "Horner Ticket." The Horner-Jarecki pairing was a fortuitous one. Horner was becoming known as a serious "reformer," a persona he had long hesitated to fully embrace. Now Horner and Jarecki were united to defend the sanctity of the ballot box. Having long regarded the tricky vote-getting procedures of Cook County as the embodiment of everything that was feared and despised about Chicago, downstate cheered the duo. Many in Cook County hissed, but others circumspectly rejoiced. Horner, the native Chicagoan, was becoming a downstate governor. He was embodying the rural ethos of his political inspiration, Abraham Lincoln, who also would have despised election fraud and machine politics.

Aside from elections, Horner also found himself at the helm of several major crises during his second term. He returned from Roosevelt's second inauguration to find southern Illinois in the grips of a devastating flood. Proving himself still the hands-on governor, he officiated over the crisis from a rowboat. In the end, thousands of people were left homeless as a result of the natural disaster of January 1937.

Another major crisis loomed with the increasing organization and activity of union protestors. In his first term, Horner had learned a hard lesson when he was unable to deal effectively with labor disputes across the state using his favored means: straightforward, "friendly" talk and mediation. With few other viable options, he had instituted a very clear law-and-order policy in the state. The desperate tactics of the laboring class were very threatening to the power structure, and Horner was not exempt from this threat. Since many new forms of labor protest were being tried out during this period, the general public had great concern about their possible outcomes.

With the scent of revolution in the air, Horner and many other leaders in the country were afraid that a skirmish on the local level could quickly grow beyond containment. In Chicago, Kelly had instituted a police policy that took a hard line against strikers. Police were given wide latitude in their treatment of protestors, and this was a cause of concern to many people. There were proposals simmering for the legalization of organized protest and the protection of protesting workers, but leaders were afraid to back any bill that might encourage uprisings or limit the ability of law enforcement to quash riots. The issues were thorny and the practices untested. If the right of "peaceful" protest were protected, who would determine what was peaceful? What about property rights and the right of owners to hire and fire at will? Horner felt torn on the matter. He had always seen himself as a defender of the underdog, and the workers clearly fit that characterization, but as much as he hated the exploitation and suffering of the poor, he hated lawlessness and violence more. Still, government leaders were realizing that they would have to invent better ways to deal with labor disputes; confrontations between protestors and law enforcement were getting out of control.

In February of 1937, workers in the Fansteel Metallurgical Corporation in Chicago conducted a massive sit-down strike. The Congress of Industrial Organizations, or CIO, had organized nearly 95 percent of the workers at this site, but the owners refused to negotiate with unions and began to discriminate against the union men. During a union meeting, it was decided that a "sit-down strike" would be implemented, a tactic that was growing increasingly common as a form of peaceful protest in locations scattered throughout the country. The workers occupied the second and third floors of the company in an effort to avoid being tear-gassed on the first floor, a typical police response. Workers on the outside provided the sit-down strikers with food and any emergency supplies they might need, and the strikers settled in for the long haul. Horner led the negotiation process, but once again this strategy was futile. With Horner's approval, the police devised a new tactic of their own in response. They built what has come to be known as the "Trojan Horse"—a platform made of ladders built on the back of a truck and then transported to the scene to give police access to the second floor. The workers were tear-gassed and quickly evacuated the building. Despite the National Labor Relations Board ruling that workers should not be discriminated against for peaceful protest or union involvement, the sit-down strikers were not rehired at Fansteel. Public unrest began to simmer against law enforcement agencies that seemed to be in league with owners.

Still, it was safer to cozy up to law enforcement than to flirt with revolution. Both Horner and Kelly were reluctant to tie the hands of the police. But they would have to rethink their positions after May 30, 1937, and the infamous "Memorial Day Massacre." At that time, a strike at Republic Steel had gripped the city. Picket lines and protests raged on for weeks. To buoy the morale of the tired and destitute strikers, the union scheduled a picnic rally for Memorial Day. After speeches, songs, and some much-needed nourishment, union leaders decided to stage an impromptu mass picket across the entrance of Republic Steel to demonstrate the solidarity and resolve of the union to the remaining workers. As they paraded toward the company from several blocks away, they met law enforcement officers carrying tear gas, clubs, and guns. The police, fearing the mob was preparing to invade the factory, opened fire on the crowd. When the dust cleared, ten men were dead and eighty-seven were injured.[5] During this confrontation at Republic Steel, a newsreel account was filmed that showed the workers peacefully protesting and the police as the aggressors. When this newsreel was finally released in the movie theaters, the public became more sympathetic to organized labor. After this incident, both city and state leaders would have to reassess their policies regarding the right to protest when they were called to account for the "Memorial Day Massacre." Mayor Kelly was especially held culpable for the bloodshed, and this incident forced him to reach out to union interests or put his own reelection at risk.

Dealing with the chaos and volatility of labor unrest was especially difficult because the impasses that caused owners and workers to war against each other were filled with gray areas and consequences. The "good guy" was not clearly demarcated in these struggles. The workers had a cause that was just and in keeping with the "common man" theme of the day, but siding with them often necessitated accepting, or appearing to accept, lawlessness. Even the most liberal politician had to take the responsibility of protecting the welfare of citizens against criminal behavior very seriously. Also, the labor protestors' loyalty to capitalism and democracy was in question in those days. Was a refusal to crack down on labor protest akin to opening a door for communism and fomenting revolution? The further breakdown of the inviolable position of business interests also troubled many in power. Where would it end?

Horner was especially caught in the crosshairs of the dilemma. His soft spot for the plight of the working class combined with his loyalty to business and his commitment to peaceful and harmonious modes of change made labor unrest his most difficult issue. His actions reflected such ambivalence. When negotiations failed, he supported police action to quash rebellion, but he usually stopped short of calling in the National Guard, feeling that such an action was an invitation to bloodshed, and that, above all else, was what would most crush his spirit. Horner's dilemma was lessened significantly, two months after the "Memorial Day Massacre," when the Supreme Court declared that the National Labor

Relations Act was constitutional. Also, the Democratic Party gradually absorbed the labor movement and adopted its goals so that the possibility of a national Labor Party vanished.

Horner found that having his own "ticket" was a time-consuming job. While he pulled out all the stops for Lucas, he pulled the rug out from under his other candidate, Tom Courtney. Courtney, who felt supported in his rebellious independence for perhaps the first time, was exercising that trait with a bit too much swagger. Horner was not one to bow to party politics on many occasions, but as a political leader, he was now seeing the necessity of "keeping things together" and behaving circumspectly, as situations warranted. Courtney, on the other hand, could not seem to put away the ax he intended to grind against the machine when the situation demanded restraint. Horner was beginning to consider Courtney increasingly unmanageable.

Determined to continue controlling the election process in Cook County, Kelly focused his attention on deposing Judge Jarecki with his candidate, the Polish circuit court judge John Prystalski. Kelly felt that Mike Igoe would easily take down Horner's conservative candidate, Scott Lucas, for Dieterich's Senate seat. And so the contest began. It would be Horner-Jarecki-Lucas versus Kelly-Prystalski-Igoe. Now that the party was split between these two camps, this contest would prove who had the upper hand in Illinois. Horner mobilized all his influence and his connections to fill the campaign treasury for his candidates.

Once again, there were charges that Horner was inappropriately leaning on those under his jurisdiction to assist in the fund-raising effort. However, this echo of scandal was drowned out by the roar of the machine gearing up to "bring out the votes" for the Kelly ticket. As had been the case in his pivotal selection of Bundeson, Kelly once again made an inappropriate choice that would be the deciding factor. Jarecki turned out to be the secret weapon in Horner's arsenal, because he anticipated every crooked move the Cook County machine was preparing to make on behalf of its candidates, and knowing his own job was on the line, he informed Horner every step of the way. Together they came up with a strategy to counter the unparalleled level of voter fraud that was about to take place in Chicago. Kelly's decision to oust the election reformer had given Horner his most valuable asset. While the returns poured in from downstate, the machine tabulated how many votes would be needed to counter the leads there and set its plans into action. Before the Cook County returns had even been tabulated, Igoe felt so confident that he delivered a victory speech on the radio. Although concerned by Igoe's self-assurance, Jarecki and Horner remained skeptical. They had dispatched a thousand police officers to guard the county's polling places. In addition, they had hired *six thousand* athletic college students to hover about, keeping an eye on things in the voting districts. It was a principled use of thuggery, a tactic that seemed somehow very fitting for the new Horner. Igoe would have to swallow his radio address. Lucas had won by a narrow margin of 75,284 votes, but he had won. Jarecki triumphed along with him. Clearly, both would have lost without their collegiate supporters. And just as surely, Horner's entire ticket would have gone down in defeat if it weren't for Jarecki. Once again, Horner had taken on the machine, and he had come out on top: a pretty remarkable feat for the "window dressing" who lacked "guts."

When Lucas won the primary in 1938, it was clear that the general election would not be an easy road for the rather conservative Democrat who was not in Roosevelt's favor. Also, as the international crisis grew, Illinois distanced itself from the foreign policy of Roosevelt. Illinois had historically favored a policy of isolationism, and that was not the direction the Roosevelt administration seemed to be headed in. Democrats feared that a growing disenchantment with Roosevelt would hurt Democratic candidates. The state Democratic Party tried to draw together to meet this challenge, despite recently inflicted wounds. Horner, with some reluctance, joined in the vision of a more united party.

Old foes of Horner's now found themselves in a position that necessitated that they extol his virtues. Although he had worked diligently to turn the Jews of Chicago against Horner, Jake Arvey was the first to take his hat in his hand and move toward reconciliation for the sake of the party. His example led others to once again stand behind the governor. Even Ed Kelly, whose party loyalty competed mightily with his personal grudge against Horner, stood up and did his duty on Governor's Day at the state fair, where he spoke glowingly of his former enemy. Kelly was always more interested in the survival of his organization than personal grudges. The machine was getting in line behind Lucas, and Horner appreciated the assistance. In return, he instructed his team to lay off the machine bashing for the present. Tom Courtney, however, didn't seem to have received his instructions. He obstinately refused to occupy the same stage with Mayor Kelly at the state fair. A short time later, the ambitious future mayoral candidate stood up in a party meeting and began leveling accusations at Kelly and Nash and their organization.

Jake Arvey went to see Horner about Courtney. Horner appreciated how the party was coming together, and he saw the necessity of it. Since Courtney didn't seem willing to abide by the strategy, Horner distanced himself from the candidate and would not give him his endorsement when it came time for him to take on Mayor Kelly in the 1939 mayoral election. It was another sign that Horner had accepted the trend toward reconciliation that Arvey had instituted. In withholding his support, Horner likely gave the election to Kelly: a generous gift to his longtime nemesis. Horner showed himself in this situation to be a man of his word and capable of some degree of forgiveness. While they were reluctant to face each other and exchange amicable sentiments, Horner and Kelly looked the other way and took a small step back into each other's good graces. It may have been strategic, and it may have been temporary, but as fate would have it, we will never know whether it might have been otherwise.

15

While the Cat's Away

Just two days before the 1938 midterm election, Henry Horner was in the midst of a campaigning blitz on behalf of Scott Lucas. He was in the back of his limousine, returning to a Chicago hotel. Horner thought Lucas's opponent, Richard Lyons, was feeding voters a lot of empty rhetoric. For example, Lyons proposed lowering taxes *and* instituting a thirty-dollar-a-week old age pension. Horner, who always despised "double talk" of this sort, was frenetically giving speeches and holding rallies to rail against the opposing candidate. He pointed out that Lyons had blocked old age pensions half a dozen times in the legislature. Clearly, the record of the Republican Party belied its campaign impression of being the party out to ease the suffering of the common folks.

Horner's mind seemed taken up with a combination of righteous indignation over the issues and a desire for personal retribution. He had been experiencing waves of crushing exhaustion, stabs of pain to his temples, and a persistent heaviness in his chest, but he had never been one to listen to the annoying demands of the human body, especially when there was campaigning to do. "When this campaign is over, there'll be plenty of time for bed rest," he had told Dr. Rosen when warned of the precarious state of his circulatory system.[1] As the limousine approached the hotel, Horner's overworked body finally reached a crisis point. When the driver opened the door, Horner was kneeling on the floor, his face bathed in sweat, muttering incoherently. His brain had finally fractured—like his grandfather's and his father's before him—giving in to the million tiny blows that he had inflicted on it. He had already given everything he had to the state of Illinois—his personal life, his stellar reputation, his peace of mind, and yes, perhaps even a principle or two here and there—and now it looked as if he might not survive his term in office.

When the driver discovered the gravely ill governor in the back of the limousine, he immediately got help to carry him into the hotel. Dr. Rosen hurried up from Springfield to discover that Horner had been struck with a blood clot to the brain, otherwise known as a cerebral thrombosis. For the next two days, the party was told nothing except that the governor had a bad cold. Horner lay helpless, unable to speak, while the election went on without him. The hard work had paid off—at least that was some consolation. Lucas won by a narrow margin. Not knowing that the governor was fighting for his life, Lucas, overcome by emotion, sat down and penned a letter to him saying, "No man in my life, except my deceased brother, has done more for me than you, and if I should live to be a hundred I should always remember your many kind and charitable acts."[2]

If Horner's health had not undermined him at this pivotal moment in his career, he would probably have enjoyed an unparalleled period of stability. Old enemies had now become firmly convinced that Horner was a leader worthy of his position. He had proven himself both as governor and as party leader. He had led the state in a spirit of straightforward hard work. Most important, he had demonstrated that he was not simply a gentleman but also a tough leader who could adapt and survive. What he could not do was to reverse time and relive his life in a way that was less destructive to his health. He had worked himself into his sickbed through toiling in a professional arena that was antithetical to his nature. In the end, only his own mortality could topple the tenacious governor.

His illness was the worst of all possible conditions for the micromanager Horner. From the outset, it gave him great anxiety to think of being unable to watch over the operation of the state and having to delegate responsibilities to anyone else. For the first few days after the thrombosis, he struggled with his speech. He was holed up in the Congress Hotel in Chicago while he and his staffers scrambled to formulate a plan. He called together those with whom he had worked most closely in the last months, men who had helped in his campaign and who now enjoyed prominent positions in his administration: Jim Slattery, Horner's campaign manager in Cook County, now rewarded with Ben Lindheimer's place on the Commerce Commission; Charlie Schwartz, who had become patronage chief in Chicago; Lyn Smith, pivotal to the success of Horner's downstate campaign, now appointed the public works director; and finally, Sam Nudelman, originally recommended by Lindheimer, who had remained by Horner's side and was now finance director. These men became his inner circle and helped him maintain contact with governance during his time of incapacity.

As soon as he could utter the words, Horner assembled this inner circle in a strategy session on the planned ousting of Mayor Kelly. The primary was right around the corner, in the spring of 1939. Since Courtney was no longer the chosen candidate, the discussion of a replacement ensued. Dr. Rosen fussed about the proceedings, alarmed that Horner would not rest but instead would insist on governing in his extremely weakened condition. Finally Rosen succeeded in convincing Horner that if there were any chance of full recovery, he would have to get away and devote himself to the task of recuperation. He would finally have to submit himself to taking a vacation. Colonel L. P. Bonfoey, chairman of the State Aeronautics Commission, offered his residence in Miami as a vacation home for the ailing governor. Horner agreed to the plan, but chiefly because he was determined to return to the statehouse and still had hopes of running for reelection or perhaps even for the White House in 1940. However, it unsettled him greatly that in his absence the lieutenant governor, John Stelle, would reign. Horner gave his cabinet strict instructions to watch over Stelle's activity and to inform the governor if Stelle should try anything funny. And so Horner set off for Miami. What, he must have wondered, would happen while he dozed?

In Miami, Horner became bedridden and emaciated. Back in Illinois, rumor and speculation began to brew about his condition and the *real* nature of his illness. Spies planted in Florida sent word northward of "Horner spottings." Eager to make a mystery of the cerebral thrombosis, the papers speculated that he was dying of cancer, that he was paralyzed, and even that he was suffering the effects of syphilis. Dr. Rosen ordered that Horner stay in Miami for six months and tried to prevent him from working. Still, Horner heard troubling stories from his regents about Stelle and the erosion of all that Horner had built in Springfield. Horner's tight reign on expenses in the state now was relaxed, and special interests from all over Illinois were eager to take advantage of the opportunity. Stelle enjoyed holding the purse strings, and the legislature seemed poised to go on a spending orgy. Slattery, Smith, Nudelman, Schwartz, and their associates set up shop in the statehouse and also seemed to be reveling in their newfound power. Rumors circulated about carousing and celebrating deep into the evening, causing those close to Horner to feel that disrespectful underlings were tarnishing his dignity. It seemed that Horner's impression that there were few politicians he could truly trust was being confirmed.

Horner's illness and his disillusionment with Courtney had taken the steam out of his plans to unseat Kelly. Having learned that he would not be receiving the crucial endorsement from Horner, Courtney was unsure whether or not the slight was personal or whether those around Horner had taken the opportunity of the governor's infirmity to give Courtney the slip. Regardless, he decided to soldier on and run for mayor anyway. As state's attorney, he used his association with law enforcement to launch a crusade against Kelly's vice-friendly administration. He honed his tough-on-crime persona by spearheading a flurry of police crackdowns on gambling operations. The theme of his campaign became a war on vice and corruption.

While Horner languished in Miami, Kelly seemed to benefit from the inadvertent "reprieve from the Governor." Kelly reminded the voters how he had helped them to weather the worst of the Great Depression and how he had stewarded the city from destitution into "the black." Kelly's association with the WPA turned out to be his best political advantage. The WPA had affected nearly every family in Chicago in its long run in the city. Thousands of jobs had been created, and millions of federal relief dollars had been funneled through the program and into the pockets of Chicagoans. Many argued that the political machine took unethical control of the distribution of such funds, but none would deny that the WPA had been a godsend to the people of Chicago.

While Horner was recuperating in Miami, the official word from his people was that he would maintain "neutrality" on the election. However, many of the cogs in what was now ironically being called the "Horner machine" distrusted the crusading Courtney and felt that the status quo of the party's power in the state would be better stabilized by retaining Chicago's incumbent mayor. Jim Slattery, in particular, came out as a Kelly supporter and made sure that the fund-raising infrastructure of the Horner ticket would be put in motion on behalf of Kelly. John Stelle was also a steadfast friend to Kelly, and he used his position as acting governor to support the mayor. He quietly introduced a bill that Horner would have despised. It allowed Chicago voters to temporarily switch party affiliations so that Republicans could vote for a Democrat in the primaries and then go on to vote Republican in the general election. Stelle reasoned that this strategy would favor Kelly, since Courtney was running as a progressive reformer.

Courtney was bitter about the loss of the support that he had expected from the now powerful governor. He accused Kelly and Stelle of taking advantage of Horner's illness but also harbored a grudge against the governor himself, as indicated by his bitter, often-quoted remark "the Jew took a dive under the bed."[3] Despite the growing strength of the war-on-crime movement, Kelly won a decisive victory in the primary. He sent a telegram to Horner stating his appreciation for the support he had received from the state government that, he acknowledged, "came indirectly from you."[4]

He may have been mistaken with that attribution, but it did seem clear that a grudge against Ed Kelly was now not primary in Horner's pantheon of concerns. He had more important political struggles to attend to, especially with the man whom Kelly had connived to place beneath him in the hierarchy. With even more assistance from the "Horner machine," Kelly would go on to win the general election against Republican Dwight Green. Green had gained notoriety as the U.S. district attorney who had brilliantly prosecuted Al Capone on tax-evasion charges. Although he had held no other political office, he was gaining much political momentum with his antivice message and with his intelligent and charismatic mode of communication. However, Chicago was apparently not yet ready for a decisive break between the government and the underworld. But Green was laying important groundwork for the final chapter of the unparalleled reign of the Democrats in Illinois; a chapter that would begin to be written only when the stubborn governor finally submitted to his fate.

On April 8, 1939, Henry Horner was on a train headed north for Illinois. He had been given the go-ahead from his doctors to return to the Executive Mansion only if he promised to work no more than one or two hours a day to allow his recuperation to continue. It was a promise that he never intended to keep. He still felt considerably weakened from his several months' stay in bed. As the train crossed into Illinois and chugged northwest toward Springfield, Senator James Hamilton Lewis was breathing his last breath in Washington, D.C. Horner's first official duty after his return was appointing a senator in his place. If Horner's train had been in Indiana when Lewis expired, Stelle would have had the pleasure of appointing Pat Nash to the position. As it was, Horner made the choice and rewarded Jim Slattery with the position. Stelle's lost opportunity magnified his exasperation with Horner's continued hold on power. He vehemently argued that Horner was incapacitated and should step aside and yield the governorship to him until election time. However, having Stelle anxious to take over made Horner more determined than ever to return to his full duties. Roosevelt, marveling from Washington over the drama in Illinois, sent Horner a telegram welcoming him back to office and complimenting him on his selection of Senator Slattery.

Stelle began actively campaigning for Horner's position the summer after his return from Miami. He announced at a Fourth of July celebration that he would run for governor in 1940. Horner also made the public announcement that he fully intended to run for reelection; he simply could not envision submitting to the vagaries of fate. He insisted that he had been down before but had surprised everyone, and he could do it again. He hoped to win the election and would then be in a position to choose his successor if he had to step down for health reasons. What drove him during this time was intense displeasure at the thought of John Stelle reversing everything he had worked for. Although Horner sometimes seemed irrational during this time because of his weakened condition, his fear of what Stelle might do was well-founded. Stelle was obsessed with the possibility of having power but had no coherent agenda or set of principles that defined how he would channel that power if it did come his way. During the months that Horner was away, Stelle had enjoyed the rush of instituting a spending spree after the tense years of Horner's control of the state's purse strings, and he brought about dramatic reversals of policy. Stelle's power base was also liberally sprinkled with anti-Semitism, and his supporters expressed their desire to "run the Jews out" of Springfield.[5] Horner knew he had to hold on at least until the election to stave off the power-hungry Stelle.

Horner's lucidity was sporadic, but frequent enough to justify his staying on as acting head of government. He had long periods of semiconsciousness, often lasting for days. At such times, the truth of his condition was heavily guarded by his regents, who provided stopgap leadership when Horner could not perform his duties. However, these men were not the sort of loyal right-hand men who would selflessly escort the governor through times of trouble. Instead, they were opportunists who fully enjoyed the power that fate had handed them—perhaps a little too freely. They camped out at the Executive Mansion, making it a sort of gentlemen's club. They drank, smoked cigars, played poker, and made liberal use of the mansion kitchen, taxing the support staff. They streamed in and out of Horner's sick chambers, puffing all the while on cigars; they brought news, questions, policy advice, papers to sign, and favors to ask, causing dangerous peaks in the patient's precarious blood pressure. Horner contributed to his own erratic health by his dogged determination to stay in the loop, to make decisions, and to try to control, as best he could, what was going on in the statehouse. There was also talk in political circles that this "bedside cabinet" was taking advantage of Horner's incapacity to pad their own pockets. There were rumors everywhere that thieves had moved into the Executive Mansion. Their behavior seemed the cruelest form of irony, since Horner's life had been spent in vigilant enforcement of honest behavior in government. He had always gone out of his way to ensure that he did not profit in any way from the wheels of government, and now it seemed especially cruel that others used the occasion of his illness to turn his very home into a haven for profiteers.

Sensing that the end was near, Horner grasped at an opportunity to extend his mortality by taking under his wing a young Jewish state senator who may have reminded him of himself in younger years. Abe Marovitz had just been elected to the state senate from the Twenty-fourth Ward in Chicago. Reversing a long-held philosophy, Horner advised Marovitz that Jews in the public eye must conduct themselves according to the highest standards as visible representatives of their people. Reflecting his lifelong insight, he urged Marovitz never to become a *politician*. As he neared the end, Horner may have regretted his decision to mix it up with the rough players to ensure his political survival. Many thoughts and reflections about his remarkable career must have spun through the governor's troubled mind. He had been forced to make many difficult decisions, and now was the time to evaluate his accomplishments in terms of the larger picture. However, despite the confusion of his thoughts, Horner could rest assured that he had done what was necessary to see Illinois through the Great Depression. Even so, he often lay in his bed in a noticeable state of mental torment.

The decisions that troubled Horner the most throughout his career were those that involved human dilemmas in which each side aroused sympathy and understanding. He had faced this burden early in his career when dealing with the coal-mining crisis and other labor disputes. Such dilemmas forced him to weigh the interests of desperate and wronged workers against those of an innocent public subjected to lawlessness and disorder. He also felt the pangs of responsibility that accompanied the governor's power to commute sentences and death penalties. Such cases always forced him to consider the humanity of both sides: the victims and their families, but also the offenders, their families, and the human narratives that explained the tragic positions in which the offenders had come to reside.

One such decision faced Horner when he was bedridden at the end of his career. Its difficulty was magnified because the offenders whose fates were now in his hands were coal miners who had committed their crimes during the painful struggle of the mining wars. These five young miners from DuQuoin had fired on the home of the local sheriff and inadvertently killed his fourteen-year-old daughter, Laverne Miller. Four of the miners had received life sentences, and the remaining one had been sentenced to forty years. Because of their youth and the tumultuous circumstances in which their crimes had been committed, a delegation of state leaders had filed for executive clemency on their behalf. Horner stayed up most of the night, reading the case file and staring up at the picture of his mother that occupied the space opposite his bed. In the morning, he personally rendered his decision. The image of the young girl whose life had been cut short by the miners' reckless disregard for human life had won out over his sympathies for the young men. He acknowledged that his mother's memory was the moral touchstone that had led him to the difficult decision.

While others were busy wheeling and dealing and strategizing about how to maintain power after the anticipated vacuum, Horner spent an increasing amount of time lying in bed, sadly reading the piles of correspondence from people around the state. Between fits of sleep, he laboriously composed correspondence to those who mattered most to him: the common people who still relied on him. Few other politicians would have spent their last hours writing letters whose only effect was probably a surprised and pleased remark that "I got a letter from the governor of Illinois today!" Now the tales of hardship and appeals for help struck him on a new level. He was no longer the benevolent leader on high who could use his power to help the vulnerable and the suffering. Now he was *one of them,* and he was beyond helping.

Most politicians in Horner's position never would have returned from retirement in Miami. But almost until the very end, Horner dismissed any talk of his stepping down and insisted that he intended to run for reelection, even though everyone around him knew that this ambition defied reality. Doctors met secretly with the Horner inner circle and impressed on them the grave state of affairs and the necessity of facing the fact that he would not last much longer. His heart had sustained permanent and extensive damage, his periods of consciousness and lucidity were growing sparser, and he was rapidly losing motor control. It was here, at the end of his life, that Horner revealed the depth of his determination to fulfill his duties. The idea of rest, leisure, and retirement were abhorrent to him. His workaholic ways penetrated him to the very core. A draft of a statement of withdrawal was passed to Horner when he was caught halfway between delirium and unconsciousness. A hush filled the room as Horner raised himself up in bed and ripped the paper to shreds. "You damned fools, don't you know that's just what Kelly wants?" he sputtered, and then fell back into bed, again submerged in a half-sleeping state from the exertion.[6]

In the meantime, the power players faced the fact that it was time to get busy. Jim Slattery and Sam Nudelman decided it was time to hash out a strategy with the Kelly-Nash machine to minimize the chance of a Stelle takeover in Springfield. Ed Kelly and Jake Arvey dashed down to Springfield to take part in an impromptu forum that included all of the factions of the Democratic Party in the state, with the notable exception of John Stelle and those loyal to him. The powwow turned into a marathon as the different interests worked to identify a figure to take Horner's place who would be amenable to all. However, it was the dying governor who got the most important say in the matter. Horner's press secretary, Pete Akers, tired himself out running up and down the stairs with proposals for the governor to consider. From the outset, everyone there had agreed that, in order to gain the important symbolic approval of the governor and to find a common ground, one stipulation had to be clear—John Stelle was definitely not in the running.

Using Akers as his messenger, Horner haggled with the Kelly-Nash contingent. Horner favored John Cassidy, the current Illinois attorney general, to replace him, while they found Cassidy's antigambling position unacceptable. They finally agreed on former Illinois attorney general Otto Kerner and summoned him to the mansion to lay the proposal before him. Kerner asked for some time to think about it, but the unruly group was getting restless and insisted that he stay and give them his answer. He found a quiet room to think and returned after some time to throw a wrench into their plans. He was clearly conflicted on the matter and turned down the nomination. The specter of Henry Horner, dying upstairs while the power players wrestled over the leavings, seemed to haunt him. He may have imagined a similar spectacle in his own future if he stepped into the governor's chambers at this time. Kerner fled to a position on a federal court, making the decision Horner probably should have made when Roosevelt offered a similar job to him before the 1936 primary. And so, the wild rumpus went on into the morning hours.

After receiving Kerner's decision, the depleted leaders settled on the state Democratic chairman, Harry Hershey. He was nobody's first choice, but he didn't send anyone into a paroxysm of protest either. And so, a deal was finally struck. Hershey was received in the governor's chambers the next day. Horner vowed that he would see him elected and asked only one thing in return—that Hershey promise to him that Carol Sanders would be supported and cared for the remainder of her life.

Meanwhile, that same night, Stelle assembled his own men to strategize a counterattack after having been squeezed out of the process. There were those who predicted that Stelle would have his turn as governor, whether he was elected or not. Horner would die any day, they reasoned, and they were eager to attach themselves to the future governor, who was sure to dispense patronage and spoils liberally out of revenge. Also, Stelle hoped that he would be able to use the temporary governor's seat as a vehicle for creating financial and vote-getting momentum for the election. During his unsuccessful bid for Chicago mayor in 1939, Dwight H. Green had gained a good deal of visibility and had planted the seeds of popular support. Now he would be the Republican candidate for governor at a very propitious time. The power of the Democrats in Illinois was unraveling. The old resentment against the Republican Party for being latecomers to the relief movement was mostly forgotten, and gratitude to the Democrats for federal dollars and funds was wearing thin.

Adding to the decline in the Democrats' popularity were rumors of the inappropriate use of funds by Horner loyalists, which reached a peak after he officially announced that he would not be running for reelection. This scandal concerned a campaign fund that was being examined by federal income tax investigators. According to Thomas Littlewood, the fund was "supplied by the 2 percent assessment of the paychecks of state employees, percentage 'dues' from contractors, a dime-a-ton tribute on coal sales to the state, and similar sources."[7] A contest between Sam Nudelman and the director of public works, Lyn Smith, for control of the fund escalated into a feud during Horner's illness. Smith came to regret his involvement in the fund when he was ordered to court to answer questions about its existence and operation. The pressure on him apparently grew overwhelming, and he began to behave erratically. His wife became concerned when she discovered him burning a briefcase full of papers in the basement of their home. Shortly thereafter, Smith became fully unhinged and stabbed himself with a butcher knife, causing a life-threatening injury. He finally committed suicide in the hospital.

As the primary election neared, Horner, whose own ambitions were at last stilled, pinned all his hopes on Hershey's winning the nomination and shutting Stelle out for good. Horner even made known his intention to actually campaign for Hershey, once again trying to ignore the elephant-in-the-room that was his health. For his part, Stelle was growing more and more insistent that Horner step aside. He argued that government should not be conducted by regency, and since the governor was thoroughly incapacitated, that he, as lieutenant governor, should be regarded as the acting governor. But in fashioning his campaign strategy, Stelle decided that he had better not attack Horner. The governor's illness and his previously earned status as triumphant underdog had made him a sentimental favorite. Instead, Stelle cast Horner as the victim of a corrupt gang that sought to take advantage of his illness. He may have overstated the case, but his spin had some merit. In the meantime, the escalating tensions abroad were beginning to factor into the elections. Reflecting the dominant view of southern Illinois, Stelle, a veteran of World War I, pledged that American boys would not be dragged into another foreign war.

While it was unclear who was in control at what time, there was still activity coming from the governor's bedside office. Horner called the legislature into special session to discuss old age pensions and public aid. The Old Age Assistance pension (OAA) had been a matter of contention between Horner and the legislature since it was adopted in December 1935. The following year, the legislature had given control of this program to the counties. Horner advocated instead establishing a system of state control so that Illinois would be able to receive federal matching grants. The federal Social Security Board (SSB) rejected the county-based Illinois system. After a second attempt to revise the OAA to meet federal standards, the SSB approved the Illinois plan anyway, and then in July 1937 withdrew federal grants until such time as Illinois came into compliance. According to historian Dwayne Cole, "Horner appointed John Weigel to straighten out the OAA administration in Illinois. Weigel's reforms restructured OAA and in less than two months the Social Security Board restored federal grants to the Illinois aged."[8]

Apparently, Stelle was not convinced that Horner was in any condition to be able to call a special session, and he assumed that someone else was making such decisions. When his protestations fell on deaf ears, he decided to take matters into his own hands. As the order for the special session was being prepared, Stelle burst through the doors of the governor's office and declared himself the acting governor, effective immediately. As his first official action in office, he sat down and wrote a letter terminating the employment of Sam Nudelman and charging him with "incompetence," "neglect," and "malfeasance" of duty.[9] The staffers in the office refused to validate Stelle's self-proclaimed status and largely ignored him as he swaggered around the office. Horner's inner circle mocked Stelle's hasty action in the press. To rebut the accusation that the governor was no longer able to effectively govern, a letter was sent out to all state employees assuring them that Henry Horner was in control of the state and would remain so until after the election. Horner's outrage at Stelle's attempt to take over the statehouse only made him more determined to hang on until after the election. Still, his condition continued to deteriorate.

Stelle's brash actions did little to endear him to other politicians or to voters. The Democratic Party had largely united around Hershey. Former Horner enemies Jake Arvey, Ed Kelly, and Pat Nash now mobilized with Horner against Stelle. Hershey had behind him the fund-raising power of both the statehouse and the Chicago organization. In the primary election, Hershey handily beat the lieutenant governor and his "rebel ticket" of Edward J. Barrett, the current Illinois state auditor of public accounts, running for another term as auditor, and Ben Adamowski, running for the Senate against the incumbent, Senator James Slattery. Stelle issued a statement suggesting that he meant to assume the role of acting governor as soon as the primary election ended. The Horner inner circle was determined to deny Stelle even the privilege of a short stint in the position, and they set up a press event to demonstrate Horner's ability to govern until the general election. They propped him up on the porch of the mansion and subjected him to a short interview regarding the special session on relief. Horner was able to manage a half-lucid reply before he was carted off back to bed. Later, Dr. Rosen testified in front of the legislature that Horner was fully in control of his capacities, but that it would be too taxing on his blood pressure for him to appear in front of a House committee inquiring into Sam Nudelman's handling of state finances.

There is much about Horner's last days that strikes a sad irony. Although he had devoted his life to scrupulous honesty in all matters financial and had hesitated to delegate anything to others for fear that the welfare of the state would be compromised, he was forced to delegate nearly all of his duties at the end. Many had thought that Horner's insistence on keeping tabs on all the record keeping was a superfluous effort, even a foolish waste of time. But in the end, his administration was tainted by accusations of financial mismanagement, all because the honest Henry Horner was confined to bed. It was as if all of his suspicions and fears were finally confirmed. He would not be allowed to go to his death in peace.

While he drifted away, the state went into a perilous confusion, and a cloud of suspicion was cast over the regency. Horner tried to at least exert what control he could over the future, but it was a fruitless effort. In order to protect him from questioning about the growing financial scandal, Dr. Rosen ordered Horner to be spirited away to a rented house on the lakeshore north of Chicago. Horner was shocked and upset when he learned about the activity that apparently had occurred during his decline. "What have they done?" he asked regarding those he had elevated to office and trusted.[10] Ensconced far away from Springfield, he began making arrangements for his death. His first action was to donate his extensive Lincoln collection to the Illinois State Historical Library. He did so with the hope that the collection would be available to all, benefiting everyone from scholarly researchers to curious schoolchildren.[11]

On September 3, 1939, Britain and France declared war on Nazi Germany in retaliation for the invasion of Poland. Roosevelt, who had stood side by side with Horner to face the Great Depression, now had a crisis of another sort to confront. In a Fireside Chat with the nation, Roosevelt appealed to the American people to understand the gravity of the matter. He assured them that the country was not heading off to war, but that Americans could not be neutral in their hearts and minds. Since World War I, the American people had adopted deep-seated isolationist and neutral philosophies, but the country was now feeling itself drawn against its will into a frightening international conflict.

On September 16, 1940, Roosevelt signed the Selective Training and Service Act of 1940, the first compulsory peacetime draft in U.S. history. Now politicians had to move from the partisan political climate that dominated a government obsessed with domestic issues to the bipartisan cooperation needed to respond to an international threat. Meanwhile, back in Springfield, the administration craved leadership as international tensions escalated and the need for local selective service boards was becoming increasingly evident. At the rented mansion north of Chicago, Horner could do little more than occasionally scratch his name across a document. He would not be there to experience the transition from the Depression era to the war period along with the rest of the nation and the rest of his old power triangle, Roosevelt and Kelly. He would be frozen in time as Illinois's Depression governor. Until the very end, Horner resisted any suggestion that he turn the reins over to Stelle. When Horner's condition turned critical on October 5, 1940, his inability to govern became undeniable to everyone, and a statement of disability was prepared that would authorize Stelle to assume the governorship. Horner bristled when he became aware of the action, but in the end this document would not be needed. On October 6, after an agonizing day of suffering, Henry Horner finally submitted to his fate. It seemed that he could not even leave this world in a restful state, that he was destined to struggle his way out of the world in death, just as he had struggled with the world in life.

When the news came of Horner's death, it was as if all of the ugly political wrangling that had so dominated his last years of life subsided in shame. No one could deny now that Horner had been a man who exemplified good government. Whatever policy disagreements people around the state might have had with him, whatever complaints they might have uttered in desperation or discomfort in the difficult times, it was roundly acknowledged that Henry Horner had worked himself to death on their behalf. When people saw the disarray that accompanied his death—the suspicion, the scandal, the loose handling of public funds, and the abuse of the public trust—they realized the extent of the protection they had been afforded by Horner's watchful eye and endless vigilance. And so, tens of thousands paraded by over a period of two days to view his body lying in state. On the insistence of Ella Cornwall, his lifelong ally, he wore the pince-nez that had become his trademark.

Scott Lucas, whose gratitude toward Horner had never diminished, delivered an address praising Horner for his ability to be the gentle humanitarian on the one hand and a lion willing to fight for what he believed in on the other. Mayor Ed Kelly, who had arrived at a tentative truce with Horner near the end, sat in the front row. He squirmed nervously, knowing that many saw him as the man who had betrayed the martyred governor. Rabbi Louis Mann, who had persuaded Horner to sign the "Eyedrop Bill" that saved so many newborns from blindness, delivered the eulogy. He used the opportunity to deliver a pointed critique of the political machine that Kelly had helmed for nearly a decade. During his address, he looked right at Kelly when he lauded Horner's battle with "graft, corruption, dishonesty, and the spoils system" and attributed Horner's death to his exhausting battle against corruption and betrayal. In the end, Kelly was made to feel that he had taken part in the murder of the man that was now a symbol of honesty and hard work. It is probable that Kelly regretted his early decision to treat Horner as his nemesis. Even in death, Horner seemed to come out on top in a battle of public perceptions that now seemed devoid of meaning.

Although Mann held Kelly responsible for the heavy burden that shortened Horner's life, the feud with Kelly had faded from Horner's consciousness during those final months. John Stelle had become Horner's chief enemy, the living symbol of all those who had tried to steamroll him during his career. Horner's distrust of the lieutenant governor had been the fuel that kept him from retirement despite the obvious breakdown of his capacities. In addition to his elected position, Stelle still operated a 769-acre farm near McLeansboro, and he was working in one of his wheat fields when he heard of Governor Horner's death on October 6. Having lost the primary to Harry Hershey, he now had ninety-nine days to be the governor of Illinois. Knowing that his term was limited and there would be little accountability for his actions while in office, Stelle launched into a frenzy of activity. He seemed motivated by the thrill of power and a desire for revenge for having been suppressed in his gubernatorial ambitions for so many months. His short reign struck a notable contrast to the modest and prudent governing style of Henry Horner. The mansion that had been so underused by Horner was suddenly filled with family. Stelle, his wife, and two children moved right in and began to enjoy the luxury. Stelle was intent on making the most of his three months there. He had the mansion itself painted and redecorated a handful of rooms in anticipation of visitors from down south who joined the Stelle family in celebration, making use of all the entertainment budget that was unused by Horner. He also ordered the purchase of two new Cadillacs for use by the occupant of the Executive Mansion.

Horner's fear for the livelihood of his staffers was soon justified. Stelle got to work gleefully deposing many of Horner's loyal state employees and rewarding his own friends with the newly created positions. Nudelman was naturally the first to go. Stelle was roundly criticized for launching into a spending frenzy. He awarded contracts left and right, spreading out the good fortune that had come to him as a result of Horner's demise. He also pardoned and paroled prisoners in numbers that shocked law enforcement. He even overturned Horner's carefully considered refusal to grant clemency to the five DuQuoin coal miners convicted of the murder of the sheriff's daughter.

While Stelle busied himself in the governor's seat, the general election between Harry Hershey and Dwight Green was underway. Although Kelly had backed Hershey in a gesture of conciliation with Horner, he now realized how much difficulty and stress the power struggle with Horner had cost him. He decided once and for all that he no longer cared to share power with a Democratic governor. It would be better to let the Republicans win. Whatever campaign momentum Harry Hershey had was cut short when Kelly turned the Chicago machine's vote-getting infrastructure against him. The Republican candidate, Dwight Green, was elected the next governor of Illinois.

16

A Test of Good Government

Harry Hershey did not become the governor of Illinois, as Henry Horner had assured him that he would, and so Hershey forgot the promise he had made to Horner to take care of Carol Sanders. In the end, she was not cared for in the manner that Horner would have wanted. The state determined that her worth was less than the late governor had thought; her I.Q. was tested, and it was determined that she did not meet the criteria for the investment of specialized care and treatment. She was remanded back to the mental hospital for safekeeping. She quickly deteriorated, losing most of the progress she had made under Dr. Gault's care. In an understaffed hospital, receiving no treatment, she soon became once again incommunicative, destructive, and disconnected from the world. The girl who had once been adored by a governor now seemed to have no purpose in the eyes of the society, and she was largely forgotten. The regression of Carol Sanders after the death of Horner seems symbolic of the unraveling of progress that can occur when a benevolent, watchful eye is finally closed. Horner wanted most of all to be a caretaker of the people. During his career, he used his power to keep an eye out for the vulnerable, to make sure nobody got fleeced, to answer the appeals of the desperate and the needy, and to do what he could to make their conditions better. This central purpose of his life was taxed to an unbelievable degree during his term in office.

As a Depression governor, he might have been wise to cultivate a harder heart. However, it was a time in which the common people badly needed someone in their corner, and he was that man. If he had only had to concern himself with watching out for the needs of the people of the state of Illinois, he probably still would have worn himself out with strain and exhaustion, but he would have died a satisfied man. Instead, he was buffeted by political gamesmanship as he tried to do an honorable job during a time of overwhelming suffering and crisis. Just dealing with the Democratic political organizations seemed to draw him and his contemporaries away from the job they were called on to do. Horner's interest in doing his job in a straightforward manner aroused suspicion; he would have been better off if he had been a "boss," his detractors seemed to think. Horner found that occupying a high office in state government was more complicated than he ever could have imagined.

Following the story of a man like Horner, a man with strong principles and good intentions, who was intelligent and capable, as he struggled in political office, can reveal to us how much our political structures have strayed from their original purpose. "A government of the people, by the people, and for the people": Horner took this philosophy at face value, and his life became an interesting test case to see whether these guiding principles actually worked. Horner was guided by simplicity. He was an egalitarian people's governor, embracing the same ideas that inspired our forefathers. If people were gambling and imbibing illegal cocktails, Horner didn't look askance at them. He didn't expect saintly behavior; he embraced real human behavior. But he valued honesty above all else and thought he could bring it to the statehouse. If one was honest and worked hard enough, that was all that should be required of any public servant. But that was simply not enough. Horner was living in the house that power built, and his hometown was evidence that as power increases, it creates complications and the potential for corruption. At its smallest unit of functioning, represented by the wards in Chicago, the political structure spun a complicated web of power relations that wove together both benevolence and avarice. Horner did not understand avarice. Dwayne Cole, in his extensive work on relief in Illinois during the Depression, sums up Horner's role well: "Governor Horner permitted political survival to interfere with what he knew was ill-advised relief legislation." Cole continues, "But had the Chicago bosses won control of the statehouse, fiscal affairs would have been in as deplorable a situation as those of Chicago." Cole believes that Illinois was lucky to have someone of Horner's "caliber" during the Depression. "Horner again and again illustrated his concern for the unemployed by permitting surplus revenue to be used for relief. But he also felt Chicago should contribute to relief financing." Cole concludes, "Horner's curious compound of fiscal conservatism and humanitarianism permitted the state to meet relief needs without deficit financing. If local units had contributed their fair share toward unemployment relief, the suffering that did exist could have been prevented."[1]

Perhaps Horner was not in the right profession. Political life seemed to wear at him more than it did others. He seemed better suited for the independent life of a judge, set at a safe distance from the sticky web of the political organization. He was also a thoughtful intellectual who enjoyed writing, discussing political philosophy, and reading books. As such, he had something in common with his role model, Lincoln. But in his day, and even more so in the contemporary moment, politicians who are too intellectual are looked upon with suspicion; we Americans don't seem to expect much deep thinking from our leaders. Perhaps Horner would have done well as a university professor or a writer. He admired the quiet, creative, and contemplative life enjoyed by his closest friends, Bishop Griffin and Carl Sandburg. Indeed, it might have been better for him not to have gone into politics at all. But the fact is, he never did seem to place much stock in what was best for him. This habit of mind was a lucky thing for the state of Illinois, for as a governor, Henry Horner was a success. With a shrewd sense of economics and policy, he dragged the state up from its knees and back onto its feet. He raised enough money through taxation and bond issues to provide relief from human suffering of unimaginable proportions. He patched up the social and economic system until it could right itself, rather than let it dissolve into the chaos of revolution. Horner may not have been cut out to be a politician, but it seems a disservice to the country that political offices are not a more comfortable fit for men of simple integrity and goodwill.

The United States has not witnessed another economic trial or another spate of human suffering to equal that of the Great Depression. We look back at our Depression-era leaders and wonder how they could cope with the demands placed on them. The American economy was still relatively new; they had no way of knowing the ups and downs of which it was capable. They could not follow precedent; they had to invent and experiment. And we have all benefited from what they learned. While today we are, as a nation, more prosperous, economic conditions are also much more complicated and potentially more perilous. It is arguable that we have lost even the hope that our leaders see themselves, or could even function, as benevolent caretakers and watchful eyes that have our best interests at heart. This is a cynical age that accepts as fact that the political structures do not simply serve as a direct link between the people and their best interests. But this is a habit of mind that begs reassessing.

What if elective office were a comfortable place for honest, hardworking, public service–oriented candidates who were more interested in doing their job than building up their own name, their own power, and their own wealth? Would we say those candidates lacked "guts"? Would we even elect them? Henry Horner seemed to many people in his time to be refreshingly naive and a bit old-fashioned. Is that the way that most Americans feel about the principles that founded our nation—despite our rhetoric about wanting honest, hardworking public servants? It seems as if these principles, embodied in Henry Horner, have been bullied, roughed up, worn down, and finally killed. Horner was by no means perfect. He was a man, in uncertain times, trying to figure out the best course of action to make things better. He was not above retribution; he played rough when he had to; he bent the rules at times. His most questionable choices, however, seemed to have been made under great political pressure. Horner's experience reveals that a politician who wants to survive and prosper must spend an inordinate amount of time playing party politics, cultivating powerful interests, strategizing elections, and building an organization to sustain his or her own interests, not simply working on the people's issues. Hard work and goodwill are not enough. And yet, upon his death, it was generally agreed that Horner had been the kind of man that most people wanted in office; he simply couldn't survive in office the way he was or doing things the way he wanted to. This is a central paradox of American politics today, I believe. What we want, we often won't elect. What is it about a good man or woman that is an impediment to the functioning of the power structure?

Horner's life has much to teach us about the challenges of "good government." He should be remembered as he is described in Robert P. Howard's history of Illinois governors, *Mostly Good and Competent Men*, as a man "with a humanitarian's compassion, an extrovert's personality, and a marathoner's determination."[2] As Illinois's Depression governor, he accomplished a great deal while in office despite the criticism and the political attacks he withstood. His two terms in office leave a solid historical legacy. His honesty was refreshing because he respected the people enough to tell them the truth. While other politicians promised that relief could be provided while lowering taxes, Horner could not bring himself to employ such dishonest, crowd-pleasing rhetoric. While his popularity suffered because of his direct approach on taxation, one of his legacies to the state of Illinois was his restructuring of an antiquated, unfair, and ineffective taxation system. He will also be remembered for his victory in passing a permanent voter registration measure, helping to bring voting practices into the more orderly and reliable state in which we find them today. He was responsible for helping to make the election process a little more dignified and consistent with its intended purpose of allowing each person's voice to be counted equally. Horner took such things seriously; he broke with the "wink and nod" tradition of politics that allowed the machine to get what it wanted. One thing that Henry Horner never seemed intent upon, which differentiated him from many of his associates, was to increase his personal wealth. While those around him seemed continually to be searching for ways to enrich themselves, Horner dedicated his life to ensuring that resources went where they were intended to.

During his lifetime, Horner contended with a partisan political structure that had organized, solidified, and crusted over through many decades. This structure did afford a remarkable level of stability to shore up the state during a crisis. The Depression-era Democratic Party reigned during the most difficult times because, despite its pursuit of its self-interests, it was perceived to be the party that placed the interests of the common people above those of business and the very wealthy. While the party leaders in Chicago got handouts from the New Deal, so too did many out-of-work and destitute families. But occasionally, the relationship between the people and the power structure needs to become more direct and more evident; otherwise, it spirals out of control and loses touch with its original purpose. World War II became the force that collapsed the entrenched distance between the American people and their government. When the Japanese bombed Pearl Harbor, the entire nation, regardless of party, dispensed with the political gamesmanship for a time and demanded a strong leader who was also a benevolent caretaker, a role that had come naturally to Henry Horner. Franklin Roosevelt would take up that position, communicating to the people with honesty and directness in his popular Fireside Chats. World War II would radically change the political organization and climate of the country. One wonders how Henry Horner would have fit into the new, postwar American political landscape. But we will never know; he will always be Illinois's Depression governor. If he was not as colorful a figure as some of those around him, hardworking, honest individuals rarely are. But he serves as a potent reminder of the function politicians were originally intended to fulfill. He reminded those around him about the ideals of Lincoln, and his life teaches us never to underestimate the power of the "good guy." Often the good guy has the tenacity of a lion.

Notes
Bibliography
Index

Notes

1. Muddy Beginnings

1. The standard work on the history of Chicago, at least to 1893, is Pierce's three-volume *History of Chicago.* A handier, one-volume work with numerous illustrations is Mayer, Wade, and Holt's *Chicago: Growth of a Metropolis.*

2. That Hannah Dernberg immigrated in part because she was orphaned is a detail from Littlewood, *Horner of Illinois,* 9. It is not clear how her parents died. Much of the specific information about Henry Horner's career in the following paragraphs is taken from Littlewood's biography.

3. Littlewood, *Horner of Illinois,* 16. Littlewood consulted court transcripts from records in the Circuit Court of Cook County.

4. For an interesting article tracing the friendship between Horner and Richard Finnegan, the editor of the *Chicago Daily Times,* see Meyers, "Henry Horner and Richard Finnegan."

2. One Foot on the Sidewalk and One in the Gutter

1. Carter's early philosophy on personal liberty is discussed in Kantowicz, "Carter H. Harrison II."

2. Harrison and Coughlin quoted in Wendt and Kogan, *Lords of the Levee,* 163. Much of the information about Coughlin and Kenna that follows is taken from this study. But see also Granger and Granger, *Lords of the Last Machine,* for another account that continues into the 1980s.

3. Quoted in Longstreet, *Chicago,* 348.

4. "Samuel Insull: 1859–1938," *Historic Figures,* Chicago Rapid Transit homepage, <www.Chicago-L.org>. The standard biography of Samuel Insull is

McDonald, *Insull.* McDonald relates his efforts in writing the Insull biography in his *Recovering the Past,* especially 14, 93–95.

5. Fremon, *Chicago Politics,* 172, 173.

6. Lincoln, "Address at Independence Hall," 87.

3. An Honorable Judge in the Age of Whoopee

1. Harrison, *Stormy Years,* 36.
2. Allsop, *Bootleggers and Their Era,* 202.
3. Quoted in Littlewood, *Horner of Illinois,* 35.
4. Quoted in Wendt and Kogan, *Big Bill of Chicago,* 95.
5. Merriam, *Chicago,* 186.
6. Bregstone, *Chicago and Its Jews,* 303.
7. Merriam, *Chicago,* 29.
8. Quoted in Littlewood, *Horner of Illinois,* 45.
9. Dobyns, *Underworld of American Politics,* 71.
10. Quoted in Merriam, *Chicago,* 190.
11. Bright, *Hizzoner Big Bill Thompson,* 291.

4. The Bottom Drops Out

1. Allsop, *Bootleggers and Their Era,* 292.
2. Quoted in ibid., 221.
3. Quoted in Bright, *Hizzoner Big Bill Thompson,* 294.
4. Dobyns, *Underworld of American Politics,* ix.

5. The Wheels in Motion

1. Gottfried, *Boss Cermak of Chicago,* 241.
2. McElvaine, *Great Depression,* 122.
3. Quoted in Stuart, *Twenty Incredible Years,* 472.
4. Quoted in Littlewood, *Horner of Illinois,* 63.

6. Judge Horner Runs the Race

1. Davis, *Prophet in His Own Country,* 185.
2. Quoted in Stuart, *Twenty Incredible Years,* 476–77.
3. Quoted in ibid., 471.
4. Campaign slogan from illustration in Wendt and Kogan, *Big Bill of Chicago,* facing 288.
5. Stuart, *Twenty Incredible Years,* 488–89.

7. A Big Hit Downstate and On to Victory

1. Quoted in Adams, *Transformation of Rural Life*, 134.

2. Quoted in Littlewood, *Horner of Illinois*, 77–78.

3. Quoted in ibid., 80.

4. Quoted in ibid., 79.

5. Quoted in Wendt and Kogan, *Big Bill of Chicago*, 338–39.

6. Quoted in ibid., 340.

7. Quoted in Strickland, "New Deal Comes to Illinois," 63.

8. Quoted in Littlewood, *Horner of Illinois*, 84.

9. Biles, *Illinois*, 217.

10. James Farley to Horner (telegram), November 9, 1932, 5:07 PM, case 55, drawer 4, box 247, Horner Papers.

8. Roll Up Your Sleeves, Governor

1. Littlewood, *Horner of Illinois*, 89.

2. Quoted in ibid., 94.

3. Quoted in ibid.

4. Stuart, *Twenty Incredible Years*, 61, 62.

5. Statistics taken from Biles, *Big City Boss*, 22–24.

6. Quoted in ibid., 23.

7. Littlewood, *Horner of Illinois*, 97.

8. Ibid., 100.

9. For the best account of the problems relating to coal mining in central Illinois, see Oblinger, *Divided Kingdom*.

10. Quoted in Granger and Granger, *Lords of the Last Machine*, 95.

11. Quoted in Gottfried, *Boss Cermak*, 318.

12. Quoted in Stuart, *Twenty Incredible Years*, 516.

13. Ibid.

9. The Crux of the Crisis

1. Watkins, *Great Depression*, 81.

2. Quoted in Littlewood, *Horner of Illinois*, 171.

3. Quoted in Meltzer, *Brother*, 68.

4. Early histories of the background to the New Deal include groundbreaking works by Goldman, *Rendezvous with Destiny* (1952); and Hofstadter, *Age of Reform* (1955). Rauch, *History of the New Deal* (1944), was the first to discuss two New Deals, insisting that the first, 1933–35, emphasized relief and recovery, while

the second, 1935–38, concentrated on reform. Like many other generalizations, Rauch's division doesn't hold up under scrutiny, but it is still used in a number of texts. Early historians saw FDR as a liberal, but Shannon, *Twentieth Century America* (1963), was one of the first to see him as a conservative and emphasized that Roosevelt preserved the capitalistic economy, but switched it to a mixed economy with the federal government playing a major role. Bernstein, "New Deal" (1968), stressed that the New Deal was aimed more toward the middle class and did practically nothing for the poor, for blacks, or for those on the bottom of the economic pyramid. For two balanced treatments, see Leuchtenburg, *Franklin D. Roosevelt and the New Deal* (1963); and Biles, *New Deal* (1991).

5. Granger and Granger, *Lords of the Last Machine*, 99.

6. Cole, "Relief Crisis," 480.

7. Quoted in Rickard, "How Dry We Were."

10. Horner, History, and the New Deal

1. This is especially a matter of inquiry for Ed Kelly's biographer, Roger Biles; see *Big City Boss*.

2. Quoted in Littlewood, *Horner of Illinois*, 115.

3. Address of Judge Henry Horner, Tuesday, October 11, 1932, case 43, drawer 1, box 5, Horner Papers.

4. Harry Hopkins to Roger Dunham (telegram), October 7, 1933, quoted in Biles, "Henry Horner and the New Deal," 41.

5. Quoted in Littlewood, *Horner of Illinois*, 111.

6. Cole, "Relief Crisis," 482.

7. Biles, *New Deal*, 103.

8. Cole, "Relief Crisis," 485; Jones, "Origins of the Alliance," 264–70.

9. Cole, "Relief Crisis," 486.

10. For some of Horner's correspondence with Mrs. Roosevelt, see case 55, drawer 4, box 247, Horner Papers.

11. Quoted in Biles, *New Deal*, 127; also quoted in Littlewood, *Horner of Illinois*, 69.

12. Biles, "Horner and the New Deal," 46–47.

13. Quoted in Biles, *Big City Boss*, 50–51.

11. The Governor Gives Himself Away

1. B. P. Alschuler to Henry Horner, March 4, 1933, case 49, drawer 2, box 11, Horner Papers.

2. Details about Governor Horner's work habits were gleaned from interviews in Littlewood, *Horner of Illinois.*

3. Quoted in Littlewood, *Horner of Illinois,* 121.

12. A Stab in the Back

1. Meyers, "Henry Horner and Richard Finnegan," 353–55.

2. Granger and Granger, *Lords of the Last Machine,* 103.

3. Biles, *Big City Boss,* 43.

4. Ibid., 36.

5. Details about the behind-the-scenes responses of the Roosevelt administration to Ed Kelly's bid for reelection are taken from Biles's biography of Kelly, *Big City Boss;* and Funchion's essay, "Political and Nationalist Dimensions."

6. Abraham Lincoln Marovitz, quoting Horner, from an interview in Littlewood, *Horner of Illinois,* 150–51; also quoted in Biles, *Big City Boss,* 50.

7. Littlewood, *Horner of Illinois,* 156.

8. Quoted in Littlewood, *Horner of Illinois,* 159. Horner's response was quoted in numerous sources.

13. Into the Snake Pit

1. Biles, *New Deal,* 126.

2. Ellis, *Nation in Torment,* 103.

3. Townsend was a retired Long Beach, California, doctor. In 1934, he called for a plan to give a $200 monthly pension to every person over sixty years old. The money would have to be spent within one month, thus restoring what Townsend called the proper circulation of money. The pension would be paid for by a 2 percent sales tax. The plan received enthusiastic support from older Americans, and millions of people joined over 5,000 Townsend Clubs. Although they failed to get the plan adopted, Roosevelt did not like it. Still, their movement on both the state and national levels is considered to be one of the forces that contributed to passage of the Social Security Act in 1935.

4. See McCoy, *Angry Voices.*

5. Quoted in Littlewood, *Horner of Illinois,* 166.

6. Quoted in ibid., 173.

7. Ibid., 179.

8. Ibid., 181.

9. *Illinois State Journal,* October 1, 1936.

10. Quoted in Littlewood, *Horner of Illinois,* 190.

11. *Illinois State Journal,* November 5, 1936.

12. *Illinois State Journal,* November 4, 1936.

13. James Farley to Horner (telegram), November 6, 1936, case 55, drawer 4, box 247, Horner Papers.

14. Election statistics taken from *Encyclopedia of American History,* 350–55.

14. The Horner Ticket

1. Biles, "Henry Horner and the New Deal," 50.

2. Patterson, *New Deal and the States,* 159.

3. Quoted in Littlewood, *Horner of Illinois,* 198.

4. Statistic taken from Biles, *Big City Boss,* 64.

5. For details of the "Memorial Day Massacre," see Newell, *Chicago and the Labor Movement,* 135–47.

15. While the Cat's Away

1. Quoted in Littlewood, *Horner of Illinois,* 205.

2. Quoted in ibid., 207.

3. Quoted in Biles, *Big City Boss,* 69; and in Littlewood, *Horner of Illinois,* 211.

4. Quoted in Biles, *Big City Boss,* 69.

5. Quoted in Littlewood, *Horner of Illinois,* 212.

6. Quoted in ibid., 217.

7. Ibid., 220.

8. Cole, "Relief Crisis," 316, 488–89, quote on 489.

9. Littlewood, *Horner of Illinois,* 223.

10. Quoted in ibid., 225.

11. Angle, "Horner."

16. A Test of Good Government

1. Cole, "Relief Crisis," 491–92.

2. Howard, *Illinois Governors,* 236.

Bibliography

Adams, Jane. *The Transformation of Rural Life: Southern Illinois, 1890–1990.* Chapel Hill: University of North Carolina Press, 1994.

Allsop, Kenneth. *The Bootleggers and Their Era.* Garden City, N.Y.: Doubleday, 1961.

American National Biography. Edited by John A. Garraty and Mark C. Carnes, 24 vols. New York: Oxford University Press, 1999.

Angle, Paul M. "Henry Horner." In *Dictionary of American Biography,* edited by Robert Livingston Schuyler and Edward T. James, vol. 22, supplement 2 [to December 31, 1940], 318–19. New York: Charles Scribner's Sons, 1958.

Bean, Philip G. "Illinois Politics During the New Deal." PhD diss., University of Illinois, 1976.

Bernstein, Barton J. "The New Deal: The Conservative Achievements of Liberal Reform." In *Toward a New Past: Dissenting Essays in American History,* edited by Barton J. Bernstein, 263–88. New York: Pantheon, 1968.

Biles, Roger. *Big City Boss in Depression and War: Mayor Edward J. Kelly of Chicago.* DeKalb: Northern Illinois University Press, 1984.

———. "Henry Horner and the New Deal in Illinois." *Mid-America: An Historical Review* 74, no.1 (January 1992): 37–57.

———. *Illinois: A History of the Land and Its People.* DeKalb: Northern Illinois University Press, 2005.

———. *A New Deal for the American People.* DeKalb: Northern Illinois University Press, 1991.

Biographical Directory of the Governors of the United States, 1789–1978. Edited by Robert Sobel and John Raimo, vol. 1 (Alabama–Indiana). Westport, Conn.: Meckler, 1978.

Bregstone, Philip J. *Chicago and Its Jews*. Chicago: Privately printed by the author, 1933.

Bright, John. *Hizzoner Big Bill Thompson: An Idyll of Chicago*. New York: J. J. Little and Ives, 1930.

Bukowski, Douglas. *Big Bill Thompson, Chicago, and the Politics of Image*. Urbana and Chicago: University of Illinois Press, 1998.

Cole, Dwayne C. "The Relief Crisis in Illinois During the Depression, 1930–1940." PhD diss., Saint Louis University, 1973.

Cutler, Irving. *Jewish Chicago: A Pictorial History*. Chicago: Arcadia, 2000.

———. *The Jews of Chicago: From Shtetl to Suburb*. Urbana and Chicago: University of Illinois Press, 1996.

Davis, Kenneth S. *A Prophet in His Own Country: The Triumphs and Defeats of Adlai E. Stevenson*. New York: Doubleday, 1957.

Dedmon, Emmett. *Fabulous Chicago*. Rev. ed. New York: Atheneum, 1981.

Dobyns, Fletcher. *The Underworld of American Politics*. New York: Published by the author, 1932.

Ellis, Edward Robb. *A Nation in Torment: The Great American Depression, 1929–1939*. New York: Capricorn, 1971.

Encyclopedia of American History. Edited by Richard B. Morris. New York: Harper and Brothers, 1953.

Flanagan, Maureen A. *Seeing with Their Hearts: Chicago Women and the Vision of the Good City, 1871–1933*. Princeton: Princeton University Press, 2002.

Fremon, David K. *Chicago Politics, Ward by Ward*. Bloomington: Indiana University Press, 1988.

Funchion, Michael F. "The Political and Nationalist Dimensions." In *The Irish in Chicago*, 61–97. Urbana and Chicago: University of Illinois Press, 1987.

Gale, Edwin O. *Reminiscences of Early Chicago and Vicinity*. Chicago: Fleming H. Revell, 1902.

Goldman, Eric F. *Rendezvous with Destiny: A History of Modern American Reform*. New York: Vintage, 1956.

Gottfried, Alex. *Boss Cermak of Chicago: A Study of Political Leadership*. Seattle: University of Washington Press, 1962.

Granger, Bill, and Lori Granger. *Lords of the Last Machine: The Story of Politics in Chicago*. New York: Random House, 1987.

Gutstein, Morris A. "Horner, Henry." In *Encyclopaedia Judaica*. Vol. 8 (He–Ir). Jerusalem: Keter, 1971.

Harrison, Carter H. *Stormy Years: The Autobiography of Carter H. Harrison, Five Times Mayor of Chicago*. Indianapolis: Bobbs-Merrill, 1935.

Hofstadter, Richard. *The Age of Reform: From Bryan to F.D.R.* New York: Alfred A. Knopf, 1955.

Holli, Melvin G., and Peter d'A. Jones. *Ethnic Chicago*. Rev. ed. Grand Rapids, Mich.: William B. Eerdmans, 1984.

Horner, Henry. Papers, 1899–1940. Abraham Lincoln Presidential Library, Springfield, Ill.

———. *Restless Ashes II*. Chicago: Trade School of Girard College, 1928.

Howard, Robert P. *Illinois: A History of the Prairie State*. Grand Rapids, Mich.: William B. Eerdmans, 1972.

———. *The Illinois Governors: Mostly Good and Competent Men*. 2nd ed. Revised and updated by Peggy Boyer and Mike Lawrence. Springfield: University of Illinois at Springfield for the Institute for Public Affairs, 1999. First published in 1988.

Jones, Gene Delon. "The Local Political Significance of New Deal Relief Legislation in Chicago, 1933–1940." PhD diss., Northwestern University. 1970.

———."The Origins of the Alliance Between the New Deal and the Chicago Machine." *Journal of the Illinois State Historical Society* 67, no. 3 (June 1974): 252–74.

Kantowicz, Edward R. "Carter H. Harrison II: The Politics of Balance." In *The Mayors: The Chicago Political Tradition*, edited by Paul M. Green and Melvin G. Holli, 16–32. Carbondale: Southern Illinois University Press, 1987.

Leuchtenburg, William E. *Franklin D. Roosevelt and the New Deal, 1932–1940*. New York: Harper and Row, 1963.

Lincoln, Abraham. "Address at Independence Hall. Philadelphia, Pa., February 22, 1861." In *The Collected Works of Abraham Lincoln*, ed. Roy P. Basler et al., vol. 4. New Brunswick, N.J.: Rutgers University Press, 1953.

Littlewood, Thomas B. *Horner of Illinois*. Evanston, Ill.: Northwestern University Press, 1969.

Longstreet, Stephen. *Chicago: 1860–1919*. New York: David McKay, 1973.

Mark, Norman. *Mayors, Madams, and Madmen*. Chicago: Chicago Review, 1979.

Mayer, Harold M., Richard C. Wade, and Glen E. Holt. *Chicago: Growth of a Metropolis*. Cartography by Gerald F. Pyle. Chicago: University of Chicago Press, 1969.

McCoy, Donald R. *Angry Voices: Left-of-Center Politics in the New Deal Era*. Lawrence: University of Kansas Press, 1958.

McDonald, Forrest. *Insull*. Chicago: University of Chicago Press, 1962.

———. *Recovering the Past: A Historian's Memoir*. Lawrence: University Press of Kansas, 2004.

McElvaine, Robert S. *The Great Depression: America, 1929–1941*. New York: Times Books, 1983.

Meltzer, Milton. *Brother, Can You Spare a Dime? The Great Depression, 1929–1933*. New York: Alfred A. Knopf, 1969.

Merriam, Charles Edward. *Chicago: A More Intimate View of Urban Politics*. New York: Macmillan, 1929.

Meyers, W. Cameron. "Henry Horner and Richard Finnegan—Footnote to a Friendship." *Journal of the Illinois State Historical Society* 55 (Winter 1962): 341–69.

Newell, Barbara Warne. *Chicago and the Labor Movement: Metropolitan Unionism in the 1930s*. Urbana: University of Illinois Press, 1961.

Oblinger, Carl D. *Divided Kingdom: Work, Community, and the Central Illinois Coal Fields During the Great Depression*. 2nd ed. Springfield: Illinois State Historical Society, 2004. Originally published in 1991.

Patterson, James T. *The New Deal and the States: Federalism in Transition*. Princeton: Princeton University Press, 1969.

Pierce, Bessie Louise. *A History of Chicago*. 3 vols. New York: Alfred A. Knopf, 1937–47.

Rauch, Basil. *The History of the New Deal, 1933–1938*. New York: Creative Age, 1944.

Rickard, Earl. "How Dry We Were: The Repeal of Prohibition." Suite 101.com, July 1, 2001. <www.suite101.com/article.cfm/us_history_1929_1945/734127>.

Sandburg, Carl. *Henry Horner, Governor of Illinois: A Tribute*. Chicago: Privately printed by the author, 1941.

Shannon, David A. *Twentieth Century America: The United States since the 1890's*. Chicago: Rand McNally, 1963.

Smith, Carl. *Urban Disorder and the Shape of Belief: The Great Chicago Fire, the Haymarket Bomb, and the Model Town of Pullman*. Chicago and London: University of Chicago Press, 1995.

Strickland, Arvarh E. "The New Deal Comes to Illinois." *Journal of the Illinois State Historical Society* 63, no. 1 (Spring 1970): 55–68.

Stuart, William H. *The Twenty Incredible Years.* Chicago and New York: M. A. Donohue, 1935.

Sutton, Robert P., ed. *The Prairie State: A Documentary History of Illinois, Civil War to the Present.* Grand Rapids, Mich.: William B. Eerdmans, 1976.

Watkins, T. H. *The Great Depression: America in the 1930s.* New York: Blackside, 1993.

Wendt, Lloyd, and Herman Kogan. *Big Bill of Chicago.* Indianapolis: Bobbs-Merrill, 1953.

———. *Lords of the Levee: The Story of Bathhouse John and Hinky Dink.* Indianapolis: Bobbs-Merrill, 1943. Reprinted as Midland Book no. 109. Bloomington: Indiana University Press, 1967.

Who Was Who in America. Vol. 1 (1897–1942). Chicago: A. N. Marquis, 1942.

The WPA Guide to Illinois: The Federal Writers' Project Guide to 1930s Illinois. With a new introduction by Neil Harris and Michael Conzen. Written and compiled by the Federal Writers' Project of the Works Progress Administration for the State of Illinois. New York: Pantheon Books, 1983. Original copyright 1939 by Henry Horner, governor of Illinois.

INDEX

Charles J. Masters is a lawyer and historian. His previous book, *Glidermen of Neptune: The American D-Day Glider Attack,* was a featured selection of both the Military Book Club and the Aviators' Guild Book Club. A member of the Society of Midland Authors, he lives in Chicago.